The Cultures and Practice of Violence Series

THE STUDY OF VIOLENCE has often focused on the political and economic conditions under which violence is generated, the suffering of victims, and the psychology of its interpersonal dynamics. Less familiar are the role of perpetrators, their motivations, and the social conditions under which they are able to operate. In the context of postcolonial state building and more latterly the collapse and implosion of society, community violence, state repression, and the phenomena of judicial inquiries in the aftermath of civil conflict, there is a need to better comprehend the role of those who actually do the work of violence—torturers, assassins, and terrorists—as much as the role of those who suffer its consequences.

When atrocity and murder take place, they feed the world of the iconic imagination that transcends reality and its rational articulation; but in doing so imagination can bring further violent realities into being. This series encourages authors who build on traditional disciplines and break out of their constraints and boundaries, incorporating media and performance studies and literary and cultural studies as much as anthropology, sociology, and history.

The War Machines

DANNY HOFFMAN

The War Machines

young men and violence in Sierra Leone and Liberia

Duke University Press Durham and London 2011

Printed in the United States of
America on acid-free paper ♾
Designed by C. H. Westmoreland
Typeset in Carter & Cone Galliard
by Tseng Information Systems, Inc.
Library of Congress Cataloging-in-
Publication Data appear on the
last printed page of this book.

Duke University Press gratefully
acknowledges the support of the
University of Washington, Department
of Anthropology, which provided
funds toward the production of this
book.

contents

illustrations

preface

> The capitalist economy functions through decoding and deterritorialization: it has its extreme illnesses, that is, its schizophrenics who come uncoded and become deterritorialized to the extreme, but it also has its extreme consequences, its revolutionaries.
> —FÉLIX GUATTARI, "On Capitalism and Desire"

The War Machines is an ethnography of war zones and war dynamics in the violent folds of capital's global empire. The events I deal with in this book took place in Sierra Leone and Liberia between roughly 1989 and 2007. But in direct and indirect ways, this is also an ethnography of wars well beyond the borders of West Africa.

The book explores how young men in Sierra Leone and Liberia are made available for often violent forms of labor. It is an argument for thinking of this region, so often described in the apocalyptic language of failure and destruction, as networked spaces of hyperproduction. The theoretical construct I use for understanding these productive forces in West Africa today is the war machine. Borrowed from the philosophers Gilles Deleuze and Félix Guattari, this concept is helpful for thinking through relations between state and nonstate forces in the African postcolony. War machines allow us to think about war and work together, to see them as resonant, even identical, activities. War machines, I argue in these chapters, are an experimental technology. They produce violence, masculinity, political subjects, and exploitative economic relations in novel configurations. War machines produce unexpected political and social possibilities—some terrifying and repressive, some revolutionary and liberatory.

War machines function (at least in part) through the way they configure labor under today's global economy. I therefore propose the barracks, with its spatial, economic, and military organization of human bodies and labor, as the *nomos*, or organizing principle, of West Africa's postmodernity. Focusing on regional militias and the lives of the young men who participated in them, I explore how the logic of postcolonial cities, border posts, refugee centers, and labor camps is increasingly the logic of the barracks: a spatial and sociopolitical configuration the purpose of which is to rapidly assemble male bodies for efficient deployment in the overlapping service of security and profit.

Locations

As I began fieldwork for this project in mid-2000, the war in Sierra Leone was almost a decade old, at least if we fix its start date as 23 March 1991. On that day the Revolutionary United Front (RUF) first crossed the Liberian border and attacked the villages of Bomaru and Sienga. The *war don don*, the official declaration by the government of Sierra Leone that the war was over, took place on 18 January 2002.[1] By that time there was serious fighting once again across the border in Liberia. Many combatants who fought in Sierra Leone's conflict subsequently took part in Liberia's, just as many of them fought in Sierra Leone as veterans of Liberia's earlier civil war. My field sites moved as the combatants did. When the war in Liberia ended in August 2003 with the overthrow of President Charles Taylor, those with whom I worked scattered. Some remained in Liberia. Others crossed the border into Côte d'Ivoire or Guinea. Still others returned to Sierra Leone.

The effective bookend for the research included here is the Sierra Leonean elections of mid-2007. By that point the two militias with which I worked most closely, the Civil Defence Force (CDF) in Sierra Leone and Liberians United for Reconciliation and Democracy (LURD) in Liberia, no longer existed as formal institutions. But the forces and pressures that assembled these young men and deployed their violence in war were still very much in evidence in the region's diamond mines, rubber plantations, city streets, and political party offices. What was surprising after seven years of intermittent time on the ground in West Africa, and continuous remote contact with combatants and ex-combatants, was how qualitatively similar their lives were on both sides of the divide between war and peace. *The War Machines* remained a work of frontline anthropology even when the front lines it originally set out to document were no longer there.

The bulk of research on which this project is based took place in the aftermath of the attacks of 11 September 2001, and in the context of the so-called Global War on Terrorism. Sierra Leone was no less a part of the post–September 11 conversation than any other corner of the world. Looming over the fieldwork were the wars in Afghanistan and Iraq and the militarization of United States foreign policy under the neoconservatives in the George W. Bush administration. This was a period of wide-ranging dialogue about new imperial projects, the uses of the armies of the state and private military contractors, and the meaning of terms like *security*, *sovereignty*, and *democracy*. In Sierra Leone, as everywhere else, conversations about September 11 were simultaneously global and local. So too were the subsequent discourses about the fundamental keywords of contemporary politics.

The book was largely written as the Bush administration and the world economy imploded in late 2008 and early 2009. By the fall of 2008 it was possible for a mainstream world publication like the *New York Times* to ask, rhetorically but without irony, "Do you still believe in capitalism?"[2] This was a period of radical thought on both the political right and left around the world about the relationship between markets and the state and the intersection of militarism and the economy. Such thinking had (and continues to have) global implications. Even at the beginning of the Obama administration in the United States certain trends in the restructuring of security and economy appear set to continue, and others appear simply unstoppable. It is in places like Sierra Leone and Liberia that this thought is tested and that its effects are most immediately felt. These are the issues that concerned me most in writing this book.

My imperative in this project is thus somewhat unusual for an ethnography of African violence. I am less interested in divining the "cultural order" (Ferme 2001b, 1) that underlies this region's recent history of war than I am in understanding the intersection of forces (political, economic, historical, and social) that set this conflict in motion, shaped its path, and will determine its relevance in the future. I do not set out to explain the Mano River War in locally meaningful terms. Instead I want to document its troubling position at the boundaries of novel transnational trends in the ordering of violence and labor. These are not necessarily mutually exclusive goals. Political economy is not cultureless, and culture is always bound to political economy. The anthropology of Africa, however, tends to be "scrupulously localized" (Ferguson 2006, 3), which historically has privileged the keywords of cultural analysis over those of politics or economy.

In recent years the anthropology of war in Africa in particular has emphasized the way culture shapes conflicts (for example, Lan 1985; Taylor 1999) or the way war zones produce a cultural community (for example, Nordstrom 1997, 2004).[3] The best of this work locates its subject in historical and political context, of course. But in much of the literature on African war there is a desire to read violence as though it were a guidebook to local "cultural values."[4] This can be a useful tool for countering the most reductive stories of violence in Africa. Explaining how the extraordinary violence of the conflict zone is related to the ordinary experiences of living can be an effective intervention against stories of African war as the eruption of primitive tribal animosities and irrational cruelties. Just as Edward Evans-Pritchard's classic analysis, *Witchcraft, Oracles and Magic among the Azande*, helped to shift debates about African witchcraft from theories of primitive minds to theories of alternative rationality, connecting seemingly inexplicable forms of violence to a culturally relevant symbolic order counters some of the worst exoticizing of African wars. Understanding acts of violence in the war zone in the terms that also describe more mundane violence based on gender, age, or ethnicity is a significant tool for depathologizing African warfare by problematizing the "normal" of nonwartime contexts. Books such as Carolyn Nordstrom's *Shadows of War* and Paul Richards's *Fighting for the Rainforest* have made a significant and positive impact well beyond the discipline of anthropology because they show a wide audience that "meaningless" violence is in fact profoundly meaningful.

But I am not convinced that this is the only imperative for an anthropology of African warscapes at this historical moment.[5] In an era when even theorists in United States military and global security circles are intent on explaining violence in local cultural terms, social theorists must recognize that this project alone may not constitute the intervention we think it is or that we want it to be. In the contemporary African postcolony, at least as it is inhabited by the young men who are the subject of this book, the keywords most in need of critical engagement are not those we normally associate with the spheres of "culture" and "the everyday."

This project also departs from a second trend in the anthropology of African conflict. At least since the 1994 Rwanda genocide, a number of studies have attempted to understand collective violence as a project of identity formation and the fixing of meaning between self and other, enemy and friend in an uncertain and fractured world (see, for example, Mamdani 2001, and the essays in Broch-Due 2005). This mirrors a growing literature in the anthropology of violence more generally, whether in specific case studies (such as Hansen [2001], writing on Bombay) or in multisited, theoretical reflections, many of which draw heavily on African examples (such as Appadurai 2006). Again, the question of identity formation is a crucial one for understanding war today, and the best of this work shines important light on the primordialist narratives that dominate popular discussions of Africa. "Tribal" identity is often assumed to be the one fixed bedrock of African social life, and there is certainly a great deal to be gained by countering that stereotype. Analyzing how identities are constructed in contemporary Africa, violently or otherwise, does a great deal to humanize the protagonists in seemingly inhuman wars.

But here again, the importance of this intervention has ebbed now that the "tribalism" narratives of Rwanda have been replaced by the Islamicization fantasies of the world media and Euro-American governments. That the identities of young people are up for grabs and are constructed by the worlds around them is integral to the logic of anti-Islamic "hearts and minds" campaigns. The United States military's Africa Command is only one of a host of new security apparatuses intent on understanding identity formation as a form of military intelligence. An anthropology too wedded to the language of belonging, autochthony, and ethnicity risks reproducing a very conservative mode of identity politics, a politics put to pernicious effects by African elites, transnational business interests, and international security forces. Moreover, work on "African identities" often occludes one of the most important and fascinating aspects of the lives of youth in the postmodern postcolony: an ability to live productively *through* the fractured, experimental, and decidedly unfixed nature of what it means to be African in the world today.

By contrast, I take my cue in the pages that follow from what Janet Bujra et al. (2004) propose as an agenda for the future of African studies. Their five areas for research and engagement combine analyses of the way globalized capitalism generates profit through African labor with examinations of new forms of solidarity and mobilizations of civil society. This is an African studies that maps emergent forms of life, to borrow Michael Fischer's (2003) phrase, and is based on the understanding that what Africa is today and what it means to be African is inseparable from the functioning of the world economy (see also Ferguson 2006, 1–23, and Piot 2010). Such analysis poses a challenge for an anthropology of African violence, and indeed for Africanist anthropology as a whole, devoted to explicating the cultural terms that make mass violence make sense. Again, in its best forms, this has been productive work. But it is not the project I undertake here. Instead I am motivated by a problem that Michael Hardt and Antonio Negri identify in their book *Empire*: "Struggles in other parts of the world," they write, "and even our own struggles[,] seem to be written in an incomprehensible foreign language" (2000, 57). Africanist anthropology has tended to translate struggles taking place "in other parts of the world" by elaborating on the local cultural orders that give them meaning. Here I ask more expressly political, less "scrupulously localized" questions: How are young men in multiple locales mobilized by forces larger than themselves? How do we take seriously a grassroots defense force as a project of postcolonial, post–Cold War democratic citizenship? What form of labor does a mercenary perform? Is it useful to think of violence today as a mode of work? What are the technologies of (post)modern occult practices and how are they connected to the global circulation of images and ideas about war, masculinity, youth, and the body? What resonates in movements like these West African armed militias with other social and militant mobilizations worldwide?

In other words, this remains a project of translation, but I shift the emphasis from terms associated with culture and the everyday to terms associated with experimentation and labor. I do so not to put these terms in opposition, but to allow us to focus on what was *produced* in the Mano River conflict zone rather than what was *reproduced* there. This is a shift in emphasis echoing that which Johannes Fabian has argued makes anthropology today "a science of forms of *survival*." The discipline is moving away, he argues, from its concentration on the "diversity and similarity of human *life* (hence the emphasis on custom, tradition, structures, and systems)." This is why "concepts such as strategies and projects seem to fit actions we observe better than habits and schemes; why resistance often describes collective action better than conformity; why production and innovation interest us more than reproduction and tradition, politics more than aesthetics, hybridity more than purity or authenticity, interactive spheres more than territories and boundaries" (2007, 12).

In an effort to make the anthropology of African violence relevant and politically engaged, scholars have privileged the more intellectually and politically conservative terms in Fabian's sequence. Culture, understood as "reproduction and tradition," becomes a way to convey the humanness of the conflict zone. The everyday, read as "habits and schemes," becomes a heuristic that allows us to see a life world that is not wholly reduced to violence. To repeat: though the goal of such work is frequently laudable and progressive, attempting to understand an African warscape vis-à-vis "the ordinary conflicts that may erupt in times of peace" (Ferme 2001b, 1) appears to me to needlessly overdetermine the peculiar present in which we live. There is a great deal about the Mano River War that is more reflective of emergent trends and experiments in living under global capital than reflective of past practices and forms of day-to-day existence. It is not enough to contextualize the war in cultural-historical terms. We need to work analytically at the outer reaches of what such conventional frameworks can tell us about violence today. The way Gilles Deleuze wrote about the nature of extraordinary events sums up this project: "History isn't experimental, it's just the set of more or less negative preconditions that make it possible to experiment with something beyond history" (1995, 170).

This means that many of the questions I ask in this book are questions that originate in various schools of political economy on the left. But if they are something of a departure from the recent anthropology of African warscapes, they nevertheless remain fundamentally *anthropological* questions in this project. Counterintuitively, perhaps, I would argue that these are anthropological questions precisely because they concentrate on those acts of subjection and experimentation that escape or exceed any cultural order and render meaningless any notion of the everyday. An anthropology of war is, after all, an anthropology of events more than it is an anthropology of a place or places (Nordstrom 1999, 155).[6] It is an anthropology of how, when, and why some things become possible and others are made impossible. A great deal of what happened during the wars in Sierra Leone and Liberia can productively be understood as an effort to grapple with extraordinary circumstances by undertaking extraordinary action. This is not a study of the reproduction of life but of its production, a study of new "forms of survival" (Fabian 2007, 12).

Which brings us back, in the chapters to come, to war machines.

Reading the Book

The topics I deal with here are fraught with complications for how one writes ethnographically. This doesn't make the project unusual; every ethnographer confronts unique challenges. The ones I face in this project stem from the peculiarities of writing about violence, writing about Africa, and writing about the two together.

Slavoj Žižek (2008, 3–4) is only one of the most recent of a long list of authors in various fields to point out that it is impossible to write satisfactorily about violence. Something about the topic eludes representation. This has been the basis of a great deal of useful theory, much of which argues that violence is by definition the undoing of language, the impossibility of representation (see, perhaps most notably, Scarry 1985). There are, nevertheless, conventions for writing about conflict zones and about the experiences of those who live in them. Novelists and other fiction writers have been historically more successful than anthropologists at working with those conventions, exploring how language grapples with the phenomenology of fear, trauma, or pain. In parts of the chapters to follow I have looked to a diverse cadre of writers for clues on effectively deploying those tropes. No writer conveys the fear of forced movement through a hostile landscape better than the science fiction

1. Riot at the Bo, Sierra Leone, disarmament center, 2001.
(All photographs by author, unless noted otherwise)

writer Octavia Butler. Writers such as Norman Mailer, Richard Price, Nuruddin Farah, and Chris Abani have worked to capture the voice of a militarized masculinity in different cultural contexts. Ahmadou Koroma's magical West African realism brilliantly captures the absurd tensions of being subject to postcolonial state authority, and Veronique Tadjo is equally powerful in examining the vexed relations of postcolonial domestic space. While *The War Machines* falls squarely into the genre of anthropological ethnography—my experiments with form have been modest—I have tried to pay close attention to the book's literary style, and to draw inspiration where I can from cosmopolitan authors (African and non-African) wrestling with the limits and the possibilities of bringing language to bear on difficult topics.

The result is an unabashedly narrative-driven ethnography. There are places here in which a story is meant not only to illustrate or evoke a place or person but to carry a great deal of empirical and theoretical weight. (Here I draw a certain comfort from Johannes Fabian's [2007,

2. Child soldiers fighting with LURD at Voinjama, 2002.

122–23] nuanced discussion of the meaning of empirical evidence in the social sciences, and Charles Piot's [2010, 16–20] examination of the centrality of storytelling to post–Cold War West Africa.) While much of what follows is theoretical analysis, metahistory, and ethnographic contextualization, much is pure narrative. This is the ethnographic form the project seemed to demand. Writers like Okwui Enwezor (2006, 12) and Binyavanga Wainaina (2005) underscore just how noncredible African realities appear when forced through the standard abstractions of documentary reportage. This sad reality, I think, we can attribute as much to lazy writing as to bald racism. Much of what I have included here may seem fantastical in other senses. But my hope is that taking storytelling seriously will at least allow for a more complex, nuanced, and ultimately convincing portrait of the lives of young men caught up in the Mano River War.

By including an extensive photographic component, I have put another tool to work in this task. I come from a background in photojournalism and have elsewhere explored more fully the implications and possibilities of the visual representation of African violence (see Hoffman 2007a, n.d.). The problems associated with the realist, documentary style of visual images of postcolonial African violence are perhaps even more troubling than those associated with writing about Africa. Whatever one might say or write in an effort to humanize young male militia fighters in Africa, the visual image of black male bodies with weapons carries a demonizing baggage that for many viewers may be inescapable. As I explore in the chapters that follow, fighters with the region's various militias are well aware of the impact their images have on a world audience and they use it to great effect. What I hope to achieve by including images of militiamen, armed and unarmed, on the battlefield and away from it, is equally strategic. In the tradition of the classic photo-essays, I have tried to put the images and text of this project into dynamic tension (see W. Mitchell 1994). In some instances, the visual imagery of armed fighters serves to contradict descriptions in the text of young men simply at work in a postmodern economy. In others, the mundaneness of images of combatants at home is a check on the excesses of narratives of violent encounters. Women, children, and noncombatant men populate the images in ways in which they cannot always populate the text, opening the space for counterreadings and contradictions. In some cases, the text directly comments on the images. In others it ignores them. In all cases, however, I intend for these images to be fully integrated into the argument of the chapters that follow.

The introduction outlines in greater detail the theoretical framework through which I approach the Mano River militia movements I study—and through which I understand their importance for the future militarization of the global economy. Deleuze's and Guattari's work has been taken up by a handful of anthropologists in recent years, but the war machine concept (like so much of their theorizing) can be difficult to put to use outside the philosophical and historical contexts in which it was written. For that reason, I am particularly concerned in this introduction to the war machine idea to elaborate on the background to their thought and to advocate for its relevance to a contemporary West African context.

The seven full chapters of the book are divided into two parts. Part I provides some of the necessary background and context for understanding the subsequent chapters. Chapter 1 is a short "authoritative" history of the two fronts of the war. Its implicit argument is that we should treat the conflict on both sides of the border between Sierra Leone and Liberia as a single, continuous war, one that exceeds the time frames normally cited for these conflicts (1989–96 and 2000–2003 in Liberia, 1991–2002 in Sierra Leone). Chapters 2 and 3 elaborate one aspect of that history by following the trajectory of the kamajor militia from a grassroots community defense organization to a national militia in Sierra Leone. These chapters intervene in specific debates in the anthropology of Sierra Leone and Liberia and in the anthropology of this war, but more important, they map the entire trajectory by which a war machine becomes an organ of the state. The chapters that follow examine facets of this process of capture, but here I cover in broad strokes the process as a whole.

Part II consists of four chapters. Chapter 4 takes up the idea of the kamajor and Civil Defence Force militia not as an army but as the militarization of the social networks surrounding young men in this part of West Africa. Written in response to the way the organization was represented by the prosecution for the United Nations war crimes tribunal, the Special Court for Sierra Leone, this chapter underscores the idea that global capital has at last realized the functionalist sociologist Marcel Mauss's fantasy of the total social phenomenon: the complete breakdown of distinct cultural, economic, and political spheres. The mobilization of a war machine in the African postcolony must be understood as the militarization of life itself; what is deployed by the barracks formation is not simply the bodies or labor power of male youth, but their very existence.

Chapter 5 is the principal theoretical outline of the barracks as the nomos of West African postmodernity. I take up two ethnographic sites in which we see the logic of rapid assembly and efficient deployment at work—and in which we see how violence becomes the critical dynamic that facilitates movement across these barracks spaces. I suggest ways in which this recreation of space is shaping not only the lives of those who inhabit the barracks but the very infrastructure of the postmodern African city itself.

Chapter 6 is an ethnographic documentation of one of those sites in particular: Freetown's Brookfields Hotel, where CDF combatants lived from 1998 until 2002. This photo-and-text essay is the book's most sustained engagement with a single field site. More experimental than other chapters in its formal presentation, it is nevertheless perhaps the most conventionally ethnographic. In the spirit of ethnography as defined by Sherry Ortner, it is "the attempt to understand another life world using the self—as much of it as possible—as the instrument of knowing" (2006, 42). Chapter 7 explores one of the oldest and most fraught topics in the anthropology of Africa: the occult. Here I suggest a vision of supernatural medicines as a form of experimental technology, akin to the research and development that goes into any other weapon of warfare. This is a parallel drawn by militia fighters themselves when they talk about their own bodies and the physical capability to repel the bullets of one's enemies. This connection underscores a great deal of recent work on "the modernity of witchcraft," though it also raises the possibility that witchcraft studies in general have failed to adequately account for both the innovativeness of occult practice and its connection to violence.

The short conclusion makes in more detail the argument that runs throughout this work: that the Mano River War matters not only because of how it helps us understand this region but for how it helps us understand our global future. The trends, thinking, and organization of modern life that made this war possible, and around which these militia groups mobilized, are fast becoming global assemblages (Ong and Collier 2005). On our current trajectory, much more of the globe will come to resemble the Mano River region and its violent recent history.

acknowledgments

THE RESEARCH AND WRITING that went into this project was supported by the following: the American Council of Learned Societies, Duke University, the School for Advanced Research through its Weatherhead Fellowship, the Social Science Research Council, the John D. and Catherine T. MacArthur Foundation, and the University of Washington. Thanks go to each of these institutions for their generous support on many fronts.

Portions of the work that follows have appeared previously in various forms. Parts of the introduction and conclusion are taken from "The Sub-contractors," in *Dangerous Liaisons: Anthropologists and the National Security State*, edited by Laura McNamara and Robert A. Rubinstein (SAR Press, 2011). Portions of chapter 4 appeared in earlier form as "The Meaning of a Militia," *African Affairs* 106, no. 425 (2007), and as "Rocks" in *Telling Young Lives*, edited by Craig Jeffrey and Jane Dyson (Temple University Press, 2008). Chapter 5 is a revised version of "The City as Barracks," *Cultural Anthropology* 22, no. 3 (2007).

A great number of people have shaped this book in ways large and small. I regret that I cannot thank them each by name, but hope that they will recognize their contributions in the work that follows. Please know that I am grateful.

I owe a particular debt to two people I am honored to call colleagues, mentors, and friends. Charles Piot and Mohammed Tarawalley Jr. had an incalculable impact on this book and on me, and I am grateful to them for both.

This project is dedicated to my family. The Grabers have been a source of encouragement and support over the past ten years. With unfailing strength, enthusiasm, and patience, the Hoffmans made everything possible from the very beginning. To Corlette Rose, Lucia Jacqueline, Martha Eve, and Julie most of all—my love and thanks.

introduction

WAR MACHINES

TRIAL TRANSCRIPTS FROM THE SPECIAL COURT for Sierra Leone dated 27 January 2006 include the following exchange about war machines.[1] Speaking are Judge Bankole Thompson; the defense attorney, Bu-Buakei Jabbi; and one of the accused, Chief Samuel Hinga Norman. Norman was indicted by the war crimes tribunal on the grounds that he bore command responsibility for crimes committed by the Civil Defence Force (CDF) militia, referred to here as the "Kamajors" or the "chiefdom hunter group."

Q. [DR. JABBI]: Now let us come to the Kamajor system as a war machine. Can you explain to the Court—let's say the chiefdom hunter group, whether that would be organized according to any command structure?

A. [NORMAN]: My Lords, I would prefer not to refer to the Kamajor system as a war machine. The Kamajors—

JUDGE THOMPSON: Is that a preference, or are you giving us factual information?

THE WITNESS [NORMAN]: That is not a preference. I would prefer to call them Kamajors rather than a war machine.

JUDGE THOMPSON: Okay.

THE WITNESS: They are not and they were not—

JUDGE THOMPSON: That's what I want to know, whether they are or they are not, rather than a preference. Right.

JABBI: Yes, carry on please.

A. [NORMAN]: Question again, My Lord.

Q. [JABBI]: As reformulated by yourself, were hunters or Kamajors constituted into any command structure within the chiefdom system?

A. [NORMAN]: Well, My Lords, I would say wherever there is control there is always leadership.[2]

Sixteen months later, I sat with Norman in the visiting room at the Special Court's detention center. A sequined Santa Claus decoration was pinned to the otherwise bare walls. Norman wore a tank top and shorts. He sipped tea while he explained his objection to calling the kamajors a war machine.

"What do you think is a war machine?" he asked. "A thing which acts without reason, its only purpose is war. It goes on ad infinitum, without stop. But these [the kamajors] are human beings, acting under their own control." This being a topic Norman did not find particularly interesting, we soon moved on.

Hinga Norman's objections notwithstanding, in this chapter I take seriously the peculiar figure of the war machine. As Norman suggests, war machines raise complex questions of agency and structure, intention and logic, command and leadership. Any movement we might label a war machine will configure these problems in different ways. But when it comes to recent efforts to think about the confluence between militarization, social movements, global capital, and the state, war machines are popping up everywhere.

I concentrate here on one of the more intriguing analyses of the war machine and suggest why it is useful for understanding recent events in West Africa's Mano River region. The blueprint laid out by the philosophers Gilles Deleuze and Félix Guattari is exceedingly complex. It represents some of the more arcane writings in Continental philosophy. And this work, like a great deal of what Deleuze and Guattari produced, has lived a strange life over the four decades since it was written. The figure of the war machine has crossed the disciplinary boundaries between architecture and military planning, postcolonial theory and the sociology of radical political movements. Deleuze's and Guattari's war machines originate in a specific sociopolitical context (urban France in the late 1960s). But since then theorists in philosophy, security studies, and modern social movements—theorists inside and outside the academy and in different parts of the world—have attempted to understand not only how war machines function but how to build them and how to make them work efficiently. Institutions ranging from the Israeli Defense Force to Al Qaeda to the Zapatistas are thinking about war machines and attempting to create them. (And in a surprising number of cases, they do so with direct reference to Deleuze and Guattari.) War machines trouble the boundary between thought and practice. They are relevant not simply because they describe an emergent form of sociopolitical organization but because writings about war machines have helped to create that mode of organization. The question Judge Thompson posed to Norman from the Special Court bench is thus more difficult to answer than it might at first appear. What is the difference between preference and fact when it comes to making a war machine?

Making War Machines

We can assume it was the popular image of the war machine that Norman had in mind when he objected to that name for the kamajor militia. The term evokes mindless, amoral violence—a machine perhaps operated by human beings but ultimately grinding away under its own steam for the sole purpose of destruction. It is an image that vaguely references a military-industrial nexus and the modernist fantasy of machines run amok, laying waste to human bodies and communities.

A second reference to war machines appears in the transcripts of the Special Court for Sierra Leone, a reference more in keeping with this commonsense use of the term. In 2005 a prosecution witness testifying against Norman and his coaccused was asked whether he agreed that the kamajors faced a "Herculean task" in fighting the People's Army rebels, a "very savage war machine." "Indeed," replied the witness, after describing how a military ambulance drove deliberately back and forth over the body of an unarmed kamajor.[3] "The corpse, whilst lying down, I saw the military Land Rover—an ambulance, a military ambulance. A sergeant was sitting on the bumper of that ambulance firing randomly all over the place saying, 'Soldiers, wives of soldiers jubilate. We are now well off. Our government has come back into our own hands.' And they drove over the corpse of the body three times and got it smashed up which was very pathetic."[4] The emphasis in this exchange was on the ruthless production of violence, the machine-like way the rebels and armed forces rolled through towns and efficiently carried out the one task for which they were designed: war. (All the more remarkable, after this earlier description, that Norman's own attorney would use the term in reference to the pro-government forces Norman led.) The war machine image here evokes an unnatural force, made by humans but beyond their control and intimately tied to economic and material production.

It is important to keep these popular evocations of "war machine" in mind while exploring the more technical definition I use here. The fantastical language that surrounds the war machine as a philosophical construct can easily eclipse the reality of the violence it is meant to describe. In "Axiom II" of a "Treatise on Nomadology," Deleuze and Guattari write that "the war machine is the invention of the nomads" (1987, 380). A few pages later, they elaborate: "If the nomads formed the war machine, it was by inventing absolute speed, by being 'synonymous' with speed. And each time there is an operation against the State—insubordination, rioting, guerrilla warfare, or revolution as act—it can be said that a war machine has revived, that a new nomadic potential has appeared, accompanied by the reconstitution of a smooth space or a manner of being in space as though it were smooth" (386). What "speed" and the "smoothness of space" mean and how we understand the figure of the nomad are key to understanding what uses we might find for the concept of the war machine. But determining such meanings is not easy, particularly when set against the backdrop of decades of war.

As the quote above would suggest, Deleuze and Guattari's two-volume *Capitalism and Schizophrenia* (volume 1, *Anti-Oedipus*, and volume 2, *A Thousand Plateaus*) must be one of the most confounding works in modern philosophical thought. It has spawned a huge secondary literature and, unusual for a work of dense philosophical theory, a group of adherents that extends across the academy and from militant social movements to pop recording artists. Its readers include, as I take up below, theorists and practitioners in both the Israeli Defense Force and autonomous Black Bloc protest mobilizations. It is a work enigmatic enough that its interpreters have referred to it as "a machine." Its authors describe it as an "assemblage," a "multiplicity," and "a body without organs." Yet despite its oddness *Capitalism and Schizophrenia* has been a remarkably generative thousand pages.

Anti-Oedipus and *A Thousand Plateaus* grew out of a very specific project: an effort "to redefine what constitute[s] 'revolutionary' politics and to rethink the terms in which we evaluate social movements" (Patton 1984, 63; see also Patton 1997, 2). The immediate context of the writing was the popular student and worker uprisings in urban France in May and June 1968. The goal was a work of usable political philosophy for an era of state collapse and the radical expansion of capitalism's logic into all manner of social relations.

The upheavals of 1968 were not limited to urban France, of course. Political organizing around the globe appeared to take on a different tenor, from the Czechoslovak "Prague Spring" and the beginning of "the Troubles" in Northern Ireland to the increasingly violent encounters between state security forces and civil rights, Black Power, and anti-war movements in the United States. The period epitomized by the events of 1968 was one in which social movements, guerrilla armies, and the dominant modes of economic production were all changing profoundly, most notably by moving away from the rigid hierarchies of high modernism and toward a more decentralized, network model of organization (Hardt and Negri 2004, 80–81; see also Boltanski and Chiapello 2005, 167–216). This is a moment that has been described as the transition from modernism to postmodernism and, in labor studies, from Fordism to post-Fordism or flexible accumulation (see summaries in Gibson-Graham [1996] 2006, 148–73; Kumar 1995, 36–65).

In Africa a number of states were officially declared independent that year, continuing the continent's transition from colonial to postcolonial regimes. The Nigerian civil war was at its height, with potentially profound ramifications for the future of postcolonial African unity and the form of new states. Reciprocal relations between African elites and the former colonial metropoles were solidified in this period and became the central tenet governing structures of the state (Bayart 1993; Bond 2006). In Sierra Leone 1968 saw the ascension to power of the dictator Siaka Stevens and the inauguration of a new mode of postcolonial governance characterized by the semiprivatization of state functions and bureaucracies; 1968 was the birth of what William Reno (1995) has described as Sierra Leone's "shadow state," a mode of sovereignty organized around the state's capacity to generate personal profits for those in power.

At least in France, the Left's intellectual response to these world upheavals had been an "uncritical synthesis of Freudianism and Marxism" (Patton 2000, 68). *Capitalism and Schizophrenia* was intended as an intervention. Where many observers were reading contemporary politics in terms of Freud's laws of the Father and a Maoist version of Marxian class conflict, Deleuze and Guattari argued for a very different understanding of the relationship between politics and desire. The volumes map the very production of social groupings, or what Michael Hardt calls the various "logics of aggregation" (n.d.). *A Thousand Plateaus* in particular demonstrated a whole new manner of writing about what makes social collectives work so hard for their own oppression—and what fissures might be opened that would allow new collectives to mobilize and escape. Though it did not break with either Freud or Marx, *Capitalism and Schizophrenia* was an effort to read both (and thus to read the contemporary historical moment) differently.

Deleuze's and Guattari's framework for understanding the political (and for understanding both Freud and Marx) was heavily influenced by Nietzsche, for whom the political landscape was divisible into active and reactive forces. The purpose of political philosophy in this Nietzschean vein was not to understand social movements, violent uprisings, or state repression in terms of class struggle or Oedipal conflicts. It was to identify the arrangement of active and reactive forces and to "promote the active ones while discouraging the reactive ones" (May 2001, 729). This emphasis on the play of forces and the subjective evaluation of their active and reactive qualities makes *Capitalism and Schizophrenia* arguably the first truly poststructuralist work of political theory. Certainly it was a departure from political thinking that saw collective struggle in terms of actually existing structures, whether those structures were internal (as in Freud) or external (as in Marx).

The result is a highly entertaining, complex, and deliberately schizophrenic work that borrows from philosophy, literature, cinema, mathematics, fine art, and, significantly, anthropology. I will return to the anthropological imagination at work in *Capitalism and Schizophrenia* at the end of this chapter. But it is important to recognize that a great deal of the theoretical work done in both volumes of *Capitalism and Schizophrenia* comes from the way Deleuze and Guattari read anthropological literature. Their approach to social movements and revolutionary impulses is informed by their engagements with French structuralists such as Claude Lévi-Strauss, Luc de Heusch, Georges Balandier, and especially Pierre Clastres, and by their readings in British structural functionalism by Africanists such as Edward Evans-Pritchard, Meyer Fortes, and Max Gluckman. (The very idea of the "plateaus" in the title of *Capitalism and Schizophrenia*'s second volume is taken from the anthropologist Gregory Bateson's *Steps to an Ecology of Mind* [Deleuze and Guattari 1987, 21–22, 159; Massumi 1992, 7].) Deleuze's and Guattari's readings of ethnography are unorthodox to be sure. But their ultimate interest was in keeping with the anthropological project of the day, which Sherry Ortner summarizes as an effort to "conceptualize the *articulations* between the practices of social actors 'on the ground' and the big 'structures' and 'systems' that both constrain those practices and yet are ultimately susceptible to being transformed by them" (2006, 2). What Deleuze and Guattari sought to create was an interdisciplinary toolbox through which to break apart the conventional theorizing of a turbulent, troubling, but potentially liberating time.

From this confusion of ideas and influences emerges the useful figure of the war machine.

The Nature of the Machine

Contrary to its name, the war machine is not dedicated to the production of war. War is simply an occasional by-product of what the war machine is really about: exteriority to the state.

Throughout the "Treatise on Nomadology—The War Machine" (chapter 12 of *A Thousand Plateaus*) Deleuze and Guattari draw from Pierre Clastres's political anthropology. Clastres argued, in part based on fieldwork in Paraguay and elsewhere in South America, that "primitive" (nonstate) society is not a precursor to the modern state but an effort to ward it off. The primary social drive is not to make war but to keep at bay structures of power that risk descending into despotism (Clastres 1989, 189–218; 1994, 139–67). For Clastres, natural sociality is small collectives organized in such a way that their leaders are accountable to the collective. Segmentary societies do not concentrate power with a ruler or an elite. Once power *does* become the exclusive prerogative of a person or institution, and is removed from society as a whole, we witness the birth of states. Clastres, in other words, turns Hobbes's *Leviathan* on its head. Where Hobbes argued that society invents the state to stave off social dissolution and chaos, in Clastres society defends itself against the chaos brought on by the state itself.

The state in this narrative is therefore a condition, not simply a historical formation. It is not limited to what we think of as the modern nation-state. "The State" is a hierarchical mode of organizing power that appears as a tendency or impulse throughout history. The usage here stands in contrast to the commonsense understanding of the state as an entity "up there" (Ferguson 2006, 92), prior to and standing above the local or the social. The contemporary nation-state is simply one expression, though perhaps the quintessential one, of a state mode of politics and organization of power. "State effects," as Timothy Mitchell called them (1991), are prior to state institutions. Indeed, the best illustrations of this argument today are found in Africa: many state functions around the continent are as likely to be performed by multinational institutions as by a sovereign state government (Piot 2010).

Moreover, statist modes of power are met everywhere with active resistance—with war machines. When necessary, though by no means always, that resistance turns violent. I will return to the problem of violence below. But first it is important to understand how these two dynamics of power and organization, these logics of aggregation, differ.

State relations operate within a "milieu of interiority" (Deleuze and Guattari 1987, 353). They are concerned with structures and codes, with stable identities and what Deleuze and Guattari call "striated" spaces (clearly mapped, delineated, and fixed). This is the space of bureaucracy, obsessed with charting its territory through cartography, conducting censuses, plotting the normal course of affairs, fixated on taxation and protocol. States dig trenches and plot straight lines. States are reactive forces; they "think" according to established principles and paradigms. A state clears paths that allow it to see and control movement around its territory. The United States interstate highway system is a state striation of space, an infrastructure designed for moving commodities and military materiel from one fixed point to another. The South African apartheid government striated space when it designed its townships with fixed points of entry and exit, creating enclosures isolated from the white city. The township could be locked down in minutes and effectively monitored and policed. The state's pass laws and identity books sought to code its citizenry in easily legible categories and assign them a place and a function accordingly. States undertake projects of distinguishing the legal from the illegal, the legitimate from the illegitimate, the licit from the illicit. States territorialize.

War machines by contrast are solely exterior relations. A war machine's properties are contingent and flexible, and its movements are those of "smooth" space, not confined to transit between fixed points or along given routes. Although it is identified at points in the "Treatise on Nomadology" with the warrior, the hunter, the prophet, even the miner, the nomad best embodies the war machine's movements and operations of power. Nomads, of course, occupy space. But unlike the state they are not concerned with fixed points or the sedimentation of routes, lines, and walls. They are more concerned with trajectories and with freedom of movement. The war machine is rhizomatic; it makes and breaks connections at any point along its network. War machines are active forces. They invent concepts. They experiment. To the striated space of the American interstate highway, smooth nomad space is the unroaded smuggling routes of the desert Southwest. To the state entrances and watchtowers of South African townships are opposed the smooth, spontaneous marching routes of student protestors and Zulu impis. To the state's fixed categories of race are opposed the war machines of "illegitimate" mixed race offspring and foreigners who do not belong anywhere in the state typology. War machines make previously unheard of or unthinkable connections. They link in illicit or illegitimate ways. Where states undertake projects of territorialization, the war machine deterritorializes.

The first comparison Deleuze and Guattari make in the "Treatise on Nomadology" is perhaps the most useful in illustrating the two dynamics:

> Let us take chess and Go, from the standpoint of the game pieces, the relations between the pieces and the space involved. Chess is a game of State, or of the court: the emperor of China played it. Chess pieces are coded; they have an internal nature and intrinsic properties from which their movements, situations, and confrontations derive. They have qualities, a knight remains a knight, a pawn a pawn, a bishop a bishop. . . . Go pieces, in contrast, are pellets, disks, simple arithmetic units, and have only anonymous, collective, or third-person function: "It" makes a move. "It" could be a man, a woman, a louse, an elephant. Go pieces are elements of a nonsubjectified machine assemblage with no intrinsic properties, only situational ones. . . . Chess is indeed a war, but an institutionalized, regulated, coded war, with a front, a rear, battles. But what is proper to Go is war without battle lines, with neither confrontation nor retreat, without battles even: pure strategy, whereas chess is semiology. (1987, 352–53)

Again, it is important not to allow Deleuze's and Guattari's fantastic language to obscure their project. Indeed, the abstractness of the language is precisely the point. It allows the play of forces they describe to be legible in a variety of ethnographic contexts. It is certainly possible, and productive, to read their analysis of the state and war machine literally—to apply those concepts to literal states and nonstate armed actors. Indeed, this is what I do in a great deal of what follows. Nevertheless, to do only this misses some of the rich potential these ideas offer for thinking creatively about the radical changes at work in today's world.

The most obvious contemporary example of the interplay of state and war machine, of active and reactive forces, is the crisis-prone process by which surpluses are generated in a capitalist economy.[5] The war machine that looms largest on today's horizon is the one identified by Karl Marx and Friedrich Engels as fundamental to the functioning of capital: the constant revolution in the means of production.

In one of the most famous passages from *Manifesto of the Communist Party* Marx and Engels (1978) argue that what distinguishes the advanced stages of capitalism is the need to deal with problems of overaccumulation by constant expansion. Expansion in space, but also in time and into domains that were formerly spaces of nonwork: kinship, sociality, tradition, even religious belief. "The bourgeoisie," they write, "cannot exist without constantly revolutionizing the instruments of production, and thereby the relations of production, and with them the whole relations of society. . . . Constant revolutionizing of production, uninterrupted disturbance of all social conditions, everlasting uncertainty and agitation distinguish the bourgeois epoch from all earlier ones. All fixed, fast-frozen relations, with their train of ancient and venerable prejudices and opinions, are swept away, all new-formed ones become antiquated before they can ossify. All that is solid melts into air, all that is holy is profaned" (476). Thinking through the implications of this constant revolution in the means of production has generated some of the most important recent debates in Marxian and post-Marxian thought. For my purposes here the crucial point is the emphasis Marx and Engels, and subsequently Deleuze and Guattari, put on capital's dependency on "constant revolution." Capital, at least in its current manifestations, generates its unique form of surplus by continuously unproducing what it produces. It must deterritorialize what it previously territorialized, only to territorialize it again. Capital needs a crisis in order to function (443–65; see also Harvey 1990, 173–88; Klein 2007).

In Marx's own writings the most thorough accounting of this process comes in his analysis of the "disposable industrial reserve army." To prevent overaccumulation, a mass of workers must periodically be thrown out of the system of wage labor so they may later be reintegrated at a lower wage (Marx [1867] 1977, 784–86; see also Harvey 2003, 140–41). In Deleuze's and Guattari's terminology, this casting out of workers is their deterritorialization. They must be uncoded from the coding of the system, temporarily relegated to the smooth space exterior to the striated space of state and capital. This is a dangerous maneuver. Crisis always poses the risk of a general revolt or collapse. The metaphor of the reserve army cannot be incidental—expulsion breeds retaliation. One of the functions of the (literal) state is to guard against such volatility, easing the devaluation of workers where it can, deploying the violence of its security forces when it must. And if all goes well, the reserve army of labor is soon brought back into the system, albeit at a reduced wage. It is captured, reterritorialized. This process of deterritorialization and reterritorialization is the engine of capital at its advanced stages. Capital "operates by conjoining deterritorialized resources and appropriating the surplus arising from their reterritorializing conjunction" (Holland 1999, 20). What is deterritorialized may be part of the labor force, but it might also be consumer goods (trends and fashions are the de- and reterritorialization of commodities) or particular labor skills (the constant rise and fall in compensation for various forms of knowledge, for example).

In the realm of Marxian political economy, this is the ground on which the war machine does its work. War machines arise in these moments of transformation. Where the metamorphosis at work in deterritorialization begins to operate under its own steam, beyond the control of the state, we find war machines. When these moments of uncoding take off in unexpected directions, we find war machines. Rebelliousness alone does not constitute a war machine, but once the consequences and conduct of that rebelliousness cannot be predicted or controlled by the usual functioning of the system, we find war machines. The war machine is the revolutionary crisis.

But a war machine does not last. It is always captured. Deterritorialized, active forces are always eventually reterritorialized, made reactive, either because they are captured by the state or because they ossify into state-like hierarchies and become the state itself (Deleuze 2004, 266; 2006a, 64–65). Though the crisis at the heart of capital's functioning is perpetual, the constituent parts of that crisis change greatly. States continuously capture the war machines around them even as new war machines continuously appear.

War Machines in the World

What I have described thus far is the war machine as it appears in the language of Marxian political economy. There are other (though related) registers in which this configuration is useful for thought and which serve to illustrate the rich potential in Deleuze's and Guattari's project.

In his ethnography of sorcery in modern Sri Lanka, for example, Bruce Kapferer characterizes war machine and state as modalities of power, descriptors of "the actual dynamics of a great diversity of structures, not particular kinds of formal organization on the ground, but rather the dynamics of their process" (1997, 274). Sinhala sorcery, according to Kapferer, expresses certain fundamental truths about the human experience and the operations of power in society. Sorcery is existential practice. As such, sorcerers embody a war machine mode of power. They move across otherwise impenetrable boundaries, forge new connections, and break down barriers. Sorcery is the operation of power that disrupts existing structures. It interrupts the normal flow of events and functioning of the state, the economy, and society. Sorcery is exteriority; it takes its victims outside the routine logic of social and political life, rearranging established hierarchies and forging new, sometimes monstrously destructive connections. Myths and rituals connected to sorcery convey the sorcerer's war machine mode of production. Suniyam, a "demon-deity," is an itinerant trader. He operates outside the relations of modern capitalism, disrupting scales of value, forever converting otherwise unequivalent things (285). Similarly Oddisa, the archetypal sorcerer in Sinhala narratives, moves through space and time consuming fixed relations in his "great maw": "Everything is drawn within him; his ever-voracious movement is a traversal of all possibility and potentiality. As bounded and ordered totalities of city and society appear before him, Oddisa becomes something like the war machine that Deleuze and Guattari describe, flattening and 'deterritorializing' them, overcoming their spatial boundaries and the internal divisions and striations of order" (79). Such sorcery is not limited to myth or to occult specialists. The International

Monetary Fund (IMF) and multinational corporations can also operate as war machines, subverting the sovereignty of the state, upending established hierarchies and continuously rewriting the fixed rules of capital (286). They, too, are sorcerers. The nationalist riots that swept Sri Lanka in the early 1980s pitted a rhizomatic, war machine youth network against the military and paramilitaries of the state. The violence of the opposition People's Liberation Front (the Janatha Vikukthi Peramuna, or JVP) was anonymous, unpredictable, spectacular. The movement was constituted along proliferating lines exterior to state logic, lines of kinship, village association, youth, and friendship.

Antisorcery rituals, by contrast, reestablish the striated space of existence. They remake the world according to the logic of the state, reterritorializing what was deterritorialized by sorcery's war machines. Antisorcery shrines are often operated by persons of wealth and power or with connections to the government; what they reimpose is not order so much as the rational state's particular coding of power (Kapferer 1997, 283). Confronted with the war machines of community-based service organizations, the Sri Lankan government sought to impose state regulations and criticized the erosion of its sovereignty. Confronted with the violence of the JVP, the state categorized its populace into abstract types—terrorists, youth, Sinhalese—and then enacted a bureaucratized form of violence that policed those boundaries and sought to remove the threat posed by dangerous categories of person.

These processes of sorcery and antisorcery, war machine and state are not mirror images of one another. They are fundamentally different modes of organization that nevertheless depend on one another. One does not negate the other. Rather, they are "two distinct positivities" (Kapferer 1997, 278).

The positing of war machine *and* state as positive assemblages is partly what makes this framing so important for anthropology. Deleuze and Guattari are celebrated in Continental philosophy for breaking with Hegelian dialectics. In anthropology, they offer a way to think about social forces without an implicit (or explicit) reference to states or to existing social orders as the ultimate positive measure of social institutions. They allow us to imagine citizenship, sovereignty, resistance, regulation, and accumulation without recourse to the language of failed states or bastard forms of belonging—the perennial problem when social science considers politics and collectivity in contemporary Africa.

In contrast to Kapferer, Janet Roitman does not explicitly draw on the figure of the war machine in her work on regimes of regulation in the Chad Basin. Nevertheless her analysis of the garrison-entrepôt (1998) is useful in imagining a productive political economy of the war machine.[6] The garrison-entrepôt is both a material zone in the border regions of Cameroon and a regulatory regime. Sited at the crossroads of trade networks that extend around the region, the garrison-entrepôt enacts an "economy of the bush" exterior to state regulations of economy and (at least officially) state models of citizenship. Combining militancy and commerce, those who inhabit the garrison-entrepôt do so without fixed address; they are *la population flottante* of nomads, migrants, traders, brigands, and mercenaries who accumulate wealth through violence. Such violent accumulation is seen as legitimate according to the garrison-entrepôt's regulatory regime, even as it is seen as illegal by the state (see also Roitman 2005; 2006).

Roitman goes to great lengths to show that the garrison-entrepôt is not simply the absence of the state or the consequence of its breakdown. It is a productive space, "positive" in the sense that it generates new formations: "Apprehending the garrison-entrepôt as a material effect means thinking about what it is producing and not just why it was produced" (1998, 321). And what is produced is "wealth . . . , regulation, violence, accumulation, redistribution, sociability, and *political and economic subjectivity*" (299). The garrison-entrepôt makes fiscal subjects. Its mode of production is not antithetical to the state; in fact, a great deal of the state form is dependent on the rents which state office holders derive from the garrison-entrepôt. But it does produce a subject whose mode of being-in-the-world is less stable, more unpredictable, and potentially more threatening than the normative vision of a state citizen.

One of the crucial dynamics underlying both Kapferer's and Roitman's analyses is the way state modalities are forever working to capture the war machine, to harness its power and potential. "The State has no war machine of its own," write Deleuze and Guattari (1987, 355), and it represents the war machine to itself as primitive, backward, illegitimate, traitorous (354, 358). Yet it needs exteriority to expand its own structuring process and perpetually strives to domesticate the nomad's modality. The state operates as an apparatus of capture. The line between the two modalities is not always easy to see, especially as it is often the army of the state that most closely resembles the war machine or is most likely to use its tactics. "Sometimes it [the war machine] is confused with the magic violence of the State, at other times with the State's military institution" (354). But the state's use of violence, and its interest in war machines, is ultimately reactive; it is not about the creation of new possibilities. The war machine's "revolution," by contrast, deterritorializes without reterritorialization. It ceases to be a war machine when its violence becomes institutional, programmatic, or exercised in the service of states.

Both Kapferer and Roitman are ultimately concerned with a historically and ethnographically specific example—Sinhalese sorcery practices for Kapferer and economic activity in the border regions of the Chad Basin for Roitman. But the sorcerer and the garrison-entrepôt suggest something more than simply a "culturally appropriate phenomenon," as Roitman puts it (1998, 301). Rather, each expresses a dynamic of power, a logic of aggregation that we might well look for elsewhere—albeit in various guises.

As a modality of power a war machine might be manifest in any given structure, system, or process. To reiterate, war machines have no specific content and thus may take various locally particular forms (hence their usefulness in a range of ethnographic settings). What matters is the symbiosis of their relationship to striated spaces of the state, their "perpetual field of interaction" (Deleuze and Guattari 1987, 360). War machines have their own creative, productive force (they are not simply the absence or negation of the state), but it is a force propelled by the existence or possibility of the state.

In the chapters that follow, I am interested in both facets of the operation of war machines. I explore those moments of revolutionary crisis in which war machines appear. I trace the revolutionary lines of flight that open new possibilities, that deterritorialize existing relationships. I explore how in its earliest days the grassroots kamajor movement functioned as a war machine against the predatory collaboration of the Revolutionary United Front and the army of the Sierra Leonean state. I look at the militarization—the machining—of economically marginal urban youth into a militia force working exterior to the state's logic of security and the statist operations of the mining economy. As the Civil Defence Force grew in number and strength it claimed to be fighting for democracy even against the forces of the democratic state, evincing a war machine's logic of society versus the actual institutions of state government. I describe more micropolitical war machines as well: How certain urban spaces were made temporary war machines by deterritorializing the logic of the state monopoly on violence. How experiments in occult technology made war machines for the protection of combatants' bodies at the battlefront by deterritorializing the logic of global popular culture, defensive military innovation, and rural hunting practices. And finally how certain spectacular forms of violence seemed those of the war machine in that they were specifically designed to decode the strictures and limits of the state and its more rational, bureaucratic modes of violence.

I am also (and perhaps even more) interested in the moments when these war machines are captured and reterritorialized. How is it that a grassroots civil defense militia is transformed into a mercenary army? I take up here the conscription of marginal urban youth into a disposable reserve army that was deployed across international borders for the overthrow of a despotic, but nevertheless democratically elected, president. By the end of the war in Sierra Leone, Hinga Norman united a previously disparate armed network into something more closely resembling a state army, and which in fact functioned in lieu of the state army and in the service of a state political party. The smooth space of the kamajors' main barracks at the Brookfields Hotel eventually became the striated space for a network of armed criminal gangs and the labor pool of the new, British-trained army. What were the mechanisms of this capture? The technologies for bulletproofing the bodies of combatants were transformed into an industry by the kamajors' High Priest and his colleague initiators, a micropolitical "state" operation. How do occult technologies designed to deterritorialize the logic of wartime terror become codified as a profit-generating ritual of violence?

These are the ethnographic details I explore in what follows. But they will make more sense if we first explore somewhat more closely the question of what the theoretical construct of the war machine has to do with actual war.

Actual War

In Deleuze's and Guattari's writing a pure war machine is more likely to emerge in nonviolent artistic or cultural movements than on the field of battle. Conventional warfare, they argue, occurs at those points in which the war machine and the state come into direct conflict, and where the state apparatus seeks to make the war machine its own (Deleuze 1995, 33; see also Patton 2000, 114). The war machine that actually takes up arms is already captured by the logic of the state. It fights on the state's terms and according to the state's logic. "War," Deleuze and Guattari write at one point in *A Thousand Plateaus*, "is only the abominable residue of the war machine" (1987, 230).

It might have been easier from the perspective of 1970s and '80s Europe to suggest that war is inherently a state enterprise. This was, after all, still the era of the great game of the Cold War, of which even civil conflicts in Africa were a part. It was a context in which the possibility of nuclear war meant that any armed conflict could become absolutely destructive. To go to war at that historical moment, whether in France or in Angola, meant to participate as a pawn in the maneuvers of the superpowers and their allied states and to risk the zero sum logic of nuclear Armageddon.

Things are less clear from the 1990s onward. What we see from West Africa and elsewhere is that the boundary between war and peace is no longer so easily fixed. Whether or not one subscribes to theories of "new war," there is no doubt that many conflicts around the world blur the distinction between war and not-war. Peacekeeping and peace enforcing in Somalia, Kosovo, and Côte d'Ivoire may lack official state declarations of war, but as military operations they are otherwise indistinguishable from it. Police activity has gone global, and domestic security in many countries has become more militarized. What's more, it is increasingly difficult to disaggregate military maneuver from the normal functioning of the global economy. While there is nothing particularly new about the military-industrial complex, or about imperialism as an economic project, we are witnessing a more generalized correlation between the use of military force and corporate profit taking (Harvey 2003; Klein 2007). In short, the zones we might today legitimately identify as war zones are proliferating. Just as one could argue that by 1968 there was no longer an outside to capital, today one might argue that there is no outside to war. Hence, contra Deleuze and Guattari themselves, it is on today's battlefields that we see the war machine most strikingly at work.

Indeed, this is the argument that lies at the heart of Achille Mbembe's writings on the contemporary mode of African sovereignty he calls "necropolitcs."[7] Politics in Africa today is not the rational exercise of collective decision making through institutions in the public sphere. Rather it is the "generalized instrumentalization of human existence and the material destruction of human bodies and populations" (Mbembe

2003, 14). In other words, sovereign authority is the absolute control over mortality, "the right to kill" or "to allow to live" (12). This is a mode of sovereignty not held exclusively by the state in many parts of Africa. The unfettered authority to kill and to instrumentalize the bodies of civilians (through, for example, forced or barely compensated labor on the battlefield or extracting natural resources) belongs to a variety of formations—a number of which we might identify as war machines. War machines are a crucial component of this new death-driven mode of sovereignty: "Necropower is wielded both by states and by what, following Deleuze and Guattari, we should call 'war machines,'" as Mbembe put it in a 2002 interview. "War machines are made up of segments of armed men that split up, merge and superimpose each other depending on the circumstances. Polymorphous and diffuse organizations, war machine are characterized by their capacity for metamorphosis. They combine a plurality of functions and operate through capture, looting and predation" (Höller 2002). In any given territory there may be competition for sovereign authority between war machine formations: state paramilitaries and community defense militias, regional peacekeepers and multinational security corporations, rebel armies and spontaneous community uprisings. (All of which we witnessed in Sierra Leone and Liberia in the 1990s and early 2000s.) Take the following bizarre, but not uncommon, story from a newspaper account of fighting in the mining regions of the eastern part of the Democratic Republic of the Congo in late 2008: "The Mai Mai [a rural militia] insist that they are Congo's true patriots. . . . The Mai Mai now seem to have a beef with just about everybody: the rebels (whom they clashed with on Thursday); United Nations peacekeepers (whom they clashed with on Wednesday); and Congolese government troops (whom they clashed with on Tuesday)."[8]

All of this suggests that contemporary armed conflict (not only in Africa, but everywhere) may now be the site par excellence for exploring the dynamics of power that characterize the war machine and state. In fact, this is exactly what is happening within the circles of military thought. Whether or not they use the language of Deleuze and Guattari, those responsible for theorizing war and its futures—whether as outside observers or as military planners—are thinking in terms of war machines and states.

At least since Carl von Clausewitz wrote *On War* in the early 1800s, the metaphor of the machine has been used to understand the functioning of war and the actions of its belligerents. Clausewitz argued that "friction" is the force which distinguishes the theory from the practice of war, a force that "cannot, as in mechanics, be reduced to a few points, is everywhere in contact with chance, and brings about effects that cannot be measured" ([1832] 2007, 66). The "ratchet wheels," "pendulums," and "counterweights" of war generate their own unpredictable dynamics and produce effects in excess of what any military theorist, general, or politician might intend (see Strachan 2007, 142–43). Human protagonists launch wars by putting into motion the machines of their armies, but this violent assemblage of moving parts soon takes on a productive logic all its own.

As we move from the analog to the digital age, however, the machine image of war has been supplemented, if not replaced, by a more contemporary metaphor: the network. John Arquilla and David Ronfeldt of the RAND Corporation, in a study conducted for the U.S. Defense Department in 2001, argued that the future of war lies in the digital formation of acephalous (nonstate) mobilizations. Their book *Networks and Netwars* builds on a decade of research in which they coined and explored terms such as "cyberwar," "swarming," and "noopolitik" to describe a mode of violent organizing that does away with the hierarchies of conventional armies. In its stead we find decentralized operations on the model of the Internet. Like Deleuze and Guattari, Arquilla and Ronfeldt are interested in rhizomes. And just as actual war is only one possibility for the war machine of *A Thousand Plateaus* (and a rather poor one at that), Arquilla and Ronfeldt contend that the new mode of "netwar" does not result in pitched battles between armies. Instead it appears as organized crime, terrorist attacks, low-intensity conflicts, or even the civil unrest of protest movements like the Zapatistas or the anti–World Trade Organization demonstrations in Seattle in 1999.

The resemblance between Deleuze's and Guattari's thinking on the war machine and debates internal to military circles can be uncanny. Consider the following from the *New York Times* in mid-2003, as military theorists debated the implications of how the initial invasion of Iraq was conducted by United States forces and what it might mean for future war. Read it against the extended quote above from *A Thousand Plateaus* on the relationship between war machine and state as reflected in the difference between the games of chess and Go.

> The surprises in Saddam Hussein's campaign were consistent with the principles of netwar, which is less about sophisticated technology than about

> playing a different game: one not analogous to Western chess, but to the ancient Chinese board game known as Go, in which equal pieces can be placed anywhere on the board.
>
> In Go, the use of massed concentrations is to be avoided, especially in the early phases of a game, because assembling them wastes time and they are vulnerable to attack. Instead of massing his forces as he did in 1991, Saddam Hussein delegated extraordinary authority to area commanders, dispersed loyalists and paramilitaries in the southern cities, and relied on small, shifting guerrilla formation to attack the long supply lines needed by American infantry units rolling north toward Baghdad.[9]

The upshot is a proliferation in military thinking that emphasizes low-intensity conflict, often waged in spaces and at times that have not been officially declared war zones. The United States military's AFRICOM, which went fully operational on 1 October 2008, is a "civilian-military partnership."[10] Its mission is a complex mix of training support, disaster and humanitarian relief efforts, development assistance, and economic projects. "Bases? Garrisons? It's not about that," said General William Ward, the AFRICOM commander, in an interview at the operational launch. "We are trying to prevent conflict, as opposed to having to react to a conflict."[11] This thinking originates in what is sometimes referred to as the revolution in military affairs, a post-Vietnam autocritique within the United States military that sought to shift the emphasis in military strategy from large ground operations to high-technology weapons systems and smaller, flexible, and autonomous troop deployments. The perception that future war is more likely to be waged asymmetrically between states and nonstate networks like Al Qaeda furthered the view that the United States doesn't need an army so much as a "counternetwork" (Arquilla and Ronfeldt 2001). The massive deployments of United States troops in Iraq notwithstanding, the future of war (at least as envisioned in the United States) is one in which security forces abandon the doctrine of overwhelming force in favor of outsourcing violence to local surrogates and mirroring the tactics of so-called enemy networks. Speed, decentralization, nodal points, swarming—this is the new terminology of global security. Strategic state thinkers see themselves surrounded by war machines, and in an effort that truly does make this century feel Deleuzian, they are working to make state militaries resemble them through a complex apparatus of capture.

In the case of the Israeli Defense Force (IDF), this parallel to the Deleuzian language of war machines and rhizomes is literal. The architect and theorist Eyal Weizman (2006) conducted a series of interviews with officers in the IDF and with Palestinian activists in the aftermath of the 2002 Israeli Defensive Shield operations. Military thinkers at the IDF's Operational Theory Research Institute had developed a line of strategic thinking that was directly connected to their readings in critical theory, notably Deleuze and Guattari's *A Thousand Plateaus*.[12] In an interview Weizman conducted with the IDF brigadier general Shimon Naveh, director of the institute, Naveh describes the role Deleuze's and Guattari's work played in formulating a new approach to urban warfare and to combating Palestinian resistance: "It [*A Thousand Plateaus*] problematized our own paradigms. . . . Most important was the distinction they have pointed out between the concepts of 'smooth space' and 'striated' space . . . [that accordingly reflect] the organizational concepts of the 'war machine' and the 'state apparatus[.]' . . . In the IDF we now often use the term 'to smoothen out space' when we want to refer to an operation in a space as if it had no borders. We try to produce the operational space in such a manner that borders do not affect us" (quoted in Weizman 2006, 11). The result was a military incursion into Palestinian territories that relied on maneuvers *through* walls, barriers, and domestic spaces that would previously have been viewed as obstacles to move *around*. IDF soldiers began to think of themselves and of space differently. They were now "operational architects" (10) who blasted holes through walls, traversed living rooms, and avoided streets as they moved through Nablus and the Balata refugee camp. They met what they saw as the rhizomatic organization of the Palestinians with their own rhizomatic war machine. This was a formation that isn't simply representative of the kind of thought we find in Deleuze's and Guattari's writings on the war machine. In an eerie extension of Deleuze's own argument that theory should be a practitioner's toolbox (Deleuze 2004, 208), Operation Defensive Shield doesn't just *look like* a Deleuzian war machine, it is directly attributable to it.[13]

In short, the strange confusion between preference and fact that crept into the Special Court exchange with which I began this chapter has characterized the career of war machines more generally. Theory and practice have begun to overlap on today's battlefields in disconcerting ways. And the reach of the battlefield has expanded to encompass all manner of social domains. *A Thousand Plateaus* has become a prescriptive work as much as a descriptive one, and the war machines it describes are being actualized all over.[14]

All of this is fairly obvious to anyone paying attention to the global discourses on security and terrorism that circulate through policy circles and the media. What may be less obvious—but is perhaps most important to understand—is the place of Africa in this new regime of militarizing the world and the evolving dance of war machines and the state.

Anti-Oedipus in Africa

If Deleuze and Guattari and their war machines have both descriptive and prescriptive relations to existing war today, they are nevertheless profoundly challenging writers with whom to think about the contemporary moment. The world as it exists in *Capitalism and Schizophrenia*, for all its extensive reference to ethnological writings, is not obviously the world inhabited by anthropologists or those about whom they write. For one thing, while these texts are political commentaries they are so by way of a philosophical tradition. When they engage the anthropological literature it is to further philosophical (not anthropological) debates.[15] What's more, Deleuze and Guattari often eschew the vocabulary of social science and the humanities in favor of a new set of terms, or they use terms familiar to social theorists but in unfamiliar ways. The result is that it is not always clear whether the "nomads" and "savages" who inhabit these texts are ideal types to be strived for or rallied against, actual beings, past or present—or somehow a combination of each.

As Christopher Miller (1998) has pointed out, considerable intellectual capital is accrued in *Capitalism and Schizophrenia* through co-opting the labors of ethnographers. "Actual" nomads give credence to "virtual" theoretics. The result, Miller argues, is a strange contradiction. On the one hand Deleuze and Guattari argue against reading their work as anthropology. They maintain that the various figures they discuss—savage, nomad, despot, capitalist—refer to tendencies that may be found in any historical moment. They are nonrepresentational in that they do not necessarily relate to any specific ethnographic context. And yet they draw extensively from anthropological writings, and from specific ethnographic examples, to make their argument. What's more, as Miller notes (22), Deleuze's and Guattari's choices of ethnographic authorities sometimes have troubling implications. Besides their references to the work of Lévi-Strauss, de Heusch, Evans-Pritchard, and Fortes, Deleuze and Guattari draw on the "anthropological" writings of figures like Paul Ernest Joset, the colonial officer and amateur ethnologist charged with violently putting down the Kitawala resistance movement in the Belgian Congo. The most troubling consequence of this curious relation to the anthropological literature is that it would appear to disavow the realities of violence. In the spirit of celebrating the nomad and writing about a war machine whose ultimate purpose is not necessarily war, Deleuze and Guattari seem to be eliding the reality of war and the violent histories that are *also* evident from the anthropological texts and ethnographic contexts they employ. "This is characteristic of Deleuze and Guattari's happy talk revolution," Miller writes. "The benefits are advertised in the text, while the bodies are hidden. . . . Nomadological immunity makes it impossible to know if Deleuze and Guattari's nomad war machine actually kills people" (195, 205). This is a critique that has been voiced in multiple (if less stark) versions since the publication of *Capitalism and Schizophrenia* by authors uncomfortable with what appears to be an optimistic, even liberatory spin on social conditions (like schizophrenia or exile) that are often experienced as trauma by existing persons.[16]

Miller's point is well taken. Certainly it holds true that anyone who would read *Capitalism and Schizophrenia* as an unalloyed celebration of nomadism, or as (to use Miller's term) a "postidentitarian" manifesto, has failed to think through the full implications of Deleuze's and Guattari's work. François Cusset has argued that, at least among their American readers, "no one has really grasped the real political dimensions of their writings, in which *A Thousand Plateaus* stands as a veritable declaration of war" (2008, 282). Too many readers and interpreters have been caught up in the performative and aesthetic qualities of the work to genuinely wrestle with the political context of the argument or its potential implications for thinking about violence and social movements. And Deleuze and Guattari *do* at times seem to distance themselves from actual violence—from "the bodies." But there is no reason to evacuate the book of its violence, even if it has become custom to do so. Certainly by applying their work to the contexts I do, one has no such luxury.

What I argue for in the chapters that follow is the profound ambivalence that surrounds movements like the militias I describe here, and indeed any formation we might describe as a war machine. It is a mistake to be too celebratory of these "active" forces, even as we might recognize that they embody a certain liberatory potential. Anthropology, like a great deal of Deleuzian thought, has tended to romanticize its subjects, finding revolutionary potential in struggles against the forces (literal or figurative) of the state. What it has had trouble accounting for is the bodies. Not those generated by the reactive forces of power, but by those who would become active against them.

I HISTORIES

chapter 1

THE MANO RIVER WAR

A Chronology

THE MANO RIVER runs between Sierra Leone to the west and Liberia to the east. It is the (in)effective boundary between the two countries for more than half their shared border. The river cuts arbitrarily through ethnic, familial, and trade ties between the two countries, linking the nations as much as it divides them.

Accounts of the wars in Sierra Leone and Liberia (as well as the periodic violence in Guinea) typically explore the influence of one conflict on the other. More rarely are they treated as the same war. I do so here, and name that war after the river boundary between the states, to reflect the seminal role that border crossing and movement played in this conflict.[1] By this I mean movements of personnel, war materiel, financing, plunder, refugees, the infrastructure of nongovernmental organizations (NGOs), tactics, and ideas. This was a war in which the same actors appear on both banks of the river, a war in which events on one side can only really be understood in the context of events on the other.

The best histories of the conflict in this region begin their narratives well before the events of Christmas Eve 1989 when the National Patriotic Front of Liberia (NPFL) launched its first cross-border raid into Liberia.[2] War broke out in both countries after long stints of repressive rule and the deliberate marginalization of the "opposition" (real or imagined). In Sierra Leone the All People's Congress (APC) party ruled for twenty-four years in the mode of a textbook African dictatorship. The long-serving president, Siaka Stevens, passed power to his chosen successor, Joseph Momoh, in 1985, leaving a legacy of sham elections, real and fictive coup attempts, a patrimonial political and economic system, and a sense of acute alienation in the country's rural south and east. Liberia was rid of its long-ruling True Whig Party in 1980 when a military coup ended the hegemony of the party (though not the dominance of the Americo-Liberian elite who composed it [Reno 1998, 80–84]). However, the new Liberian president, Samuel Doe, put in its place an even more ethnically divisive and criminalized mode of politics that set the stage for war a decade later.

Structural forces facing both countries appear now as obvious predicates to the war to come. The relationships these two small but resource-rich West African states maintained with their colonial and neocolonial metropoles hardly lent themselves to long-term stability. The diamond industry in Sierra Leone, rubber and iron ore production in Liberia, and timber harvests in both nations were structured to concentrate most of the earnings in the hands of a small in-country elite and their partners overseas. Both countries were severely wracked by Cold War–era geopolitics, including the end of superpower patronage and the disastrous reforms demanded by international financial institutions in the 1980s. As A. B. Zack-Williams puts it, "In an ironic way, Foday Sankoh's infantile revolution [in Sierra Leone] aided the flight of skilled personnel out of the country by finishing the job begun a decade earlier by World Bank and IMF structural adjustment programs" (2002, 310). In both countries the deliberate impoverishment of much of the country by its domestic elite, combined with international interventions that were incompetent at best, exploitative at worst, guaranteed tragic outcomes for the majority of the region's population.

What follows is a brief chronology of key events in that tragic history. It is hardly exhaustive. The Mano River War was long and complex. There are others better positioned than I to tell that story in detail. What's more, a great deal of the book that follows is an effort to recount the history of the war in terms that are frequently omitted from narratives of this region. Like that of many anthropologists, my interest in history lies partly in telling it differently, partly in analyzing how various histories are deployed in the present. What may be most important to understand about the subject of this book, the region's militia movements, are the ways in which they escaped history. I am most concerned in the chapters that follow with the innovations and the experiments that could not necessarily have been predicted by history or existing cultural orders.

Nevertheless, as Stephen Lubkemann has argued, anthropologists (especially anthropologists of war) cannot help "actually 'doing history'" in the conventional sense of reconstructing a past (2008, 31). The alternative is to begin only with the violences of the present, to write ethnographies of war that treat violence ahistorically and reduce the nuanced life trajectories of existing people to characters in a just-so story of violence. Despite the valid critiques anthropology brings to the study of history, at some level the project of relating what happened, event by event, must be a central concern of the anthropology of war.

I therefore have two specific imperatives for "doing history" in this chapter. First, because the history of this war is so little known outside the region. Although Sierra Leone and Liberia briefly dominated the international news section of various world media outlets in the 1990s and early 2000s, for the most part this was not a war that was well covered or well understood. Even basic facts about the conflict are largely unknown outside the region and to a small group of experts and expats.

The second imperative behind including an "official" history chapter in this volume is that even among those who are familiar with the details of this conflict, those details are very rarely read synchronically across both sides of the Sierra Leone and Liberia border. While most observers acknowledge that events in Sierra Leone influenced those in Liberia, and vice versa, most studies focus on one conflict and present the other as background material. Yet as Morton Bøås and Kevin Dunn have argued, the way in which this war was "regionalized" tells us a great deal about the nature of postcolonial West Africa (2007, 36). It is only when we consider them together that we begin to understand the larger implications of this war for the future of this region and the future of the modes of militarization we find there.

The Invasions

This history of regional exploitation was the context in which Charles Taylor and the NPFL crossed the Ivorian border and attacked the town of Butou in Liberia's northern Nimba County at the end of 1989. The ethnic politics of Nimba County had grown increasingly violent in the preceding years as President Samuel Doe stoked ethnic tensions and marginalized Nimba County's Gio majority. If the particulars of the NPFL invasions were not predetermined, the likelihood of violence was.

Nimba was rife with rumors that major conflicts were coming (Ellis 1999, 72–73). There were clear signs that politicians and community leaders were prepared to fight back against Doe's government, and at least three factions or splinter factions outside the country were training recruits for armed assaults.

Taylor, a former bureaucrat in Doe's government, had been in exile since 1983. He was well positioned to launch an anti-Doe campaign. Taylor had spent the years before the invasion moving through a network of West African dissidents and interventionist politicians prepared to assist an armed effort in Liberia, a circle of anti-Doe actors that included Ivorian president Félix Houphouët-Boigny and Burkinabe president Blaise Compaore. Libyan president Moammar Gadaffi hosted both Taylor and Foday Sankoh, the eventual leader of the rebels in Sierra Leone, as well as other key figures in both wars, as part of an effort to establish a West African sphere of influence. Taylor benefited further from efforts by French businessmen in Côte d'Ivoire and members of the Lebanese diaspora throughout the region to solidify relations with Liberian exiles who might one day give them in-country access to Liberia's natural resources.

Though the NPFL has over the years become synonymous with Charles Taylor (an elision Taylor himself encouraged), in its earliest days it was a more amorphous, chaotic affair. As Stephen Ellis notes it is probably more accurate to call the NPFL a "network of armed dissidents than a political party or a guerrilla army . . . united by little except their dislike of Samuel Doe" (1999, 74).

Still, one of the keys to the NPFL's success is attributable to Taylor: a canny media strategy. Despite the relatively poor military quality of the NPFL, Taylor garnered early support in Nimba by announcing that the invasion was an extension of a popular but unsuccessful 1985 coup attempt. Taylor routinely phoned the BBC to update Liberia and the world about his advances across the country and his plans for Samuel Doe. With these phone calls, Taylor set a precedent that would become integral to the logic of this war for the next two decades: his most important weapons were the video camera and the satellite telephone.

The NPFL retained the character of a loosely coordinated network in these early days. Though it made rapid progress across Liberia, and had Monrovia surrounded by early July, there was already a splintering of forces. Prince Johnson, one of the more highly trained members of the leadership, broke with Taylor early on in the invasion and by July was leading what he called the Independent National Patriotic Front of Liberia (the INPFL). Johnson's INPFL was considerably smaller than Taylor's forces but better trained and more disciplined. Taylor by contrast had a larger contingent of foreign fighters, civilian supporters, and child soldiers, including his infamous Small Boys Unit. What's more, Taylor had extensive contacts with Liberians in the diaspora and non-Liberian supporters outside the country. By the time he laid siege to Monrovia in mid-1990, Taylor had brokered deals with companies interested in the timber, rubber, and iron ore resources that lay in territory he controlled and could be exported through the recently captured port.[3]

On 24 August 1990 a contingent of West African peacekeepers led by Nigerian troops arrived in Monrovia. The Economic Community of West African States (ECOWAS) voted to send in forces to stablize the country; at least in the opinion of ECOWAS's Anglophone members, the toppling of the Doe regime could potentially destablize the entire region.[4] The staging ground for ECOMOG (ECOWAS Monitoring Group) was the Sierra Leonean capital, Freetown, from which they entered the INPFL-held Freeport area of Monrovia. Unlike Taylor, Prince Johnson welcomed the intervention and agreed to work with the foreign troops, while ECOMOG and the NPFL immediately clashed on the city streets.

The relationship between Prince Johnson and ECOMOG set up one of the most surreal moments in a generally surreal war. A few days after a cease-fire agreement was brokered between Johnson and Doe, the Liberian president left the Executive Mansion and drove to ECOMOG headquarters. In what was either a carefully orchestrated plot by international forces, or "a tragic catalogue of misunderstandings, misjudgments, and coincidences" (Ellis 1999, 5), Doe was captured by INPFL forces. Over the next several days, the Liberian president was tortured and eventually executed, an ordeal famously captured on videos that still circulate around West Africa.

In the wake of Doe's killing an ECOWAS settlement established an interim government under President Amos Sawyer. Taylor, meanwhile, set up a capital for what he called Greater Liberia at the northern city of Gbarnga, and for the remainder of 1990 consolidated his grip on the majority of the country.

Life for civilians in Greater Liberia could be terrifying. The NPFL presence was most evident at the numerous "gates" erected on major roads, checkpoints through which civilians had to pass Taylor's poorly trained and undisciplined troops. This, too, was a pattern to be repeated through much of the next two decades. Roadblocks and ambushes were the primary sites of encounter between civilians, rebels, and security forces, and it was here that much of the violence of the war took place. Regular "taxation," outright looting, violence, and arbitrary executions were a part of the logic of these barriers. Given the relatively small number of large-scale operations (relatively few, at least, given the length of the conflict), these microencounters made up the fabric of the war on both sides of the border.

The regional impact of the Liberian war was evidenced not only by the ECOWAS intervention. Refugees from Liberia fled the fighting across the borders of Sierra Leone, Guinea, and Côte d'Ivoire, and expatriates from those countries who were living and working in Liberia moved back across the border. By October 1990 there were rumors in Freetown of the recruitment of Liberian Mandingo and Krahn youth living outside Liberia to join an armed resistance to Taylor. In February 1991, a Liberian politician in Conakry, Guinea, Alhaji Kromah, announced the formation of the Movement for the Redemption of Muslims (MRM), a nakedly Mandingo nationalist project dedicated to the defeat of Taylor. Taylor himself fanned the regional flames as he continued to strategically deploy the BBC as a weapon. He announced, for example, that he was prepared to attack and destroy Freetown's Lungi Airport as a legitimate military target for its use as a staging area by ECOMOG forces. And in the final days of 1990 and the early months of 1991, there were at least three NPFL attacks on villages within Sierra Leone itself.[5]

It was the cross-border attack on 23 March 1991, however, that truly inaugurated the Sierra Leone front of the war. A group calling itself the Revolutionary United Front (RUF) launched assaults on two border villages in the Kailahun district. As with Taylor's NPFL assault on Liberia, the RUF entered Sierra Leone with a small group of fighters, a mixture of Burkinabes, NPFL-affiliated Liberians, and Sierra Leonean exiles. Foday Sankoh, the Taylor associate who would emerge as the RUF's leader, had foreshadowed the attack in a call to the BBC a few weeks earlier. He promised listeners a revolution if President Momoh refused to step down. Drawing on the populist, revolutionary rhetoric that he would invoke throughout the war, Sankoh announced that the "people's armed struggle" against the APC had begun (quoted in Gberie 2005, 59).

Within a week the RUF had attacked much larger towns in the east and within a month had captured virtually all of Kailahun. As with the NPFL in Liberia, the RUF initially had significant popular support in the rural Kailahun District. Though its ethnic politics were not as divisive as in Liberia under Doe, the APC was viewed as a party of northerners that had deliberately marginalized much of the south and east. Popular RUF support did not last, but even late in the war Mendes from the Kailahun region (including many who fought against the RUF) maintained that the initial RUF invasion was necessary and justified.

As soon as word reached Freetown of the RUF attack, the former Liberian ambassador to Sierra Leone under Doe, General Albert Karpeh, offered to assist the Sierra Leonean government in the defeat of the RUF and NPFL in Sierra Leone. Karpeh mobilized Liberian refugees and Armed Forces of Liberia veterans who had scattered throughout Sierra Leone with the fall of Doe, naming his new force the Liberian United Defense Force (LUDF). With some assistance from the government in terms of weapons and materiel, the LUDF began to deploy alongside Sierra Leone Army forces.

By the end of May 1991, the LUDF had merged with Alhaji Kromah's MRM and other dissident Liberians. The combined force, United Liberation Movement for Democracy in Liberia (ULIMO), was to be a major factor in the war on both sides of the border. In its early days, ULIMO received support from the governments of Sierra Leone, Guinea, and Nigeria (via ECOMOG), as well as from Liberians throughout the region. Under the military leadership of General Karpeh and the political leadership of Alhaji Kromah, ULIMO forces were more or less headquartered in the eastern Sierra Leonean town of Kenema but deployed around the country.

Repeating the pattern in Liberia, the Sierra Leonean government's initial responses to the poorly organized and untrained RUF were haphazard. It was not until the end of 1991 that President Momoh launched a concerted counteroffensive. The small Sierra Leone Armed Forces (deliberately kept small by the APC to prevent it becoming a threat to the state) was rapidly expanded by the conscription of urban youth sent to the front with little training or support. Not unlike that of the NPFL or the RUF, the picture that emerges at this point is of a state security force best described as a network of semi-independent operators rather than a highly structured and centralized fighting force. Many frontline troops acted independently from military headquarters in Freetown. Some of the more innovative (or desperate) commanders like Captain Prince Ben-Hirsch in the Segbwema region recruited local youth to serve as guides, support personnel, and even irregular combatants. With the armed forces undermanned, underresourced, and largely unfamiliar with the areas in which they were deployed (another government tactic to prevent the army from achieving credibility or strength), the use of irregulars was almost inevitable.

Which is not to say that it was popular with the military as a whole. Some of the most successful operations conducted by the anti-RUF forces relied heavily on nonprofessional or at least nonstate troops. By October 1991 ULIMO forces, many receiving extra weapons and training from the Guinean military, had pushed the RUF out of Pujehun District in the southeast. Captain Ben-Hirsch's "Airborne Division" of irregulars was at least moderately successful further north. Whether by design or simple ineffectiveness, the Sierra Leone Army itself made more modest progress, and at least some within the military began working actively against the pro-government forces. In late 1991 Ben-Hirsch was murdered by enemies within the armed forces.

Eyewitnesses to attacks throughout the east of Sierra Leone routinely comment on the large numbers of Liberians involved, and many (including, somewhat disingenuously, Foday Sankoh himself) attribute some of the worst violence to Liberian mercenaries. Taylor is said to have committed his fiercest troops to the RUF, whether to protect himself from them or to make the undertrained Sierra Leonean recruits in the RUF more effective. By the early part of 1992, however, Taylor had recalled most of the NPFL fighters operating with the RUF in response to an incursion by ULIMO into Liberia itself.[6] From that point forward, the RUF was primarily a Sierra Leonean force, though one that received considerable support from Charles Taylor.

The Coup

On 29 April 1992, President Momoh was ousted. The military coup ended the APC's long reign and installed Captain Valentine Strasser and the National Provisional Ruling Council (NPRC) as the new government. The overthrow was a haphazard affair, largely the work of junior officers from a single battalion based in Kenema. It is a measure of the discontent with Momoh that the Special Security Division (SSD), the specialized security force that straddled the military and police and served as the president's paramilitary, seems to have backed the military rather than attempting to protect the president (Keen 2005, 94). At least in Freetown, the NPRC coup was met with a certain amount of enthusiasm (Opala 1994), heralding a new dawn for the country that would be unfortunately short lived.

In theory, with the APC overthrow the RUF lost its reason for war. The rebels had been pushed back from many of their initial conquests and support from Taylor was not as forthcoming as it had been due to his preoccupations with ECOMOG and ULIMO in Liberia. In May the RUF declared a cease-fire and it seemed as if the war, at least in Sierra Leone, might be over.

Yet the NPRC elected to step up attacks on the rebels and the RUF soon renewed its own offensives. The army's ranks had swelled dramatically under Momoh's efforts to recruit youth for the battlefront, and ULIMO had similarly grown with the mobilization of Liberian refugees. By some accounts the RUF was genuinely taken aback by the NPRC's refusal to negotiate, suggesting that even at this early stage of the war there were informal agreements and collaborations between the military and the RUF (see, in particular, Keen 2005, 94–96). Others have noted that the RUF's continuation of the war belies whatever claims Sankoh and others made about the purpose of their "revolution"; theirs was never an ideological struggle or a political project of reforming the government of Sierra Leone (Abdullah 1998; Kpundeh 2004).

Whatever their purpose, the rebels in both Sierra Leone and Liberia were aided by intense factionalism in the opposing forces. ULIMO, which had been operating on both sides of the border, split into two factions when Alhaji Kromah orchestrated the murder of General Karpeh at his Kenema home. One of Karpeh's loyalists, Roosevelt Johnson, soon emerged as the leader of ULIMO-J, while a pro-Kromah faction came to be known as ULIMO-K. The split occurred along ethnic lines (Kromah leading the Mandingo faction and Johnson the Krahn), and both sides received assistance from patrons within the Sierra Leone security establishment. One of the major fault lines between the two groups was control over the cross-border diamond trade that ULIMO leaders used to pay for weapons from their Sierra Leonean military supporters (Ellis 1999, 96).

In Liberia, the interim government and ECOMOG managed to keep a hold on Monrovia while Taylor consolidated power in the countryside and fought the ULIMO incursion. Although supposedly a neutral peacekeeping force, ECOMOG favored the anti-Taylor coalition. In response, on 15 October Taylor launched a devastating assault on Monrovia. Operation Octopus unleashed a massive wave of violence throughout October and November. Taylor and a small contingent of INPFL forces battled a coalition of ECOMOG troops, rearmed AFL fighters, pro-interim-government militias, and the bulk of the INPFL faction. Together the latter managed to drive the NPFL from the city, but ECOMOG's counterinsurgency measures throughout November became even more highly partisan in opposition to Taylor and devastating to the civilian population of the city and its surroundings.

Late 1992 was also a confusing period in the relationship between factions in Sierra Leone. The state security forces, swollen by new recruits and bolstered by ULIMO and other foreign factions, became increasingly predatory. Civilians, especially in the resource-rich areas of the country, were routinely rounded up and displaced, allowing for a high level of mischief by soldiers. Looting and illicit mining were widespread. The government continued to rely on the inexpensive ULIMO fighters (who were supported financially in part by Liberian expatriates [see Keen 2005, 97]) and on other irregular troops who did not receive a fixed salary. The result was a relatively cost-effective fighting force, but one which could be unpredictable and untrustworthy in the extreme.

Both explicitly and through tacit agreement, poorly supported front-line troops collaborated with the RUF, leading to the Krio colloquialism *sobel*, or soldier-rebel. Illicit diamond trading, informal war "taxes" imposed on the civilian populace, and outright looting erased the difference between members of the state security force and the rebels they supposedly fought against. This relationship would become stronger in the coming years, but already by this early stage in the war it was clear that this was not a war between a recognizable rebel faction and the forces of the state.

For civilians in the rural parts of Sierra Leone, this obvious fact generated countermeasures that would prove crucial in the coming years. Captain Ben-Hirsch's Airborne Division was only one of a number of efforts to draw local men into auxiliary forces that could support (and in some cases replace) the Sierra Leone Army. The most successful early deployment of pro-government irregulars occurred in the northern Koinadugu District, where an NPRC lieutenant by the name of Komba Kambo collaborated with occult specialists to mobilize area men as trackers and gunners. The *tamaboros*, as these fighters were known, were prepared for their encounters with the RUF by rituals intended to combat the rumored occult powers of the rebels. Once the protections proved effective, a local occult expert, Daembaso Samura, was pressed upon along with a few others to begin "washing" groups of fighters in protective medicines (Gberie 2005, 82; M. Jackson 2004, 143–44).

The tamaboros were not a large force. Caspar Fithen estimates that they could not have numbered more than a few thousand (1999, 207), and one former tamaboro described to me a handful of units of a few hundred men. Yet they were surprisingly successful. Tamaboros played key roles in taking the Njaima-Seawfe Bridge near Koidu in late 1992 (Tostevin 1993) and in offensives in Kailahun in early 1993 (Muana 1997, 81).

In December 1992, a second civil defense group was formed in the Kenema district. With the assistance of the NPRC's secretary of state east, Tom Nyuma, the Eastern Region Defence Committee (EREDCOM) was established by local elites intent on creating their own defensive body. Dr. Alpha Lavalie, a university lecturer and Mende nationalist who had long advocated for stronger Mende independence from the APC-dominated state, was named the head of EREDCOM, with the assistance of Joe Demby, a Kenema-based doctor who would go on to become the vice-president of Sierra Leone.

EREDCOM was set up to mobilize Mende *kamajoisia*, the southeastern counterparts of the tamaboro in the north. Like the tamaboro, the *kamajoh* or *kamajo* (sing.) was an existing social category prior to the war. Empowered to carry firearms in the bush and to draw on occult knowledge and protective medicine, the kamajoisia historically had a role protecting rural communities from the threats of the forest. (I take up this prewar history in greater detail in the next chapter.) EREDCOM and similar efforts elsewhere in the south and east were early attempts to bring these figures together and to coordinate their efforts with those of loyal elements in the state military. The result was significant military gains. By January 1993 the RUF in Pujehun was limited largely to a single chiefdom. By March a combined NPRC and tamaboro force had taken an important rebel base at Woama outside Koidu, and a month later drove the RUF from Pendembu in the east.

However, as David Keen (2005) makes clear in a detailed analysis of the role of the security forces in Sierra Leone, it is one of the peculiar dynamics of this conflict that at exactly those moments when government forces were most successful, the tide of the war turned in favor of the rebels. There were those in the state military for whom a continued war and a continued relationship with the rebels was simply more profitable than peace. In early 1993 a land mine planted at Mano Junction killed Alpha Lavalie and severely hampered the EREDCOM initiative; it was widely suspected that Lavalie's death came at the hands of his "partners" in the Sierra Leone military. When pro-government fighters began to move against the last rebel stronghold in Soro Gbema chiefdom, the result was serious tensions with the military in Pujehun (113). When a tamaboro unit in Tonkolili arrested a group of soldiers on the grounds that they had deserted the army and begun preying on local communities, tensions with the army deepened in the north as well. A few months later, a massive RUF attack on Kabala, the main headquarters of the tamaboro, all but ended the movement when two of its major occult leaders, Samura and Mariama Keita, were killed. The Kabala attack was almost certainly facilitated by the Sierra Leone Army (Gberie 2005, 83; M. Jackson 2004, 144).

Just as the RUF seemed to succeed when its prospects looked most dim, so too did the NPFL in Liberia. In early 1993 ECOMOG retook the port of Buchanan from Charles Taylor's forces, while ULIMO and a new force, the Liberia Peace Council, claimed more and more of Taylor's territory. Apparently recognizing that absent an intervention and cease-fire he risked losing completely, Taylor and other NPFL leaders orchestrated a massive execution of civilians at Carter Camp in the Firestone Plantation and at Duport Road in the suburbs of Monrovia. Some six hundred people were killed in the attacks, which were initially (and erroneously) blamed on AFL forces. The upshot was exactly what Taylor hoped for: a cease-fire negotiated the next month under international pressure. According to the agreement, the interim government would be dissolved in favor of a Liberian national transitional government which would include both the NPFL and ULIMO; United Nations military observers would monitor the agreement and preparations would be made for elections and for a constitutional government. The cease-fire, however, did little to stop the fighting. The factions recognized in the Cotonou agreement negotiated with one another over the terms of peace, while simultaneously waging a proxy war through surrogates like the Liberia Peace Council (supported by ECOMOG and the AFL) and the newly formed Lofa Defense Force (supported by the NPFL).

Surrogate forces had become the order of the day. Throughout 1994 increasing numbers of kamajoisia were mobilized in the south and east of Sierra Leone. Communities in the far south set up patrols and checkpoints to secure villages against attacks by both the RUF and the military, and chiefs and other elites within the internally displaced persons (IDP) camps of the east began to organize men into civil defense units. These were not necessarily coordinated efforts, though a number of key figures were associated with these mobilizations and carried word of the successful organization of defense throughout Mende country.

One of these key figures was the regent chief of Jaiama-Bongor Chiefdom, Samuel Hinga Norman. Norman was appointed regent of the chiefdom not far from Bo by the NPRC in 1994. A graduate of British officer training and a former captain in the Sierra Leone Army, Norman claimed that the NPRC tapped him to serve as regent precisely because of his military background and ability to coordinate the defenses of the chiefdom. As in so many instances, however, this did not protect Norman or the pro-government forces. On 30 June 1994, a combined force of RUF and soldiers from Bo and Koribundu attacked the chiefdom headquarters of Telu, where Norman was overseeing the training of a group of kamajoisia from neighboring chiefdoms, killing a majority of the new recruits.

Mobilizations of the kamajoisia were not the only community defense efforts during this period. In the later months of 1994, residents of the eastern city of Kenema organized patrols and checkpoints, largely to defend against the abuses of government forces. Villages around the country mounted nightly patrols and erected checkpoints around their communities. Among the best known of these so-called vigilante operations were the apparently random uprisings in Bo in December 1994 and a mobilization a few months later in Kenema during which a variety of civic organizations (ranging from the Poro men's society to local youth football clubs) served as the basis for organizing community defenses against both RUF and military attacks.[7]

1995–1996

Over the course of 1995 both fronts of the Mano River War changed significantly. Sani Abacha, less hostile to Charles Taylor than his predecessor in the Nigerian presidency, General Ibrahim Babangida, brokered a power-sharing arrangement between the various Liberian factions in anticipation of national elections. In a strange twist, Taylor returned to Monrovia at the end of August, now under the protection of ECOMOG troops.

Taylor's political machinations in the capital resulted in massive fighting in Monrovia in April 1996. By the time his main opposition, Roosevelt Johnson's loyalists in ULIMO-J, had been reduced to one major holding in the capital, two thousand to three thousand people had died. It was clear that if Johnson was defeated there would be no opposition strong enough to prevent Taylor from taking over the entire country. Factions within ECOMOG, assisted by the United States through the Pacific Architects and Engineers logistical support teams, began to arm ULIMO-J against Taylor and the NPFL. In a development that seemed perfectly in keeping with the cynical logic of this war, at this point Nigeria was supporting both sides of the conflict. (See Ellis 1999, 108, for a detailed account of the battle for Monrovia.)

The first months of 1995 were also significant in Sierra Leone. The civil mobilizations to protect rural communities continued, especially in the south and east. Hinga Norman escaped the attack on his training base at Telu and became a galvanizing figure for kamajoisia mobilizations throughout Bo, Bonthe, and Kenema districts. As 1995 progressed, more and more young men were nominated by community leaders to take part in efforts to protect civilians at the chiefdom level and within the region's IDP camps. In addition to the increasing prominence of community leaders like Norman in organizing civil defenses, a group of ritual specialists in the south grew more visible for their role in preparing occult protections. Men like Allieu Kundewa in Bonthe, Saddam Shariff in Pujehun, and Brima Bangura in Kenema were invited to various chiefdoms to wash local fighters with powerful medicine (*hale* in Mende) that would protect them in battle.

While rural irregular mobilizations had some success they did not stop a series of high-profile RUF attacks. On 18 and 19 January, RUF fighters, apparently working closely with members of the military, attacked and looted Sieromco and Sierra Rutile in Moyamba District. The two sites were among the last of Sierra Leone's mining operations (bauxite and rutile) still held securely in government hands, and among the last sources of foreign capital from which the government could draw funds for the prosecution of the war.[8] January also saw a noteworthy attack on the campus of Njala University College, long perceived as a bastion of opposition to the APC and NPRC. A month later, rebels took the town of Mile 38, very close to Freetown. They were quickly repelled by an overwhelming NPRC assault, aided by Nigerian ECOMOG troops and a helicopter gunship manned by Ukrainian pilots. As Lansana Gberie (2005) notes, it was the last time (at least until the 1997 coup) that the RUF attempted to take and hold a major town on the route in and out of Freetown. Instead, "the tactic was now to hit, destroy and run," Gberie writes. "The carnage was unrelenting" (92).

In May, the Sierra Leonean government tried yet another source of foreign intervention. Executive Outcomes (EO) was a South African firm employing former soldiers with the South African Defence Force 32 Battalion. The bulk of EO's personnel were black Namibian and Angolan veterans of the apartheid government's campaigns in southern Africa. EO's officers were primarily white. EO made its reputation in the private security business by successfully protecting diamondiferous regions in Angola. In fact, Strasser was apparently made aware of EO after reading about the company's Angola work in *Newsweek* and *Soldier of Fortune* magazines (E. Rubin 1997), and was encouraged to hire it by international mining interests with complex financial interests in EO and its partner corporations.

EO helped the pro-government forces make rapid advances in Sierra Leone. Its 150 troops conducted training exercises with members of the Sierra Leone Army and the kamajoisia. It coordinated attacks on the RUF with the army and with Nigerian and Guinean troops. Relying heavily on its helicopter gunships, EO allowed the alliance of state security forces, foreign troops, and local militias to challenge the RUF on multiple fronts at once. The private security contractors brought a level of communications and intelligence coordination that had largely been missing from the conflict to that point.

EO also brought a great deal of complicated politics to an already complex political situation. One of the Sierra Leonean government's principal liaisons to the company was Brigadier Julius Maada Bio. On 15 January 1996, Bio led a successful coup against Valentine Strasser. EO's fifteen million dollar contract was a significant investment for the cash-strapped Sierra Leonean government, and much of the payment was made by redirecting funds from the World Bank and International Monetary Fund and by granting the company a large diamond concession in the east. EO's activities proved to be a complicating factor in cease-fire talks between the NPRC and RUF and in the efforts to return Sierra Leone to civilian rule; under international pressure the NPRC had agreed to hold elections in 1996, but apparently hoped that the cease-fire and continuing peace talks would allow it to postpone the vote. EO's corporate leaders have claimed, implausibly, that they insisted on democratic elections as a condition of their contract, while the RUF refused to support a full cease-fire and elections unless the EO contract was terminated and its forces withdrawn.

Despite the RUF and NPRC efforts elections did take place and in March 1996 Ahmed Tejan Kabbah and the Sierra Leone People's Party (SLPP) took power in a new civilian government. The SLPP had a long history in Sierra Leone, having been the party in power at Sierra Leone's independence in 1961. During the APC period the SLPP was relegated to the provinces and identified primarily with Mendes in the south and east. Its victory in the 1996 elections was not particularly surprising given the disastrous record of the APC and the NPRC, but it did put the government at odds with its own military, which was still dominated by northerners and Freetown-based elites.

The distrust between the SLPP and the army was exacerbated by the SLPP's support of the kamajoisia as a security force. President Kabbah named Norman his deputy defense minister (the president himself being the constitutional minister of defense), and Norman made no secret of his efforts to mobilize and train kamajoisia for every chiefdom in the south and east. Throughout 1996 there were clashes between the military and these irregulars, a situation that worsened considerably as the year wore on.

In November, Kabbah traveled to Abidjan to sign yet another peace accord with the RUF. Signing the accord did nothing to lessen the tensions between the Kabbah government (including the kamajoisia) and the military. By early 1997 the ranks of irregular fighters had swelled considerably; by some estimates there may have been as many as fifteen thousand to twenty thousand pro-government militia fighters by March. In April the Sierra Leone parliament voted to legalize the use of arms by hunter militias, a move the military deeply resented. The army chief of staff is alleged to have issued "shoot-to-kill" orders to army personnel in situations of conflict with irregulars, and there were very public, violent confrontations between the forces in Kenema, Kambia, and

Pujehun districts. A conflagration in the town of Kenema on 1 May resulted in over a hundred combatants killed, apparently after soldiers attempted to block the wedding procession of a militia leader (see Fithen 1999, 223; Gberie 2005, 100; Henry 2000, 42).

Even as tensions with the military increased, under Norman's leadership the kamajoisia were becoming a more coherent organization. The Mende terminology for irregular fighters became more Anglicized and standardized. Kamajor (sing.) and kamajors (pl.) became the conventional reference for the force in the local and international press and in government documents. The process for joining the movement was also more standardized. Where the use of medicines to make the bodies of kamajor fighters immune to the bullets of their enemies had always been part of kamajor practice, joining the movement was increasingly marked by initiation by a ritual specialist. Beginning with the appointment of Norman to the SLPP government, the sense of joining a collective body, albeit a decentralized one, grew increasingly important.

The Armed Forces Revolutionary Council

At the end of May 1997, the tensions between the SLPP and the military came to a head. Government troops from upcountry, especially the Tongo Field diamond region, had been returning to Freetown over the previous weeks. On 25 May a group of soldiers broke into the capital's Pademba Road Prison and released some six hundred inmates, including Major Johnny Paul Koroma, who became the new head of state when the soldiers announced their takeover of the government and President Kabbah fled to exile in Guinea.

The Armed Forces Revolutionary Council (AFRC) immediately suspended the constitution, banned demonstrations, abolished political parties, and outlawed the kamajors.[9] In a move that finally made official the relationship between the RUF and factions within the military, the AFRC invited the RUF to enter into a power-sharing agreement. Foday Sankoh was named as the vice-chairman of the AFRC and the combined force was named "The People's Army" (though this was a title little used by anyone outside the combined force itself).[10] Sankoh was, however, prevented from taking up his new post when he was placed under house arrest in Nigeria.

The AFRC immediately went on the offensive against the kamajors and other civil defense bodies. In June AFRC forces razed Telu to the ground. A peaceful demonstration in Freetown by unions and NGOs was violently put down in August, and there were clashes between AFRC forces and mobilized students and faculty at Fourah Bay College. In parts of the rural south and east, kamajors and a small number of loyal army units were able to guard territory against the AFRC/RUF, but communication and coordination between these forces was weak.

Not long after the AFRC took power violently in Sierra Leone, an equally stunning turn of events took place in Liberia: Charles Taylor and his newly christened National Patriotic Party (NPP) won national elections, giving Taylor the presidency and the NPP a majority in both houses of the National Assembly. In what international observers grudgingly acknowledged was probably a legitimate electoral victory, Taylor at last took his seat in the Executive Mansion in Monrovia.[11]

By this point the always porous border between Sierra Leone and Liberia became even more so. Taylor, who despite periodic tensions with Foday Sankoh had never ceased to support the RUF, continued to act as a conduit for weapons and materiel flowing into Sierra Leone and for diamonds and other resources flowing out. Sanctions by the Commonwealth and a general international refusal to recognize the AFRC meant that this relationship with Liberia was crucial to the AFRC as a source of foreign cash.

Conversely, Liberia became the staging post for the armed resistance to the Sierra Leonean junta while the political leadership remained in Guinea. ECOMOG forces still controlled a great deal of Liberia, including the southwestern border at the Mano River Bridge. It was here that kamajors from inside Sierra Leone gathered to prepare a coordinated effort to reinstate the Kabbah government with materiel and training from ECOMOG. Operating from the villages of Gendema on the Sierra Leonean side and Bo Waterside (or Bo Njala) on the Liberian side, kamajor forces attacked Zimmi and made forays further into Pujehun District. Hinga Norman traveled between Conakry, where Kabbah and his government in exile were based; Monrovia, where he liaised with expatriate Sierra Leoneans and with ECOMOG officers; and the border. These travels generated the funding and military hardware used to bolster the growing number of kamajors who came to "Base One" at the Mano River Bridge. Some stayed for extended periods, others came as representatives of community mobilizations throughout the south and east attempting to organize resistance to the brutal AFRC forces. The kamjors were made part of a larger umbrella organization, the Civil Defence Force, a broad coalition of ethnically based militias which included what remained of the Kuranko tamaboros, the Temne *gbethis* and *kapras*, and the Kono *donsos*. Of these, the kamajors remained by far the largest and most influential force.

In September, Norman relocated to the village of Talia in the Yawbeko Chiefdom of southern Bonthe. Bonthe had seen some of the earliest and most successful community mobilizations against the AFRC. Paramount chiefs, elites, and fighters from throughout the south began to assemble at Talia at the invitation of local chiefs, and Norman was called to join them and coordinate the resistance.

There were a number of reasons for Norman to relocate to Talia, or what soon came to be known as Base Zero. In testimony before the Special Court, British colonel Richard Iron maintains that Norman was advised by ECOMOG to operate from a more strategic location than the far eastern border area if he hoped to overthrow the junta. CDF personnel at Gendema maintain that Norman grew frustrated by the kamajors' failure to capture the town of Zimmi, and that tensions between Norman and the popular regional commander Eddie Massalley had reached a boiling point. Fearing that he might lose control over the movement, Norman attempted to move the center of the resistance outside of Massalley's sphere of influence. These tensions were apparently exacerbated by the presence at Gendema of a growing number of Liberian fighters connected to Massalley who did not share the Sierra Leoneans' allegiance to Norman.

Throughout late 1997, kamajors from the south and east traveled to Base Zero and Base One to meet with Mende elders, ask for material support, and, to the extent possible, coordinate their activity. Although there were large-scale assaults on some of the major towns in the region (Zimmi was eventually taken by the kamajors, and there were assaults on Koribundu, Tongo, Bo, and Kenema), the most concerted effort on the part of the CDF to remove the junta was a campaign called Black December. Working with ECOMOG and with South Africans who had stayed on in Sierra Leone after the Executive Outcomes contract was canceled (and who continued to use an EO helicopter gunship), the CDF attempted in Black December to shut down the major roadways, preventing the

AFRC from moving logistic supplies out of Freetown and isolating its upcountry units.

Estimates of the strength of the CDF at this point vary. Norman and the CDF leadership routinely claimed that the CDF had ninety-nine thousand men under their control, a figure that is no doubt wildly exaggerated. Other observers have speculated that there might have been thirty thousand to thirty-five thousand CDF fighters across the country at this time (Fofana 1998, 12–13; Zack-Williams 1999, 152). Testimony before the Special Court and reports of other eyewitnesses suggest that there were between one thousand and five thousand CDF fighters at Base Zero alone, though this number would have fluctuated greatly given the rapidity with which young men cycled in and out of Talia Yawbeko. This points to a larger problem in estimating the number of kamajors throughout the war: many young men, especially in the rural areas, mobilized to defend their communities for short periods, even going through some variation of a kamajor initiation. But the vast majority then demobilized just as quickly and were never formally recognized by either the government or the CDF hierarchy.

Although Norman was coordinating efforts to return the Kabbah government to power, the coup strained the already tense relationship between him and the president. Norman complained bitterly that Kabbah did not provide sufficient support to the kamajors, and hoped instead for a negotiated end to AFRC rule. Though he did authorize some funds for Norman's efforts, Kabbah in return seems to have feared that Norman was raising a private army and would simply replace the AFRC with the CDF, with Norman himself the new president. Norman stoked these fears by nakedly discussing his desire to "someday" be president of Sierra Leone and by telling multiple audiences that the CDF would need to impose three years of martial law before it would be safe to fully restore the constitution.

This was evidently a concern for the ECOMOG force commander, the Nigerian general Maxwell Khobe. Khobe made at least one trip to Talia to coordinate the Black December operation with Norman and to plot an airlift of kamajors to Freetown. As it happened, when Khobe and the Nigerians did launch their attack on the city in February, they did so largely without the CDF. By some accounts it took Norman by surprise when he was not included in the liberation of the capital, but in any case the simultaneous CDF pressure on the AFRC and RUF upcountry does appear to have kept the junta from bringing in reinforcements to defend the city. On 10 March 1998, President Kabbah returned to Freetown. Johnny Paul Koroma, many of his AFRC soldiers, and the RUF fled the capital, some retreating across the Liberian border and others dispersing throughout Sierra Leone.

The Restoration and 6 January

Shortly after his reinstatement in Freetown, President Kabbah took two important steps to bolster state security. First, he named Khobe as his army chief of staff, placing him in charge of the loyal remnants of the army. Second, he formally placed the CDF under the control of ECOMOG (Hirsch 2001, 123).

The United Nations entered the political landscape in a more significant way after Kabbah's return. Security Council Resolution S/RES/1181 was adopted in July, establishing the United Nations Observer Mission in Sierra Leone (UNOMSIL). The unarmed mission was meant to assist ECOMOG in disarming combatants, which it did with limited success over the subsequent months. (Only 2,145 combatants were officially disarmed and registered by the time phase one of the process was declared complete in September.) Shortly thereafter, however, RUF and AFRC fighters began once again making major advances across the country. ECOMOG troops in the town of Koidu in the diamondiferous east were soundly defeated, apparently caught unawares as they mined diamonds. By Christmas the town of Makeni was once again controlled by the rebels, and attacks had been launched on Waterloo and Benguema, not far from the capital.

The single most violent campaign of the entire Sierra Leonean front of the war may have been the three weeks of fighting inaugurated by the AFRC and RUF in Freetown on 6 January 1999. The goal of Operation No Living Thing does not appear to have been the recapture of Freetown, but its destruction.[12] Despite the presence of some fifteen thousand Nigerian soldiers in Sierra Leone, and a large contingent of CDF fighters barracked in Freetown (albeit many of them disarmed), the rebels moved rapidly through the eastern half of the city. In the aftermath of 6 January, there has been speculation that ECOMOG commanders knew the rebels were planning a massive attack. There were serious tensions between the former ECOMOG commander, Maxwell Khobe, and other top ECOMOG officials, and combatants involved in the defense of the city have long maintained that ECOMOG allowed the invasion as a way to discredit Khobe in his new role as the army chief of staff.

In any case, the level of destruction in the Kissy and other eastern neighborhoods was staggering. Units known as "Cut Hands" or "Burn House" brigades lived up to their names. The amputation of civilian limbs, a practice engaged in by the rebels throughout the war, seem to have been most widespread during the 6 January invasion. And not surprisingly, given the history of the state military in Sierra Leone, much of the most horrific violence was committed by former soldiers.

There was also foreign support for the attack. Charles Taylor allegedly committed two thousand NPFL commandos to the operation (Keen [2005, 229], citing *Africa Confidential* reports from 12 May 2000 and 22 January 1999). Herbert Howe writes that the attack bore the trademark tactical planning of South African military strategists, and suggests that former Executive Outcomes personnel had begun working for Taylor training the NPFL and RUF (Howe 2001, 221). Eyewitnesses to the events of 6 January reported seeing white mercenaries, apparently Ukranians, directing units in the city center.[13]

Rebel forces managed to push their way through Freetown as far as the Congo Cross Bridge, where a combined ECOMOG and CDF force finally halted their progress. CDF fighters from upcountry were airlifted to the capital to bolster defenses. A former United States Embassy official described watching as planes chartered to fly embassy staff out of the country first offloaded CDF fighters before filling them with expatriates from the United States and Europe bound for Guinea. Others arrived on a leftover EO helicopter. Former EO personnel also played a decisive role by ferrying supplies in support of the ECOMOG defense. The progovernment forces successfully held the western sector of the city, and after a prolonged standoff eventually began to retake downtown and then the city's east.[14]

The movement of troops across the Liberian border at the behest of President Taylor was answered by a new opposition force entering Liberia. Liberians United for Reconciliation and Democracy (LURD) was formed in Guinea and Sierra Leone by Liberian expatriates. Just as the NPFL began as a loosely affiliated network of armed groups united primarily by their opposition to the president, so too with LURD. The official announcement of LURD's existence in February 2000 in Freetown was preceded by smaller armed incursions by a disparate array of factions (Reno 2007, 76).

LURD's first forays into Lofa county were not particularly successful, but they touched off a series of cross-border raids in which LURD and NPFL fighters took turns attacking positions within Liberia and Guinea. In July 2000 LURD captured Voinjama, the first major town across the Liberian border from Macenta and the political seat of Lofa County. Over the coming years the city would trade hands frequently.

Though pushed out of Freetown, the rebels in Sierra Leone had not yet been defeated. One group, mostly former AFRC soldiers, retreated to the Occra Hills outside Freetown and began calling themselves the West Side Boys.[15] Others retreated to the far east. Sam Bockarie allegedly moved back across the border into Liberia, apparently in response to internal schisms in the RUF (Pauw 2006, 214) and to assist Taylor in defending against further LURD attacks.

Despite the setbacks to the People's Army, on 7 July 1999 an extraordinary agreement was signed in Lomé, Togo. At talks sponsored by ECOWAS, the Organization of African Unity, the United Nations, and the ambassadors of the United Kingdom and United States, a comprehensive peace agreement was reached. The Lomé Accords established a national unity government which recognized the RUF as a political party (the RUFP) and gave the rebels four ministerial posts, four deputy ministerial positions, and—in a bizarre twist—named Foday Sankoh the chairman of a new Commission for Mineral Resources. The post gave Sankoh vice-presidential status and essentially put him in charge of the nation's diamond resources. Lomé also stipulated that the CDF was to be disarmed and that there would be no prosecutions of the AFRC and RUF for war crimes.

Blame for the outrageously generous treatment given the rebels in the Lomé Accords has been widely cast on the United States and in particular on President Bill Clinton's special envoy, Jesse Jackson. Jackson was vilified in West Africa for comparing Foday Sankoh to Nelson Mandela, and the RUF to the African National Congress. United States ambassador Joseph Melrose, who participated in the talks, has argued that the Lomé agreement was the best that could be negotiated under the circumstances. But critics of the plan assert that international brokers in Lomé simply did not understand the rebels or the war, and that they strongarmed Tejan Kabbah into signing the agreement (see, in particular, Lizza 2000).

In response to the Lomé Accords, the United Nations Security Council expanded the role and personnel of UNOMSIL. The small group of unarmed observers was replaced by a full peacekeeping contingent. The United Nations Mission in Sierra Leone (UNAMSIL) was to implement the Lomé provisions and take over peacekeeping duties from ECOMOG. The handover was far from smooth, and the process left many locations undefended except by local CDF forces (Jaganathan 2005, 214–15). What's more, Sam Bockarie broke with Foday Sankoh and refused to accept the Lomé provisions or the United Nations peacekeepers; in November and December he led assaults against ECOMOG positions outside of Freetown.

By April 2000 UNAMSIL had officially replaced ECOMOG as the peacekeeping force for Sierra Leone, making the blue-helmeted United Nations troops the new object of attack by recalcitrant units of the People's Army. On 1 May fighting broke out between the RUF and UNAMSIL at the Makeni Disarmament Camp. A few days later some five hundred peacekeepers were abducted by rebels in the east.

The mayhem of the period escalated when on 8 May a peaceful demonstration outside Foday Sankoh's Freetown compound turned violent. Shots were fired from a ring of Sankoh's personal RUFP bodyguards and UNAMSIL peacekeepers, leaving more than twenty people dead. Foday Sankoh fled the house, only to be arrested a few days later by a local kamajor. Once again rebels began marching on the city. As they drew closer to Freetown, eight hundred British paratroopers were sent to Freetown to evacuate British citizens, secure the airport for the United Nations, and head off another devastating assault on the city. The British presence had a stabilizing effect. When eleven British soldiers were abducted by the West Side Boys in late August, a commando force attacked the Occra Hills and ended the last major AFRC presence in Sierra Leone.

The New Liberia Front

The effective end of the RUF came not long after. In September 2000 the RUF launched a series of cross-border attacks in Guinea, mainly into sites with heavy Sierra Leonean refugee populations and, not coincidentally, diamond reserves. Gberie (2005, 172) and contemporaneous accounts by Human Rights Watch suggest that these attacks were at the instigation of Charles Taylor.[16] Guinea's response was to assist in the training of a force of donsos from Kono who were living in the camps and to send its own armed forces across the border.

By May of 2001 Sierra Leone's disarmament program had resumed. The new Sierra Leone Army, under British supervision, deployed to RUF-held territory and the RUF officially became the Revolutionary United Front Party, an unarmed political (rather than military) organization. An unknown number of RUF fighters slipped back across the Liberian border to join Taylor's hodgepodge of security forces, but they no longer had an armed presence in Sierra Leone. On 18 January 2002 the war in Sierra Leone was officially declared over with the symbolic burning of weapons outside the country's main airport. The *war don don* ("war is over") declaration was attended by representatives of all the major parties. When elections were held in May of that year, the RUFP presidential candidate, Alimany Paolo Bangura, won just 1.7 percent of the popular vote, and the RUFP took no seats in parliament.

The Guinean government's other major intervention in the Mano River War at this stage was to step up its support for LURD forces making incursions into Liberia from a rear base in Guinea. LURD was, yet again, a rebel force that succeeded because of its allies and its access to resources, rather than its organization or its ideological vision. LURD's leadership was shockingly inept at formulating a political vision, and its plans for a post-Taylor Liberia were vague at best (see Reno 2007). LURD commanders echoed Norman's argument about the need for a three-year period of extraconstitutional rule. The ostensible leader of LURD was Seykou Conneh, a Liberian exile living in Conakry when the LURD rebellion started. The more critical figure was Conneh's wife, Ayesha. Ayesha Conneh was Guinean president Lansana Conteh's dream interpreter and the main conduit for materiel flowing from the Guinean government and Liberian exile community to LURD forces in-country. At least some of that support was funding that originated with the United States government, meant as military assistance for the Guinean army.[17] The poorly trained and ill-disciplined LURD became somewhat more "professional" under the guidance of Guinean authorities after mid-2001 (Reno 2007, 77), but it remained an organization whose tactics were calculated to cause spectacular damage in a bid to attract international attention (Hoffman 2004).

Both LURD and Charles Taylor recruited heavily from among Sierra Leonean ex-combatants, some of whom had just finished the Disarmament, Demobilization, and Rehabilitation (DDR) Program in Sierra Leone, a process meant to ensure that these fighters did not return to the bush. A sophisticated underground railroad brought many former

CDF fighters, as well as RUF and West Side Boys combatants, to the CDF base at Freetown's Brookfields Hotel. From there they were sent by boat or road to Ayesha Conneh's compound in Conakry and then up to the Liberian border at Macenta. Despite efforts by LURD operatives in Sierra Leone, the Kabbah government could not be persuaded to allow LURD to move personnel and materiel across the eastern forests and directly into Liberia, so LURD was forced to concentrate its movements through Guinea and Liberia's Lofa County, an arrangement that slowed their progress across the country. Only in the final days before Monrovia fell was the Mano River Bridge opened to LURD, and then primarily as a smuggling route for looted property.

As the war in Sierra Leone was officially ending, Taylor declared a state of emergency in Liberia. The slow burn of the LURD rebellion continued throughout 2002, with LURD forces (much like the RUF in Sierra Leone) holding onto very few of its territorial conquests. Other than parts of Lofa County, LURD quickly retreated from towns and villages that it captured, replicating the RUF's hit-and-run strategy in Sierra Leone. Only in February 2003 did LURD definitively capture the town of Tubmanburg, a month before it reached the outskirts of Monrovia. Concentrated primarily in the west and north of the capital, LURD was mirrored in the east by a smaller faction, the Movement for Democracy in Liberia (MODEL), a loosely affiliated group with backing from forces in neighboring Côte d'Ivoire. In a strange reversal of history, Monrovia—and Charles Taylor—were surrounded.

Though Liberia was the center of the violence by the summer of 2003, it was still influenced by events across the border. The end of the Sierra Leone front saw the creation of a war crimes tribunal, the Special Court for Sierra Leone (SCSL). A hybrid court, it was the joint effort of the United Nations and the government of Sierra Leone, the third ad hoc tribunal following the International Criminal Tribunal for the former Yugoslavia and the International Criminal Tribunal for Rwanda. Charged with trying "those who bear the greatest responsibility for serious violations of international humanitarian law and Sierra Leonean law committed in the territory of Sierra Leone since 30 November 1996," the court handed down thirteen indictments.[18] Some of the indictees never made it to court. Foday Sankoh died in prison in July 2003, and Sam Bockarie died in Liberia, apparently executed on Taylor's orders. Johnny Paul Koroma disappeared following his indictment, and though he is presumed dead his case remained open as of the end of 2008. Three other leaders from each the RUF, the AFRC, and the CDF were arrested, including, in March 2003, Sam Hinga Norman, then serving as Sierra Leone's interior minister.

The final indictment was for Charles Taylor. With Monrovia encircled, Taylor flew to Ghana for peace talks in June. The SCSL prosecutor, David Crane, announced Taylor's indictment during the talks, apparently in an effort to prevent Taylor from negotiating a settlement with the rebels and under the mistaken assumption that the Ghanaian government would apprehend him. Instead, the talks immediately ended and Taylor was flown back to Monrovia by Ghanaian authorities.

The result was a deadly siege of the Liberian capital. Much as Doe had done a decade before, Taylor refused to leave office, vowing to fight until the end unless guaranteed amnesty. Also repeating events of ten years before, the United States flirted with the idea of sending troops to prevent a major catastrophe in Monrovia, but elected not to make a serious commitment to the country. After two months of devastating urban warfare, including a long standoff at the New Bridge on the edge of downtown, ECOWAS agreed to supply peacekeepers to keep the city from being overrun. Nigerian troops were again deployed in Monrovia and the Nigerian political establishment once again intervened in a regional war. On 11 August Charles Taylor held a ceremony in which he installed Moses Blah as president of Liberia and boarded a plane for exile in the southern Nigerian town of Calabar. It took three more years for Taylor to be handed over to the SCSL and another two years for his trial to begin at the Hague.

Moses Blah's Liberian government was quickly replaced by a transitional government under Gyude Bryant, a power-sharing arrangement that included representatives from LURD, MODEL, and the previous regime. A United Nations peacekeeping force, larger even than the one in Sierra Leone (which until 2003 was the largest United Nations mission ever) deployed to Liberia in advance of elections in November 2005. Nine years after she was defeated by Charles Taylor at the polls, Ellen Johnson-Sirleaf was elected the new president of Liberia and the first African female head of state.

To the extent that it ever really ended, the Mano River War fizzled. By the time of Johnson-Sirleaf's election, there was a low-intensity war in neighboring Côte d'Ivoire, one which drew former Sierra Leonean and Liberian fighters across that border. The instability of Guinean president Lansana Conteh's regime led to a series of mass strikes and clashes which also drew ex-combatants prepared for a full-scale conflagration that may yet come. In September 2007 the APC party candidate, Ernest Bai Koroma, defeated the SLPP's Solomon Berewa in Sierra Leone. The change in power was peaceful, but it uncovered frightening dynamics in the way ex-combatants were utilized by the country's elites and the kinds of social and economic pressures which continue to face those living in the subregion (Christensen and Utas 2008). After two violent decades it seems that the dynamics that led to war in the Mano River region have not changed. What drew young men to join the various factions continues to lead them to participate in all manner of deployments, from labor at resource extraction to labor on the political campaign trail.

These are the subjects of the chapters that follow.

chapter 2

HUNTERS, LUMPENS, AND WAR BOYS

A Social History of the Kamajors

BY THE THIRD HOUR we ran out of things to talk about. We had exhausted the topics of my research and the bonding banter of young men. The younger boys at the Bandajuma Sowah checkpoint drifted to the dirt pitch behind the guard hut where they played soccer under a light rain.

On women: a kamajor warrior-hunter cannot touch or be touched by a woman while "prepared," or in the purified state that makes him impervious to enemy bullets. He cannot touch his protective garments after sex without first taking a purifying bath.

On drugs: a kamajor cannot smoke *djamba* (marijuana) without losing the immunization bestowed by Allah or the bush spirits and administered by human initiators. This despite the furious drags one young man sucked off a large spliff while we spoke. He was, the others assured me, not a kamajor. Just a local youth with nothing better to do than hang about the checkpoint all day.

We worked our way through the dangerous terrain of conversation I came to expect with each new group of kamajors: offers to douse my body with holy water and then fire from close range with automatic weapons—proof, they said, of the efficacy of protective magic. There were the joking threats to slice off my ear for wearing the single earring that symbolizes the Avondos, a unit of kamajors whose sweat is said to make them impenetrable to bullets. And the crowd at Bandajuma added new challenges. From an older man came the offer to remove my kidneys; a demonstration, he suggested, of the powers of the local hunters from whom the kamajor name is drawn. A young man with a hunting knife teased that he might cut off my head and mount it on a pole, a common tactic for scaring the enemy. There was an invitation to be boiled for two days or smoked for seven, later explained to me to be a veiled reference to protective hunting magic and the curative powers of smoke—things which could only be spoken of allegorically, because they reference the techniques for initiating new kamajors. As with every group of kamajors I interviewed collectively, this part of the conversation was part ritual and part lesson. It was a test of male bravado, theirs and mine. It was an exploration of the limits of discretion, me pushing toward forbidden terrain, them titillated by the power of secrets partly revealed. Mostly our conversation underscored that to be a kamajor was a performance. The phenomenology of joining and fighting with a secret society must be shown. It is not easily explained.

Bandajuma Sowah is a small town on the Bo-Pujehun highway in Sierra Leone's southeast. As the British expanded their colonial authority into the interior in the 1800s they made Bandajuma a regional police headquarters. There was intense fighting at Bandajuma during the anticolonial Hut Tax War, and as a chiefdom headquarters and garrison town, Bandajuma was an early target of the RUF. The rebels fought the Sierra Leone Army there in April 1991, killing a number of civilians. Much of the town was burned in late 1997 when kamajor fighters drove out an AFRC contingent, and during the Black December push toward Freetown at least one woman was decapitated by the kamajors for her alleged collaboration with the junta.

In mid-2000, Bandajuma was relatively quiet. Two groups of kamajors occupied the town. The one under the control of a young initiator named Sheik Kallon operated the checkpoint on the highway. Another, smaller group was led by a local imam, Abraham Kekula. Kekula and his men had largely demobilized. They had returned to farming and running Kekula's tiny Islamic primary school, and were vocal in their resentment of Sheik Kallon's group.

There were no vehicles traveling from Pujehun to Bo all afternoon, and as the day dragged on it seemed increasingly unlikely that any would come. Sheik Kallon wandered down from town to check on his men. After an unpleasant meeting with him earlier in the day I was uncomfortable seeing him at the checkpoint. My interview with him about the initiation process was frustrating. For over an hour, he performed mystical feats to prove his power. Most were transparent parlor tricks involving cleverly folded paper or disappearing ink. I was disappointed. His ineptitude undermined my determination to accept, without skepticism, whatever occult practices I might encounter. It was only when

Sheik Kallon rubbed a spot of holy water on my palm, then instructed me to turn my hand over and find the back wet that I was at a loss for alternative explanations for his magic.

Not long after Sheik Kallon's arrival at the checkpoint, a large transport vehicle rumbled down the highway toward Pujehun. The truck was packed with goods and passengers. Petty traders, mostly, bringing commodities from the larger town. Grabbing the weapons stacked inside the hut, two Russian Kalashnikovs and a German automatic rifle, the kamajors began their routine. Those with weapons circled the vehicle. Those without ordered the passengers down and checked their documents, or began to press the driver for a donation to the cause of democracy. Others jumped onto the now abandoned vehicle and began the search.

Ten minutes passed. I wandered back from the parked vehicle toward the guard hut, approaching a slowly expanding knot of people forming around the initiator, who was seated on a bench under the eaves of the hut. To his side sat a few of his kamajor initiates. In front stood three men. Around them gathered the passengers, hawkers, and hangers-on. The mood was tense.

A protracted debate was under way about an incident with the same vehicle at the same checkpoint the previous week. The driver and his assistant were lodging a complaint with the initiator, claiming the kamajors' search on the earlier trip took more than three hours and put the truck at risk by forcing it to travel the Pujehun highway after dark. What's more, when they reached Pujehun, a passenger complained that the kamajors had stolen three cartons of cigarettes during the search. The passenger refused to pay the fare for the trip, claiming it was the driver's responsibility to safeguard the goods of his passengers—in this case from those charged with safeguarding the truck from attacks on the road.

Sheik Kallon listened to the men's complaint, then to his kamajors' defense. They had, they agreed, detained the truck and ordered it searched. But the search had been conducted by the police, whose guard hut sat some twenty yards from that of the kamajors. The lone officer posted at the checkpoint had been friendly enough to me earlier in the day, but it seemed clear that he had no practical authority at the Bandajuma checkpoint. His clean uniform and reflective yellow vest emblazoned POLICE only mocked his powerlessness next to those with real control, the young men in shorts, sandals, and shades.

After both sides of the case were repeated several times, Sheik Kallon began to speak. He worked out a compromise. The kamajors would bear no responsibility for the alleged theft, and in return would not subject the truck to such stringent scrutiny in the future.

At this point, the third man from the truck, silent to this point, broke in. With a seemingly unwarranted aggressiveness, he insulted the kamajors of Bandajuma for their criminal activity. They were not real kamajors like himself, but petty thieves.

The young man seated next to Sheik Kallon, who I later learned was not even on duty the day the alleged crime took place, answered for Sheik Kallon's men. He was, he said, content to sit silently and be subjected to false allegations before his initiator. Sheik Kallon could arbitrate those matters. He would not, however, stand for personal insults. The exchange grew louder, and the spectators pressed close.

When the verbal sparring crescendoed to a shouting match, Sheik Kallon interrupted. Turning to his initiate, he asked: "Do you believe that you can beat this man?" When his kamajor replied that he could, he

3. The kamajor checkpoint at Bandajuma Sowah, 2000.

turned to the kamajor from the truck. "And do you believe that you can beat *this* man?" Again, the answer was yes.

"All right, then. Go over there, and do not come back until one of you begs for mercy or one of you is dead."

The two young men stripped to the waist and circled one another as the crowd, in turn, circled them. Both the stranger and Sheik Kallon's champion had the prize-fighter physiques so many rural Mende men acquire from labor on the farm and in the mine. But the misty rain and deep muck of the impromptu ring gave the fight the feel of an absurd—if grave—parody. The two fighters struggled to grab one another as the mud made them clumsy.

I ran through the inventory of weapons I had seen at the checkpoint. The three firearms I was aware of were stacked inside the hut. The kamajors at the truck had returned them when the argument with the driver began. (Not, I think, out of any sense of military protocol. I had earlier witnessed kamajors throwing loaded weapons back and forth, or napping with their foreheads on the gun barrel mouth.) The kamajor with the hunting knife compulsively drew and sheathed the blade as he watched.

The fight was short. The two men each locked hands around the other's throat and slipped down into the mud. Standing toward the back, I could hear more than see them kick at one another while they tried to wrench free. It took the police officer nearly a minute to wade through the throng of spectators, and minutes more to wiggle his body between the two fighters. No one made a move to help, but neither did they stop him. By the time he pried the two apart, it was clear that the physical confrontation was over, and the conflict quickly degenerated into the kind of inane insults that schoolboys hurl at one another, without conviction, because they don't know how else a fight should end.

There is one thing about the pro-government militia on which everyone agrees: God loves Sierra Leone, and so he sent the kamajors. Everything else about the movement is open to interpretation.

The movement has its time of history, and it has its time of the gods.[1] There is, therefore, no single story of the Sierra Leone front of the war or the kamajors' involvement in it. We know that when historians tell the story, the rebel war begins on 23 March 1991 with the RUF invasion of Kailahun. The war ends on 18 January 2002 when a collection of government ministers, international peacekeepers, journalists, and aid workers set fire to a symbolic pile of weapons and declare the fighting done. When kamajor combatants narrate their own history they often do so with more attention to divine providence or state failures than to dates or specific events. As with any history, there are infinite ways to tell the story of what happened during the Mano River War, and limitless possibilities for painting the picture of what came before and for recounting what comes after.

In the previous chapter I told that story as a chronology of major events. In this chapter and the next I tell the story as social history. I divide the life of the kamajor movement into four parts. These are not distinct phases so much as loose groupings of significant events. There is no fine line between them, and the trends or traits I associate with one moment are sometimes evident in others. I therefore follow Deleuze and Guattari (1987, 21–22) in calling these "plateaus" rather than phases—a collection of events, problems, and questions that share characteristics and can be linked together thematically, not just chronologically. What these plateaus trace is an arc from grassroots mobilization to institutionalization, from community defense to full incorporation into the logic of contemporary global capitalism.

I begin with the mythical origins of the movement and a series of key figures in the poetics of the militia: the hunter, from whom the militia draws its name and to some degree its ethos; the urban masquerade troupes that were a central component of city social life prior to the war; the rural "war boys," mercenaries in the colonial era who played a part in the violent consolidation of the chiefdoms as they exist today; and the so-called lumpen youth who have historically been the foot soldiers of Sierra Leone's rough brand of politics. How much we can understand the evolution and character of the kamajors through these mythical metanarratives of manhood, responsibility, and marginality are the questions that dominate the first plateau.

I mark the second moment of the movement by the disparate defensive formations that appeared in the early years of the war across the south and east, a region dominated by ethnic Mendes. The rebel advances and the treacheries of the military were met with grassroots resistance. Communities formed civil defense committees and armed local youth to secure the roads leading into villages and the bushpaths to outlying farms. These were decidedly local efforts informed by events elsewhere and by rumors of resistance around the country, but uncoordinated at the national level. What was clear across Sierra Leone was the need to take defensive measures in the absence of the state's willingness or ability to do so. Mobilization, then, is our second plateau.

By the period just prior to national elections in 1996 and the change from a military junta to the Sierra Leone People's Party government, a marked transition occurred with the consolidation of community defense committees into a more proper paramilitary. Here again there are questions to be answered about the relationship of the kamajors to the state and to democracy as a form of postcolonial politics. In such contexts, who exercises the monopoly on legitimate violence? We confront here the difficult issues of ethnicity and international trade. How do we understand the intersection of state and nonstate forces in a context where the economy has for decades been dependent on a subtle ambiguity between the formal and informal institutions of governance? This is our third plateau: institutionalization.

Our fourth plateau begins roughly with the Lomé Accords of 1999 that brought the RUF into a power-sharing agreement. It continues to today. It is the axiomatization of the movement—the point at which the militia's logic is indistinguishable from the logic of the global economy. The point at which all "transactions" (political, social, and economic) are governed by the peculiar rules of capital today. The kamajors at that point raise in a profound and disturbing way the question of what it means to live in the violent folds of a global economy.

By mid-2000, on the Bo-Pujehun highway, all of these questions could be asked of the kamajors. None of them had simple answers. But we begin before the war—before the beginning, as it were.

First Plateau: Mythopoetic Origins

Abraham Kekula, the imam and militia leader at Bandajuma, tells the kamajor story like this:[2]

> The first kamajoisia were wanderers in the bush. They killed the wild animals disturbing their people. If they happened to kill a big animal—an elephant, a bush cow, a deer—they paid a token to the paramount chief or the town chief, and parceled out the remaining portions or sold them at market. When they came to a village, they asked to see the paramount chief and pre-

sented themselves as his wards. Whatever a kamajoi did in the chiefdom, the paramount chief was responsible. Even the late father of Bandajuma, where we now sit, had a kamajoi whose name was Lahai.

If a kamajoi is based in one place, and he chases an animal across the boundary to another chiefdom before he kills it, the paramount chief in that place must consult with the paramount chief who is the hunter's host. In those days, things were nice. People were more honest, and they worked within their boundaries. Not like kamajoisia today, who move to other places.

These early kamajoisia provided cheap meat to the populace. They made their own cartridges, these kamajoisia, with the aid of the blacksmiths, and the chiefs gave them gunpowder.

The kamajoisia who killed large animals had supernatural powers. They called the animals to them, they became invisible, they flew. The powers came sometimes from the sheiks, the powerful *mori-men*, who could give hunters the powers to be brave in the face of wild animals and become famous. Some hunters got their powers from the animals themselves. Elephants and bush cows have medicine in their bellies and bladders; the kamajoi who removes it enhances his powers—and that is why women must not be present when the stomach and the bladder of the elephant and the bush cow are removed.

In those days people respected and honored such kamajoisia.

The terms associated with the kamajor militia draw important connections to Sierra Leonean histories and Mende cosmologies predating the Mano River War. Kamajor, kamajoi, and hunter; medicine and hale; society, Poro, men, *hindo*; youth, *rarray*, lumpens, and war boys—each of these Krio, Mende, and English terms evokes some facet of the contemporary militia movement and makes some reference to the historical or mythical past. Everyday warscape encounters like those at the Bandajuma checkpoint and narratives of war like Kekula's telling of the kamajoi story are animated by these terms. And by how the meanings of these terms change. Understanding the mythopoetic origins of the movement, and understanding the evolving character of the kamajors, means reckoning with the histories of these terms and asking what relation they have to the present and to the recent past.

Hunters

We can begin with the most obvious. *Kamajor* (sing.) and *kamajors* (pl.) are Anglicized versions of an older Mende word, *kamajoi* (sing.) and *kamajoisia* (pl.). As the kamajor militia movement grew the Anglicized version became the standard, a product of both the international media and the movement's own internal documentation. (In what follows I use the Anglicized *kamajor* or *kamajors* when referring to the institutionalized militia, and *kamajoi* or *kamajoisia* in reference to their prewar namesake.)

Both *kamajor* and *kamajoi* are generally translated as "hunter" or "traditional hunter."[3] The translation is not a particularly good one. Not every man who hunts is a kamajoi. There were relatively few of these figures, whose command of the bush paths, the gun, and the secrets and medicine (hale) of the forest distinguished them from other hunters and other men. Unlike the kamajor militia fighters, the kamajoi is a solitary figure. He hunts at night and often alone. Many rural Mendes in Sierra Leone today remember only a handful of these specialists, and they are often recalled with a certain awe. Musa Brima is a kamajor from Bo, an older man who knew kamajoisia hunters prior to the war and knew a great deal about kamajor fighters during the war. Reflecting on the difference between the old kamajoisia and the new kamajors, he made the distinction based on community: the kamajoi hunter had no "society" to which he belonged. Unlike hunter figures in other Mande groups, Mende kamajoisia of recent memory learned their craft through long apprenticeship rather than initiation into a collective or a fraternity.[4] Yet ironically, despite his solitary occupation, it is the hunter who is most often associated with the founding of new Mende communities (Hill 1984; Little [1951] 1967, 26; Muana 1997, 85–86). And it is the kamajoi hunter's responsibility to protect the village from the threatening forces of the forest. A kamajoi blurs the distinction between the hunter and the warrior-protector (Abraham 1978, 10), not least because threats to the village come in all forms—human, animal, occult.

It is therefore no small thing to be a kamajoi. As Abraham Kekula tells it in his story, the kamajoi's medicine and his secret knowledge were prized, but given the other forces capable of flight, disappearance, and shape shifting—witches and forest devils, for example—they were also feared. Anything closely associated with the forest carries its taint of chaos and threat. Through his unique access to the resources of the forest the kamajoi often finds power outside the usual channels and is therefore "not opposed to seriously disrupting social harmony and cohesion to achieve [his] ends" (McNaughton 1988, 71; see also Leach 1994, 167; 2000). So not surprisingly, in the Mende imaginary, as is true across the span of West Africa's Mande diaspora, the hunter's position in the social milieu is ambiguous (see Cosentino 1989; Leach 2000, 581; McNaughton 1982, 1988; and the essays collected in Hellweg 2004). He is a hero, but a volatile one.

While he is associated with esoteric knowledge passed down from more experienced practitioners, the kamajoi is at the same time characterized in Mende villages by his access to the most modern of technologies: the gun (Ferme 2001a). This, too, contributes to his ambivalent place in the community. The kamajoi's right to firearms was a privilege carefully limited and regulated by the colonial and postcolonial state as well as by chiefdom authorities, each of them cognizant of the threat posed by civilians with access to guns (Alie 2005, 57).

This combination of knowledge and weaponry marks a significant boundary embodied by the kamajoi, the divide between women and men. The kamajoi as hunter operates in an expressly male domain. The gun in the kamajoi hunter's hand is both linguistically and symbolically phallic (Leach 1994, 161). And the hunter's activities are often dependent on a careful attentiveness to their counterpart, the excessive and unpredictable power of women. Rather than simply excluding female power, the hunter proscribes it (Leach 2000, 589–91). Women's power is volatile and chaotic, like the forest itself. Contact with women, particularly sexual contact, threatens the hunt and the hunter's safety in the bush. The possibility of hunting secrets falling into female hands and deployed by women is a danger not because women lack power but because their power lacks control (see Leach 1994, 161–73; see also Moran 1995).[5]

By the start of the war in the early 1990s, it was not at all clear what the future of the kamajoi as a social institution might be. In her ethnography of Mende communities in the Gola Forest region of eastern Sierra Leone, Melissa Leach describes an institution that seemed increasingly antiquated given the expansion of commercial hunting, declining stocks of certain bush animals, and an aging population of kamajoisia whose social standing among young people was rapidly eroding (Leach 1994, 168–73). Nevertheless, the symbolism of the community defender, his knowledge of the physical and imaginative landscape of the forest, and his practical access to weaponry makes the kamajoi a logical catalyst around which to mobilize and militarize community defense. For the state army of Sierra Leone looking for assistance in unfamiliar rural terrain, and for community leaders looking for figures to spearhead and to embody an armed resistance, the kamajoi was an obvious choice.

Hunting Societies and War Boys

Though the kamajoi has no "society," as Musa Brima put it, the hunter has been an important icon for other collective mobilizations in Sierra Leone. The hunting or hunters' society is a Sierra Leonean institution dating to colonial Freetown.[6] In the capital and in upcountry towns, hunting societies were social clubs for elites (notably Krios) that utilized both West African and British colonial hunting artifacts and maintained a stock of collective armaments for group hunts (see Cohen 1981, 101–2;

4. Hunting society mural, Freetown, 2003. (Photograph by Julie Graber)

Little [1951] 1967, 270; Nunley 1987). A related movement, the ode-lay, was more populist, more youth oriented, and more urban. Ode-lay troupes also drew on the iconography of the hunt, notably in the public masquerades for which they are best known (see Nunley 1983).

Far from simply leisure organizations, the hunting societies and ode-lay troupes served as political forces as well. The hunting societies were often made up of bureaucrats and civil servants and have historically been important conduits for Sierra Leone's flows of political patronage. Ode-lay youth mobilizations were a key part of the APC government's expanding power in the late 1960s when candidates and politicians rallied the youth vote and deployed ode-lay members to campaign on their behalf (Nunley 1987, 207–13). "Secret societies" performed a variety of tasks for the politicians who supported them and against those who did not. Though they were often referred to as cultural or artistic troupes, violence and secrecy were central components of their performances both in the service of, and in opposition to, the state. The "thug labor" of such youth has been a staple of party politics in Sierra Leone for the past few decades (see Rashid 1997; see also Ferme 1999), and the ode-lay collectives were an important part of this political infrastructure. They worked the streets in politicized performances, clashed with opponents, and were a conduit for politically sensitive and important knowledge (see Hecht and Simone 1994, 22).

In the 1970s and '80s such urban groups were effective because of the way they mobilized what scholars have called "lumpen" youth (see Abdullah 1998; Abdullah and Muana 1998; Bangura 1997), known in Krio as *rarray man*, *savis man*, or *dreg man*. These are the marginal youth Marx labeled the lumpenproletariat, "thieves and criminals of all sorts, living off the garbage of society, people without definite trace, vagabonds, *gens sans feu et sans aveu* [people without hearth or home]" ([1850] 1974, 52). The political infrastructure of Sierra Leone drew heavily on such marginalized youth to serve in the violent brand of politics practiced in the postcolony (Abdullah 2002). Outlets like the ode-lay offered a pool of thug labor for politicians. But they also produced one of the few spaces of possibility for oppositional politics. Sierra Leone's one-party state effectively quashed progressive labor movements and radical political parties. So when university students began to oppose the APC government in the 1970s, their fellow travelers were underemployed marginal youth with whom they shared an interest in politicized music (notably reggae), anticolonial and revolutionary rhetoric from around Africa and Latin America, a burgeoning drug scene, and informal but distinct youth spaces within the city. In short, a politically unsophisticated youth culture became the only effective form of political opposition, though one that had only moderate success.[7]

One result of a political opposition restricted to youth mobilization such as the ode-lay was the emergence of the RUF and what Zack-Williams calls its "infantile revolution" (2002, 310; see also Abdullah 1998; Rashid 2004). How this mode of youth mobilization relates to the evolution of the kamajor militia is more complicated. In some parts of the country, notably in Bo and Kenema, existing hunting society or ode-lay relationships were no doubt the basis for mobilizations that eventually became kamajor units (for one example from Bo, see Richards 1996, 389). And late in the war the leadership of the Civil Defence Force promoted the Organized Body of Hunting Societies (OBHS) as a Freetown, Krio equivalent to the kamajors, though in truth the OBHS was never much of a factor in the war.

What is significant about the hunting societies and ode-lay troupes for understanding the kamajors is the tradition of giving political weight to an overlapping iconography of the rural hunter—with his volatility, his violence, and his extraordinary power—and the popular culture of a global black underclass. Tupac Shakur, Rambo, and Bob Marley were rallying figures for the kamajors just as they had been for other youth mobilizations since the 1970s. These are iconic young men whose exploits upset the existing order, who achieve an ambiguous greatness not only because of their political platforms but through rebellion and often through violence. Michael Jackson and Bob Marley in the early 1980s and Sengbe Pieh (of the *Amistad* antislave rebellion) in the early 1990s were all figures analogous to the hunter and representative of what youth who participated in the hunting and ode-lay societies hoped to become (Cosentino 1989, 34–35; Opala 1994; Osagie 1997, 2000). The current that runs through all of these stories is the potential of male youth to seize power when the existing order denies them recognized forms of authority. They invent, sometimes violently and sometimes tragically, a different future. The way these various discourses come together in the mobilization of male youth for political engagement is a recurrent theme in the life of the kamajor movement.

The outsourcing of political violence to collectives of young men in Sierra Leone has even deeper roots than the masquerade societies under the APC. As historian Joe A. D. Alie points out, militia mobilizations were frequent in conflicts in the Sierra Leone Colony in the late eighteenth century and early nineteenth century (2005, 52; see also Schama 2006). In the latter part of the nineteenth century, the Mende regions of southeastern Sierra Leone were almost continuously at war as small polities consolidated into the chiefdoms of today (Fyfe 1962; Wylie 1969). Arthur Abraham links much of the violence to a professional mercenary class moving across the region in the late 1800s (1976, 13–14). Like that of the hunter, their effectiveness was in part a product of occult protections that guarded them against the bullets of their enemies (Abraham 1976, 20–21; Little [1951] 1967, 35–36). The documentation of these mobilizations is much thinner than for the later deployments of youth violence in politics, but it is clear that these mercenaries provided a violent resource to local elites for settling disputes and expanding their influence—a system sufficiently entrenched that "buying

5. Tupac Shakur mural, Brookfields, Freetown, 2001.

war" in the form of mercenaries became a recognized term of political practice (Abraham 1976, 11). In a pattern that we saw repeated throughout the Mano River War, these "war boys" or "war men" waged war primarily through ambushes, and were often paid through the spoils of their activities (Fyfe 1962, 403; see also Abraham 1976, 18; Little [1951] 1967, 29).

Images of the Past

Very few of the young men who joined the kamajor movement were hunters prior to the war. Even fewer were kamajoisia. Over the years, some of those kamajor fighters with whom I worked drew a direct connection between their own activities and their kamajoisia namesakes. Others did not. Some of the military tactics used by the militia seemed to draw on both the techniques of the hunt and older forms of Mende warfare.[8] But a great deal of the militia's tactical planning came from lessons taught by the veterans of contemporary armed forces and from popular culture representations of guerrilla war. In other words, in virtually every facet of the contemporary militia's existence, there is both resonance and disconnect with these mythopoetic origins. Fighters themselves were aware of the complexities of their own genealogy, and there was little about their relation to historical antecedents that was broadly accepted within the movement. My questions to militia fighters about the connections between themselves and the kamajoisia of old invariably sparked interesting and intense debates. Debates about the relative bravery required to stand alone before wild animals of the forest versus the heavy artillery of a modern army, debates about the authenticity of occult knowledge and the role of men in the protection of a community. These debates sometimes split along generational lines. Older men tended to see the hunter connection as integral, and to see the RUF as prey; younger men not surprisingly saw in the kamajors a new movement, a novel youth-led organization. Urban fighters, too, more often highlighted the novelty of the movement while their rural counterparts were more likely to draw connections to the past.

The desire of outsiders to explain the kamajors in terms of a prewar past is a strong and understandable one. The language of a great deal of media coverage of the movement connected the kamajors to rural hunting traditions, even if it did so in only a vague and unnuanced way.

Special Court testimonies about the kamajors often delved into the "ancient" roots of the kamajoisia. What little anthropological treatment there has been of the militia has primarily explored the cultural continuities that kamajor fighters share with the specialized hunters from whom they draw their name. There is more than just history at stake here. Connecting the kamajors to "tradition" has a political edge. For some, locating the kamajors squarely in the kamajoisia tradition or in the hunting societies and ode-lay troupes exemplifies the prison house of culture that dooms Africans to repetitive violence. For others, it rationalizes the seemingly irrational, making "local" sense of the most fantastic elements of this war.

Certainly these mythopoetic origins are illuminating for what they tell us about the conceptualizations of power, violence, gender, youth, and political organization at work in the militia movement. They constitute a repertoire of tropes and a reservoir of knowledge. And by tracing the trajectory of the kamajors we can see how these factors unfolded in the life of the movement. But the desire to find explanations for what the kamajors became by looking to the ethnographic details of village kamajoisia, early colonial mercenaries, or even to revolutionary youth culture in the postcolony is, I think, misplaced. The kamajors's historical antecedents are not explanatory in the ways we might like them to be.

In the work that follows, then, I am less interested in how images of the past—images of kamajoisia, of war boys, of secret societies, and of popular youth culture—constitute a structural foundation for the kamajor movement than I am in the way they became available for strategic deployment in the creation of new futures. Other writers have also explored the inventiveness of Sierra Leone's violent mobilizations. Mariane Ferme (2001b), Michael Jackson (2005), and Paul Richards (1996) have each written about the way the "cultural infrastructure" (Richards 1996, 30) of communities in Sierra Leone was reimagined and creatively deployed by the various factions. Both Jackson and Richards write of the centrality of initiation metaphors during the war (initiation being a key sociological process in rural life), as young men sought to make themselves into new kinds of social beings and as the RUF as a movement sought to give birth to an entirely new sociopolitical world. "Thus," writes Jackson, "armed rebellion and revolution spring from the same imperative of rebirth that underlies such rites of passage as birth, initiation, and death" (2005, 63). These ethnographies highlight the ways in which the cultural material that made up the prewar, everyday habitus in Sierra Leone was frequently reworked in the "rituals" of warfare, albeit often in perverse or unmoored ways. Many theorists have explored the grotesque or carnivalesque aspects of warfare, explaining how historical cultural tropes circulate within the war zone and give acts of violence their meaning (see, for example, Gluckman 1963; Guha 1999; Owusu 1989). What the Mano River War makes clear, however, is the extent to which the possibilities for these creative reworkings of the imaginary have changed at this historical moment. Grounding an analysis of the violence of war in historical, cultural antecedents risks eclipsing what is unique about warfare today.

One mark of the postmodern moment is that images of the past are available for combination and recombination almost without limit, and without carrying the full weight of their historical meaning. They can be deployed, exchanged, and combined in an infinite variety of configurations. "[T]he random cannibalization of all the styles of the past" is how Fredric Jameson defined the postmodern aesthetic (1984, 65–66), and the play of images from the mythopoetic past of the kamajor movements was capricious indeed. Kamajor identity was constructed from a pastiche of images of kamajoisia, revolutionary postcolonial youth culture, legacies of mercenary labor, and masculine responsibility, and these images were combined differently across the span of the movement and the war. The consequences of these configurations and reconfigurations of images could never have been predicted, even if they were oriented in certain directions by prevailing notions of what it means to be a man, the social ambiguities of the hunter, or the revolutionary potential of youth. But in the end, what mattered were the experimental possibilities for the future opened up by these mythopoetic origins. As I noted in the preface, Deleuze argued that "history isn't experimental, it's just the set of more or less negative preconditions that make it possible to experiment with something beyond history" (1995, 170). What we see in the chapters that follow is that as the kamajors moved across the plateaus of the Mano River warscape, they experimented with their own origins in very different ways.

Second Plateau: Mobilization

Abraham Kekula continued his story:

> The initiated kamajors today are also highly regarded and honored in the community because of their braveness in defending the motherland, having realized that the constitutional army connived with the enemy to destroy the land. In the beginning, there were two kinds of kamajors: those who were initiated and prepared by the initiators to face the enemy, and those who were just brave men offering themselves for the fight. They were initiated later, when they saw how the initiators could immunize a man against the bullets of his enemy. With the help of Allah, they drove the rebels from the region.
>
> The soldiers were the ones who called for the establishment of the kamajoisia as an association. They requested that the paramount chiefs present their old kamajoisia to fight alongside them, since they knew the terrain. And so all the paramount chiefs in this region gathered their kamajoisia and presented them to the soldiers. But each time they went to the battlefront, the soldiers turned their guns on their helpers, and in this way killed many of them over time. The soldiers told all the people in the region to gather at Bandajuma Sowah, and they went into the houses of the people and collected the goods they left behind. Having discovered that the constitutional army was not genuinely pursuing the war, we all came together to hail the initiation of the kamajoisia to drive out the soldiers and their allies the rebels, and formed the people's militia, the kamajors.

"[E]ach time there is an operation against the State," Deleuze and Guattari write, "it can be said that a war machine has revived, that a new nomadic potential has appeared" (1987, 386). The appearance of the kamajor movement onto the warscape of the Mano River War was the birth of a resistance movement. That resistance was directed at the RUF rebels, of course, but in a more profound way it was directed at the Sierra Leonean state—or at least at the failure of the state to protect its civilian populace. The government and its military spurred to action an array of disparate forces in a broad effort at mobilization for the defense of rural communities. As I explore in this section, these mobilizations put into action a network of social relations deeply rooted in the logic of rural communities in Sierra Leone's southeast. But these mobilizations were a novel configuration of forces. They were not simply the mobilization of existing social institutions; rather what gave these early mobilizations their "structure" was the need for experimentation with the technologies of defense and a growing sense of collective exclusion from the state.

Community Defense Committees

Irregular combatants were a fixture on the Sierra Leone front of the Mano River War from its inception in March 1991. The poorly supported Sierra Leone Army routinely drew on local volunteers to serve as logistical support, guides, and auxiliary gunners. By April of that year, the army captain Prince Ben-Hirsch was recruiting and arming local civilians in Segbwema. The Kuranko tamaboros and the Kono donsos, the first of the "hunter" groups, appeared soon after. Fearing the military as much as the rebels, many communities organized civil defense committees or civil defense units, mostly groups of local youth manning roadblocks, interrogating strangers, or conducting defensive patrols.

These earliest mobilizations lacked a central command and fixed organizational structure. Instead they were dominated by a few strong personalities and regional collectives of elders and patrons. These were decidedly local efforts, not yet organized into a coherent movement, and they represent a variety of interests and of action styles. For example, in the south, chiefs from the Pujehun District chiefdoms of Mano Sakrim and Yakemo-Kpukumu and from the Bonthe chiefdom of Kwamebai Krim organized the Krim Civil Defence Unit. Town elders and regional chiefs established the Civil Defence Committee in Bo, and in the far east there was a mobilization known as the Kailahun District War Effort.

One of the largest and most successful of these civil defense efforts, the Eastern Region Defence Committee (variously referred to as the ERDC, ERECOM, or EREDCOM) in Kenema, was closely affiliated with members of the Sierra Leone People's Party, the party ousted and marginalized by Siaka Stevens and the APC. Dr. Alpha Lavalie, the lecturer at the University of Sierra Leone and staunch anti-APC activist, had at least since the early 1980s been interested in the potential mobilization of Mende youth to combat APC election violence (see Lavalie 1985). Lavalie sought to catalyze as political forces some of the social institutions associated with Mende traditionalism, notably the Poro and rural chieftaincy. When the NPRC removed the APC from power, the NPRC's Tom Nyuma worked with Lavalie and other SLPP officials in the region (including the future SLPP vice-president Joe Demby) to coordinate and support these grassroots security efforts.[9]

In an early analysis of the kamajor militia, anthropologist Patrick Muana outlines how the "politics of displacement" (1997, 83) influenced many of these mobilizations of community defense bodies. RUF incursions and the unreliability of the Sierra Leone Army (SLA) generated massive populations of internally displaced persons in camps and larger towns. There were especially large concentrations of displaced people around Bo and Kenema, the major urban centers of the southeast. These IDP camps were zones of state retreat. Regulation and governance of these populations therefore largely fell to the chiefdom authorities, whose position was strengthened by their role in allocating and coordinating NGO resources (82–83). Local leaders procured armaments from military officers sympathetic to the community defense effort, but most importantly they coordinated the organization of men willing and able to fight and shaped what these mobilizations would look like.[10] Not surprisingly, as with the tamaboro to the north, the Mende kamajoisia were the locus of that organization.

The early recruitment of youth into the growing civil defense effort was therefore intimately connected not only to the kamajoisia mythos but also to the logic of Mende chieftaincy and elite patronage.[11] Common practice at this early stage was for committees of community leaders at the various levels of organization (section, village, town, chiefdom) to request from the community a given number of young men to be conscripted to the expanding force. In some cases these were youth with access to family weapons or with occult garments associated with war and with the hunt. Community leaders putting forth young men were expected to "stand for" them in the new force, and the community as a whole was responsible for provisioning these youth as they conducted the war effort. The ambiguity surrounding the soldier-rebel identity made the politics of local recognition at work here doubly important: to be spoken for by the community was a testament to the loyalty and character of new recruits and it bound fighters to the community and its defense. (Again, as Alie [2005, 57] points out, this practice of vouching for those empowered with community defense has precedent in rural areas, where at least since the Chiefdom Council Act of the 1960s chiefs were required to testify to the moral character of anyone granted a firearm license by the state.)

Muana highlights the importance of this grounding in the chieftaincy for the kamajors' "superior myth" (1997, 85), the psychological power the force brought to bear against the seemingly invincible RUF. This association with the rural institutions of cultural nationalism was indeed a potent psychological weapon. It was also important, however, because it meant that the early mobilizations were allied most closely with chiefdom councils, town elders, and the local elites rather than with a national war effort, the governing party, or the state army. Even when displaced from their home communities, these were decidedly "local" forces.

Other social networks were also mobilized and militarized during this early period when the state army was an ambiguous force. In late 1994 the RUF first appeared in the Gondama refugee camp up the road from Bo and launched a "recruitment" drive into Bo itself. When it became clear that there were only a few rebels in the force, and that at least some of their weapons were wooden fabrications of AK-47s, social organizations ranging from the Poro to youth soccer clubs called on their members to resist the RUF and drove them from the city, killing those they could catch (see Gberie 2005, 87–88; Richards 1996, 152–55; 2005b, 388–92). Also in December 1994, civilians mobilized through a Poro call-up in Kenema routed an army contingent. Soldiers barracked outside Kenema had been patronizing a local hotel restaurant and raising security concerns for the local populace. Rumors spread that the unit was expecting a large consignment of weapons from the garrison town of Daru, and soldiers were alleged to have shot a twelve-year-old boy outside the hotel. Poro members assembled at night and drove the military out of town, tearing down the hotel in the process. Other Kenema "youth organizations" accompanied refugees to outlying farms during the day as protection from both the RUF and the army, and confronted soldiers who attempted to extort war taxes on those returning to Kenema town for security at night.

Word of such civil defense efforts spread throughout the south and east in the early 1990s. Officers in the NPRC government sympathetic to the irregulars carried the blueprints for civil defense to different communities. Travelers, traders, and internally displaced populations brought with them news of efforts to resist the RUF incursions, or warnings about the predations of certain military units. Far from the central government in Freetown, knowledge of grassroots efforts to provide security circulated rhizome-like through the upcountry territories. At this stage of the development of community defense and the kamajor militia, rumors, storytelling, and other forms of traveling knowledge were more important to the mobilization effort than any central coordination or institution, whether of "society" or the state.

By focusing on the localism of these various mobilizations we begin to get a picture of a war best seen as the conglomerate of many localized conflicts. Obviously this is true to some extent of any war—a war comprises individual encounters. But this localization is especially pronounced in conflicts in the Mano River region, where politics at the district, chiefdom, and town levels has a much greater impact on the average person's daily existence than do events at the national level.

Thus, local narratives of the war are generally made up of references to smaller-scale conflicts. The Ndogboyosoi Rebellion is only the most commented on of a number of examples. Ndogboyosoi was a series of mid-1980s conflicts between APC and SLPP strongmen in the Pujehun District, motivated both by party politics and (allegedly) control over trade routes.[12] The RUF found some initial support in the Pujehun region by exploiting the factionalism and resentment still associated with Ndogboyosoi. This led many people in the region, both combatants and observers, to conclude that the RUF invasion was simply an extension of the Ndogboyosoi conflict (Richards 1996, 91). As Lansana Gberie has pointed out, even the chief of staff of the Sierra Leone Army declared in 1993 that the RUF invasion was an extension of Ndogboyosoi (2005, 66).[13]

The upshot is that now, in the aftermath of the conflict, it is possible to step back and cast the war in national, meta-analytic terms. From a postwar vantage one sees the national character of the movement that eventually became the CDF. As I have argued, it is of course important to keep both the national and transnational dimensions of the war in mind. But it is critical that in the process we do not lose sight of the countless disparate and only tenuously connected local dynamics that together gave this war its meaning.

Initiation

One of the most important narratives to spread through the network of expanding knowledge about community defense efforts came from the far southern Bonthe region. These were stories about protective medicines (*hale*) administered to the new defense forces. Though hale was always part of the kamajoisia tool kit, and was certainly part of the tamaboro stories in the north, the efforts of occult specialists in Jong and Yawbeko chiefdoms were of a different order. A local herbalist named Allieu Kundewa was alleged to be washing recruits, or preparing them in ways that made them invulnerable to the bullets of their enemies. Not only the kamajoisia but now any young man could draw on occult forces when mobilizing for community defense. (See chapter 7.) Soon other ritual experts gained reputations for their abilities with protective medicines. Mama Munda Fortune, the only female kamajor, was widely recognized in Bonthe and Bo; Kemoh Muniro became an important figure in Pujehun; and Brima Bangura rose to prominence in Kenema. Regional defense committees sent recruits to these occult specialists for preparation before being deployed, or funds were raised to bring Kundewa, Mama Munda, Muniro, and others to a community for ceremonies of military preparation.

These preparations or "initiations" (*ngiyei*) spread quickly and changed the nature of the movement. In Mende *hale* connotes not only a medicinal artifact but the collectives associated with its use (see Henry 2000, 143; Jędrej 1974, 40–42; Little [1951] 1967, 228). The overlapping mythos of the kamajoisia, the discourses of male civic responsibility, and the advancing occult technology began to coalesce in a heightened sense of united effort. The kamajoi name was now synonymous with participation in these irregular bodies, at least in Mende regions of the southeast. Though these disparate mobilizations lacked an administrative structure, they were increasingly thought of and referred to as a "society" into which new recruits were inducted or initiated. Initiation became the standard form of mobilization. The ritual preparations performed by Kundewa and others were not simply personal protections in most cases but the marker of membership in the new collective. Some *kemohs* or initiators were identified most closely with specific units (Mama Munda's Kasela War Council and Kemoh Muniro's Born Naked Brigade) but collectively they were understood to be operating within the broad range of the kamajor movement. In short, by the end of 1995 the movement still lacked coherence of structure, but had achieved a certain coherence of identity.

The process of initiation was a society secret. Those who possessed the knowledge of society secrets were distinguished from those who did not, and possessing secrets became a more significant marker of identity than any particular knowledge the secret contained. (This is true of secret societies throughout this region, as Bellman [1984] illustrated in his classic study of West African secret societies; possessing secrets distinguishes those in power more than does the actual content of the secret possessed.) Throughout the movement initiates policed themselves and guarded their secrets by observing restrictions on their behavior, restrictions that would guarantee a purified state and thus a bulletproofed body. Some of these taboos were universal: prohibitions against contact with women while in combat dress, for example, and admonitions against looting civilian property. Others were particular to various initiators, and could be esoteric or seemingly random: sitting on overturned rice mortars, or stepping over a banana peel.[14]

What was stressed in every instance, however—initiates often said it was the most fundamental, inviolable rule—was expressed as *baa woteh*, roughly translated as "do not turn." One implication was that the ini-

6. Mama Munda Fortune and her apprentice, Bo, 2000.

tiate should show no fear and should not run from combat. But more important was that he was not to turn on his companions or the civilian populace.[15] In other words, the kamajors' collective identity coalesced around an ethic of betrayal. Although it was ostensibly the RUF against which the war was being waged, it was the untrustworthy and predatory state army that posed the greatest threat to Mende communities and against which the kamajors defined themselves. The kamajors became those whose first principle was to behave not as soldiers do.

There are no accurate accounts for how many young men were initiated into the movement by early 1996 when the national elections brought the SLPP back to power. Muana makes a rough estimate of a hundred fighters per chiefdom in the south and east by October 1996 for a total of twenty-five hundred men, though as he points out this number was rapidly growing at this point and no centralized records were kept (1997, 90). But by the time of the Black December operations, the estimates of the number of kamajor (or CDF) fighters were an order of magnitude higher, into the tens of thousands. In other words, the vast majority of militia recruits came into the movement at a time when the state army, even more than the RUF, was the enemy. Their understanding of who they were (a nonstate force) and what they were fighting for (a legitimate, democratic government) was defined in contradistinction to the government of the contemporary postcolony. Initiation, as it became the principal determination of who a kamajor was and what he stood for, was initiation into opposition to the state.

The Poro Society

In sum, by mid-1996 a growing sense of a collective mobilization across these grassroots community defense organizations in the Mende south and east of Sierra Leone was engendered through initiation, the kamajoi name and mythology, and an anti-RUF and antistate identity. The "Mendeness" of the movement was pronounced, though ethnic nationalism was only one point in a much broader constellation of discourses about the state, civic responsibility, self-defense, and masculinity. Nevertheless, the kamajors' sense of themselves as a secret society has led many to question whether the militia should be seen as an armed manifestation of the quintessential Mende institution, the Poro secret society. This is a question deeply rooted in the ethnographic particulars of rural Sierra

Leone, but it has more broad implications: it raises the possibility that what appeared to be a novel and organic mobilization of community defenders, patched together from a host of influences and needs, may simply have been the product of a much more coherent and pre-existing social institution.

Poro is not an easy subject. The anthropologist Kenneth Little, who did the most extensive ethnographic research on Mende social practices in the 1940s, explains that "the primary function of the Poro is to equip every Mende man for the part he is to play in community life" ([1951] 1967, 243–44). Poro is often referred to as a compulsory "bush school" through which men pass en route to marriage and adulthood. Once initiated, men participate as Poro members in activities that influence a given community's social and political life. Poro members convene in secret and exercise power through the manipulation of secrecy and revelation (see Bellman 1984; Ferme 2001b, 161; Little 1965).[16] The strength of Poro varies across Sierra Leone, with relatively more importance in certain rural areas and much less prominence in urban settings or locales governed by strict Islamic authority (R. Shaw 1997, 44).

Historically, Poro played a significant role in Mende wartime mobilizations, notably interchieftaincy conflicts in the nineteenth century and the Hut Tax War with British colonial authorities in 1898 (Leach 2000; Little [1951] 1967; Malcolm 1939). Poro has also at times influenced the conflicted national political landscape of Sierra Leone, particularly in relation to SLPP intraparty politics (Kilson 1969). It does not seem unreasonable to ask, then, whether the kamajors might be considered a "Poro thing" (a Sierra Leonean English colloquialism for matters influenced by the machinations of the society). Indeed there is a great deal of evidence for a link between the two societies. Ellis (1999, 249–52) and Sawyer (2005, 62–64) each suggest that Poro was an important factor in the Liberia front of the war and in that country's exercise of political control (though for a partial critique see Utas 2003, 93–95). Paul Richards describes a Poro role in the Christmas 1994 resistance uprising in Bo (1996, 153) and, together with Fithen, identifies a Poro role in Ben-Hirsch's mobilizations (Fithen and Richards 2005, 128). Kenema residents also described their uprising against the military at the end of 1994 as a Poro affair. Those men who did not participate were fined in the same way that a Poro man who failed in his obligations when called upon by the society would be fined. In Kenema and in other defense mobilizations,

7. The red net top of a kamajor, reminiscent of the clothing of Poro initiates, near Bandajuma Sowah, 2000.

men were called together with cries of *hindo hindo* (man man), which is also used to summon Poro members. Kamajor war songs incorporated phrases from songs that mark Poro appearances or reference Poro activities. Kamajors I spoke with in the Kenema area claimed that Alpha Lavalie's mobilization efforts were also known as hindo hindo, and it was Lavalie's belief in the efficacy of Poro mobilizations against the APC government that served as one of his inspirations for Mende defensive organizing. What's more, Poro iconography was evident in kamajor mobilizations. In his work on Poro, Little notes that a "garment of red netting" marked the initiate in the Poro bush ([1951] 1967, 120). Such garments were a common enough sight at kamajor highway checkpoints in mid-2000.

Certainly many non-Mendes in the armed forces seem to have felt there was a link between the Poro and kamajor societies. In security operations in the Kenema region soldiers often questioned, beat, or detained any man with scarification, one mark of Poro membership, convinced that such marks implied kamajor initiation. Bizarrely, RUF leader Foday Sankoh is said to have appealed to the Poro in Kailahun for assistance in ridding the area of the very Liberian mercenaries he brought with him in his 1991 invasion (see Henry 2000, 67).

Kamajors themselves, however, were mixed on the importance of a

Poro link to the kamajor mobilizations. Some claimed a direct connection. Others denied it. Charles Moiwo, the national public relations officer for the CDF, vehemently disavowed any Poro involvement in the kamajors, claiming instead that the kamajors were on their way to becoming a more popular organization than Poro. "Even women and children," he said in a July 2000 interview, "would join the kamajors if they could." Many kamajor combatants drew the distinction between the two sodalities as a question of agency: the Poro and kamajors could not be the same because the former was compulsory for all men while the latter was a volunteer force (though they also argued that no self-respecting Mende man would decline to join the kamajors if the opportunity presented itself).

Others suggest that the mass dislocations in the southeast had all but suspended Poro initiations, which are tied to specific geographic locations. The Poro bush is the collection point for Poro initiation and assembly, and the Poro bush does not travel. Prominent Poro leaders were among those targeted by the RUF in a general campaign against community leaders and elites, and by the mid-1990s Poro was said to be in disarray. Alie writes that a similar fate befell the Wunde institution (a Kpaa Mende society akin to Poro) during the war years, and that the kamajor initiation largely replaced Wunde (Alie 2005, 56).

In the end, however, the question of whether or not the kamajors are a "Poro thing" is probably the wrong one to ask. To suggest that Poro underlies the kamajors as some kind of orchestrating institution gives both the kamajors' early mobilizations and Poro itself too great an institutional coherence. As Little writes: "There is, actually, no permanently existing Poro in the sense of a continuous and uninterrupted round of society activities. Members are called together at indefinite times for the attainment of specific objects, and when these objects have been gained, the 'poro' breaks up or dissolves" ([1951] 1967, 244).

Poro, in other words, is less an institution than a mobilization of (male) agency. Though it has status offices, practices, traditions, and modes of communication, Poro epitomizes Nietzsche's performance theory of power: "there is no 'being' behind the doing, acting, becoming; the 'doer' has simply been added by the imagination—the doing is everything" (Nietzsche [1872] 1956, 178–79; see also Deleuze 2006b, 85). Poro is a flexible network, a rhizome in Deleuze's and Guattari's (1987, 3) formulation. It does not seem to have controlled or given birth to the kamajor militia as much as exemplified a set of dynamic functions which in the context of war the kamajors came to fill. Increasingly kamajor initiation became the determiner of adult Mende masculinity, not so much replacing the Poro as becoming it—or, said differently, becoming the form of such becomings. The exercise or potential exercise of violence through the militia became the determinate of manhood. Musa Brima, the Bo kamajor, once told me that any Mende man who was not a kamajor initiate would be "just like a woman," a discourse of masculinity very much in keeping with that of the Poro. What's more, kamajor membership (like Poro) became a mediating force in social relationships between men and the state. The kamajors, in short, were a "Poro thing" only in the sense that they mirrored the Poro's function and many of its tropes. To see the two as synonymous is to give too much coherence to either one.

The Mobilization of Sodalities

This second plateau of the kamajors' trajectory—mobilization—is intriguing for what it suggests about nonstate militarization. What I have argued for here is a view of the kamajors at this stage as the militarization of an existing network of social relations (especially patronage) rather than the militarization of an existing social institution (the kamajoisia or the Poro). The collective identity of the kamajor militia grew, rhizome-like, from a complex mixture of experimentation and need, meaningful histories and social categories, localized conflicts and experiences of violence. Through these bits and pieces the mobilization and militarization of young men began to develop an "institutional" logic and identity all its own. This is the subject of the next part of the book, but we see its genesis in the formation of community defense committees and the proliferation of initiations into a secret society.

What I am suggesting is consistent with what other anthropologists studying the parties to this conflict have found: that the fighting factions developed their own institutional logics over the course of the war, and that much of their violence springs from how, in Mary Douglas's terms, "institutions think."[17] But here I want to pursue somewhat different implications that relate not only to the Mano River War but to how we think and talk about militarized, nonstate collectives more generally.

Underpinning a great deal of the culturalist turn in international security studies, especially within military circles of the United States and its allies, is the fantasy of an indigenous network "ideally suited for covert use by criminals, terrorists, and insurgents" (Simons 2005, 334). Consider the following from a 2004 report submitted to the U.S. Office of Net Assessment and the secretary of defense. The report calls for greater emphasis on gathering "ethnographic intelligence" (EI) on nonstate adversaries: "What we mean by EI is information about indigenous forms of association, local means of organization, and traditional methods of mobilization. Clans, tribes, secret societies, the *hawala* system, religious brotherhoods, all represent indigenous or latent forms of social organization available to our adversaries thoughtout the non-Western, and increasingly the Western, world" (Simons and Tucker 2004, 5, cited in Renzi 2006, 16–17). Such "ethnographic intelligence" is increasingly desired by the United States military and the militaries of other nations not simply to understand those against whom it is waging war but as the basis for outsourcing violence to surrogate forces. The way to combat such "latent" indigenous institutions is, according to this line of thought, to co-opt and militarize them in the service of security.

This military fantasy mistakes the mobilization (and militarization) of social networks for the mobilization of indigenous cultural institutions. It fails, in other words, to recognize that the sodalities being mobilized are the creation of that very mobilization. The kamajor militia was a novel creation whatever its connection to prewar images or categories. As deeply enmeshed in the logic of the kamajoisia and the Poro as the kamajor militia might have been, it was never simply the armed wing of either one.

The figure of the militia commander is perhaps the best illustration of the difference between the militarization of social relations and the deployment of a militarized social institution. From the beginning, the practices of patronage ran through the militia. Young men recruited into the expanding community defense patrols were nominated by community leaders who vouchsafed their identity and their trustworthiness. To join the ad hoc force was to participate on behalf of others, to be the responsibility of one's backers or patrons and to in turn be responsible for them. (This in marked contrast to the RUF and even to irregulars within the SLA, for whom participation was initially the severing of ties with those who might otherwise stand for them in the community.) Throughout the early 1990s these relations were closely tied to chiefs and other localized elites. But as the force expanded, that patronage relation was increasingly invested in the militia's commanders. The responsibility for protecting and provisioning combatants, for standing for them before the community and the militia itself, fell to an ever-greater degree on the men who were seen as militia leaders and big men, rather than as community leaders and patrons. There was, of course, a great deal of overlap; many elites, especially rural leaders affiliated with the SLPP, rose to prominence in the kamajor forces. But the role of the commander as patron created an institutional logic that was the militia's own. Young men previously marginalized from the structures of rural authority became powerful in ways they could not have before, given the patriarchal gerontocratic governance of rural communities. Violence, access to armaments, and the wherewithal to profit from providing "security" opened new pathways for patronage and building unconventional networks of influence and wealth. The kamajor militia was not simply putting to new uses an "indigenous form of association" or a "latent form of social organization." It was the emergence of a war machine, a novel force built from the material of existing social relations but put toward new ends and generating its own institutional logic as it evolved. (I explore the patronage relations at work in the movement more fully in chapter 4.)

Beginning from the assumption that kamajor mobilizations were mobilizations of an existing social institution makes it much more difficult to understand how and why the movement changed over time. As the militia expanded and the war progressed, kamajor fighters became increasingly involved in violence directed against civilians and in behavior that replicated that of the forces against which the kamajors were arrayed—the army and the RUF. (Though the level of these abuses never approached that of either of those two factions.) The discourse of the movement continued to emphasize the militia's opposition to the state military and its predations. *Kamajor baa woteh* remained an important mantra for the movement, and its claim to be the true defenders of "life and property" and democratic governance became more central to kamajor identity. But there is no question that the kamajors grew to be an ambivalent mode of community defense, ever more so as time went on. The civilian noncombatant population found themselves increasingly wary of the kamajors as they became more prominent on the Sierra Leone warscape.

There is, in other words, an evident paradox at the heart of the project of militarized community defense as embodied in the kamajor movement: the force which arose to defend communities against the state and its occasional allies, the RUF, was simultaneously a threat to those very communities. It is easy to say in retrospect, therefore, that there is no qualitative difference between the various parties to the war—and indeed, many observers have said just that (most notably the Special Court and the Truth and Reconciliation Commission). But such a reductionist view erases a more nuanced history and fails to account for some dramatic changes taking place within the militia over the course of its existence.

The common explanation for this increasing violence is the shift in deployments of kamajor units away from their "home" territory. Perhaps the most consequential analysis along this line was the "Military Expert Witness Report" submitted by the prosecution to the Special Court. The British colonel Richard Iron (2005) argued that the nature of the kamajors changed, as he put it in his testimony before the court, once they began to be "driven from many of their traditional areas" and their "chiefdom structure broke down."[18] He (and he is not alone in this) equates the "traditional" authority of the chiefs with a specific geography, namely, the village. Like a classic Africanist anthropologist, Iron equates movement—especially movement away from the village—with a loss of authentic African culture and control. Mobility and change inevitably result in a bastard and dangerous form of "cultural" (i.e., non-state) institutions.[19]

Such interpretations misread the kamajor movement empirically and conceptually. The movement was, after all, born out of dislocation and diaspora. It was in the IDP camps around Bo and Kenema, and in towns swelling with forcibly relocated villagers, that the movement recruited most of its new initiates and began its initiations. It would be a mistake to equate the kamajors, even at these early stages, exclusively with a "home territory." Certainly relationships to chiefdom authorities were critical, and the kamajors' sense of identification with their chiefdom and its terrain was strong. But this was only one factor in a web of identifications that included their status as displaced persons and as citizens of a national community betrayed by its own state army. Those who insist on seeing the kamajors as the deployment of existing social institutions are inevitably drawn to the conclusion that what the kamajors eventually became is understandable only in terms of the way these institutions ultimately failed.

Equating the changes in the kamajor militia with a loss of ties to the village and its governing structures is therefore misleading for another, more subtle reason. It is certainly true that the prominent role played by chiefdom authorities eroded in many cases, though local elites of various stripes were important players throughout the life of the movement. But the implication in these narratives of eroding "villagization" tends to misunderstand what happened next. Again, Colonel Iron's report for the Special Court is exemplary. As control of chiefs over the kamajors waned, he argues, there was a power vacuum at the center of the movement. Into the break stepped a handful of charismatic leaders who took over the militia and turned it into a private army: "The just cause of a civil defence force in Sierra Leone," said the chief prosecutor of the Special Court in his opening statement, "became perverted and was twisted beyond measure by Norman, Kundewa and Fofana. Under their leadership, these Accused war criminals turned what should have been a just cause into an unjust effect, serious breaches of the laws designed to protect humanity. These so-called defenders of the nation were really offenders of the nation looking out for their own self interests."[20] In essence, according to this argument the kamajors were deinstitutionalized, severed from the institutions of traditional chiefly authority, and then coopted by the political aspirations of a few persons.

What I take up in the next chapter is an alternative way to understand the changing nature of the movement. The kamajors' third and fourth plateaus were not its deinstitutionalization but its increased subsumption in a different institutional logic—the institutional logic of the state. It was *increased institutionalization* rather than the *absence* of controlling institutions that blurred the boundary between licit and illicit violence and helped to draw the exercise of violence into the sphere of exchange and ultimately into capital's logic of surplus production.

chapter 3

STATES OF CONFLICT

A Social History of the Kamajors, Continued

SMALL DENNIS IS A BIG MAN. He fidgeted while we sat in his black SUV parked on the main street in Duala, Monrovia. Dennis answered my questions in distracted fragments, a mountain slowly crumbling under the weight of many concerns. He compulsively checked his rearview mirrors as though expecting to see an angry mob shouting his name. Dennis never looked directly at me, and never asked why I wanted to speak with him.

In the summer of 2005 Small Dennis's concerns were serious indeed. Dennis was a veteran of the CDF Special Forces, a Liberian commander who joined the push against the AFRC in Sierra Leone and spent time in Freetown when the SLPP government was reinstated. In 2001 he joined a new rebel movement back in Liberia, the Liberians United for Reconciliation and Democracy. For two years Dennis took part in LURD's slow march on Monrovia to overthrow President Charles Taylor. When they succeeded in 2003, Dennis took his men and occupied a rubber plantation west of the capital.

The occupation was a financial success. Dennis allocated small plots to his fighters, who in turn tapped the rubber trees or hired casual laborers to do it for them. Every day the road through the plantation was lined with bundles of congealed white sap. Buyers from the domestic rubber company and from international producers drove the road and paid cash for whatever the combatants could harvest. Dennis received a cut from each plot. After two years he was a modestly wealthy man.

Now the owners of the plantation were putting pressure on the national transitional government of Liberia to rid the plantation of its squatters. The government in turn put pressure on the United Nations Mission in Liberia (UNMIL) to drive the ex-combatants out. Dennis and his associates claimed to have some three thousand ex-combatants living in camps on the plantation, and the rumor among United Nations officers was that they were heavily armed. If the ex-combatants were unwilling to go, forcing them off the plantation would not be easy.

Clearly, the ex-combatants did not want to go. The first phase of the Disarmament, Demobilization, Rehabilitation, and Reintegration Campaign (DDRR) was complete. All weapons were supposedly turned in to military observers, and all combatants registered to receive their benefits. There were no appealing alternatives for future income. The plantation was it.

As a commander Dennis was the link between his men and the United Nations. When United Nations officers decided to conduct a weapons sweep and check identities on the plantation, they contacted Dennis. So Dennis had problems. First, there were not three thousand fighters living on the plantation as he had claimed. In fact only a few hundred actually lived there, and a small number more had financial interests in the operation. There were limited firearms stashed among the rubber trees, but not the heavy artillery that a small group of fighters would need to keep from being overrun. Nor was it clear that his men would support a pitched battle with United Nations peacekeepers anyway. There was no way to stop the census and sweep, and once it began it would be clear that the plantation was virtually undefended. The ex-combatants would be moved out.

Dennis's second problem was more immediate. Once the men living on the plantation learned that Dennis had inflated the number of fighters in the forest they would assume he was chopping ("eating") the disarmament benefits of thousands of fictitious ex-combatants. A certain level of profit taking from the rents of the plantation was Dennis's prerogative as a commander, but pocketing all of the money from a DDRR scam would go a step too far. Once Dennis was accused of that level of graft, whatever justice he could expect from his men would be rough indeed.

I met Dennis when he showed up at the Monrovia home of a friend to beg for help. Mohammed was a well-known figure in both the CDF and LURD, someone who had helped bring Dennis into both organizations. What Dennis needed from him now was simple: approximately two thousand registered ex-combatants who could make it to the plantation in time for the United Nations sweep. Dennis could be slightly low on the final body count. But he needed thousands of fighters with DDRR cards to back up his claims both to the United Nations and to his

8. Rubber production outside Monrovia, 2005.

men. Mohammed could put out that kind of call and quickly draw men from around Liberia. The same good roads that move rubber from the plantations to the ports could move bodies the other way. The challenge was to get the word out, and to do so through channels that were both legitimate and discreet.

Mohammed arranged for me to speak briefly with Dennis before he turned down his request. When the occupation of the plantation began two years before, Mohammed was excluded from the profit-sharing scheme. He bore a grudge, and though he could deliver the men to protect Dennis's investment, he chose not to. He seemed to enjoy breaking the news to Dennis as I concluded my interview, and together we watched the black SUV pull back into the thick Duala traffic. Dennis looked smaller as he sped off toward downtown Monrovia to beg for bodies from sources elsewhere in the city.

The two plateaus covered in the previous chapter describe a field of forces that could only just be called a movement. They were disparate responses to a problem, the problem of protecting rural communities from the predations of both the rebels and the state army. Word of efforts from various parts of the country spread rhizome-like through the south and east of Sierra Leone. Certain figures traveled the region to share their experiences. Successful experiments in defense sparked experiments elsewhere, and gradually a common set of practices, and then a common set of identities, began to take shape. But through the middle 1990s the kamajors remained an ad hoc mobilization.

In this chapter I outline the next two plateaus in the trajectory of the kamajor militia movement. These are the further steps in what we might call, following Deleuze and Guattari, the state's capture of the kamajor war machine. What we witness here is gradual institutionalization. Institutionalization under a recognized leadership with close (if sometimes ambivalent) ties to the government of Sierra Leone, but also an institutionalization of practice and collective identity, a striation of social space (to draw again on the language of Deleuze and Guattari) in contrast to the smoothness of the war machine's early mobilizations. By the late stages of the war in Sierra Leone and the rise of the LURD rebel movement in Liberia, that institutional logic had reached its conclusion. Its apex is the fourth and final plateau of the trajectory, a plateau on which combatants still find themselves. This plateau is defined by axiomatization under the totalizing logic of capital today. At this point the process of capture by the state was complete, and the young men who participated in the militia movement were fully enmeshed in the violent logic of the contemporary global economy. There are, of course, moments of rupture. The state is always spawning new war machines. But by the nominal end of the Sierra Leone front of the Mano River War and the beginning of the LURD insurgency in Liberia, the movement as a whole was a creature far removed from its origins.

Third Plateau: Institutionalization

A report from the National Consultative Conference for the Restructuring of the Republic of Sierra Leone Civil Defence Forces (RSLCDF 2000) held in Freetown from 12 to 14 September 2000 includes this account of the pro-government militia movement from 1996 onward:

> The democratic process came in 1996 and Alhaji Dr. Ahmed Tejan Kabba leading the SLPP party won the general elections and a government of national unity was formed in February 1997 [*sic*].[1]
>
> The union of the Sierra Leone Army and the Civil militia broke up when after the general elections—November 1996 [*sic*][2]—the army then conspired against the civil populace and went into an unholy marriage with the common enemy (RUF/NPFL) fighters and turned their weapons against

> the tax payers (the civilians) whose taxes were used for the purchase of fighting logistics, uniforms, etc. for the army. This unholy marriage was unveiled on Sunday, May 25, 1997 when the army overthrew the democratically elected government led by H.E. Alhaji Dr. Ahmed Tejan Kabba, there and then the marriage partners, (the RUF/NPFL) were invited to form an illegitimate government named, the Armed Forces Revolutionary Council (AFRC) headed by the now retired Lt. Col. Johnny Paul Koroma.
>
> The AFRC government did not only throw the legitimate constitution into the dust bin, but caused the worst atrocities ever recorded in the history of mankind. The governance of AFRC sent every patriotic Sierra Leonean into hiding, including the legitimate SLPP led government in exile in Guinea.
>
> On Thursday, June 9, 1997, a small man—Mr. Eddie S. Massalley—in a very small but loud voice, shouted from the Mano River Bridge, in the Pujehun District, in the Southern Region, "I crave the indulgence of every Civil Militia: Tamaboroh, Kapras, Gbethis, Donsos, Donsuras, OBHS, Kamajors, etc. to take their fighting equipment to say no [to] the AFRC fugitives and join me at the Mano River Bridge by breaking through whatever defenses these AFRC usurpers may put up." On Sunday, June 12, 1997 thousands of Civil Militia across the board adhered to this call, thus fresh battle broke out between AFRC and the Civil Militia.
>
> Honourable Chief Sam Hinga Norman was the first government Minister to join Eddie S. Massallay at that Bridge to start organizing and co-coordinating the Civil Militia that aided ECOMOG to kick out AFRC from ruling this country in February 1998.

The history recounted in the Consultative Conference Report marks a new epoch in the kamajors' historical trajectory. The kamajoisia's ambiguous, ambivalent relationship to the military was codified in March 1997 as a relationship of armed opposition. What had been a loose network of activity took on greater coherence, both because of a more solid infrastructure for the movement and because the object it was arrayed against was also solidified. The meaning of community defense changed. Once the SLPP had been ousted from power it was no longer possible to disaggregate national concerns from those of the village, or the defense of individual rural communities from the reinstatement of a functioning, elected government. What we see in this, the kamajors' third plateau, is the institutionalization of a movement.

9. The hat and NPRC-era kamajor identification card of a village kamajor outside Bandajuma Sowah, 2001.

A De Facto Army

Early in 1996, despite the ongoing war, the NPRC military regime bowed to international and domestic pressure and held elections, handing power to an elected government. In two rounds of voting in late February and early March, the SLPP under the leadership of the former United Nations official Alhaji Tejan Kabbah became the dominant force in a new government.

The election occurred against a backdrop of heightened tensions between the armed forces and the irregular militias. Clashes between the two groups continued in the southeast and in the diamond regions farther north. Though President Maada Bio of the NPRC promised closer ties between the government forces and the kamajors, Brigadier J. O. Y. Turay announced that the army was too preoccupied with the war to offer security for the elections, leaving the kamajors to serve as the primary election-time security force throughout the southeast. Theirs was a volatile sort of security. At least twenty-four people died in the first round of elections, and in Bo "hundreds of youths danced through the streets with the severed heads and limbs of several 'rebels' who had tried to stop the election" (Riley 1996, 543).

The SLPP election victory only made tensions with the army worse.

From the party's perspective, the army remained a northern-dominated, APC institution. From the military's point of view, the SLPP affiliation with the kamajors and its close ties to key patrons in the southeast, rather than those in the capital, threatened the army with further marginalization (on this point, see Fithen 1999). The "Mendeness" of the militia grew more pronounced with the SLPP victory, creating a sense across Sierra Leone that the kamajors were becoming an "ethnic praetorian guard" (Zack-Williams 1999, 152). Vice-President Joe Demby's influential early participation in the mobilization of the kamajors furthered the perception that the militia was deeply intertwined with the new government, and President Kabbah's appointment of Regent Chief Samuel Hinga Norman as deputy minister of defense antagonized the military further.

Samuel Hinga Norman was born in 1940 in Mongeri, Bo District. Norman was regent chief of Jaiama Bangor Chiefdom, having been asked to take the position by the NPRC. An ex-military officer, Norman served in the preindependence Sierra Leone regiment and then the postcolonial Sierra Leone Army. He was known as an SLPP activist, and in 1967 was imprisoned for his part in a coup attempt against President Stevens (see Cox 1976, esp. chapter 7). Norman's role as the leader of the kamajor movement was the product of his military background and a deft ability to navigate the overlapping political worlds of the Mende chiefs and the SLPP. Though other figures emerged in the national consciousness as leaders of the irregular fighting forces, notably the kamajors' "High Priest" Allieu Kundewa, by the time he was named deputy defense minister, Norman was the face of the kamajors.

Once the SLPP was in power, its actions confirmed the military's concerns. In March 1996 the government ordered joint kamajor and military anti-RUF operations, and by October 1996 it was an open secret that the government was planning to send massive arms supplies to the kamajors (Muana 1997, 93). Press coverage of a May 1997 shipment of five thousand assault rifles intended for the kamajors made it generally impossible to consider the kamajors a supplement, rather than an alternative, to the state army (Richards 1998, 171). As peace talks with the RUF stalled, Kabbah threatened to launch kamajor-led attacks on the rebels. Rice subsidies to the military were cut in 1997, and in his Myohaung Day Parade Speech in the same month, Kabbah gave the kamajors legitimacy (and implicitly denigrated the army) by associating them with international norms of civilian defense: "Several countries maintain civil defense forces as auxiliary units to be called upon in time of need. Britain has its Territorial Army and the United States maintains the National Guard. These forces are not standing armies or rivals to the national armies of those countries. Their roles are no different than what is now intended to be assigned to the kamajors" (quoted in Bundu 2001, 55–56).

Events on the battlefront also heightened the antagonism between the militia and military. The army was generally assumed to be behind the death of Alpha Lavalie. Mwalimu Sherriff, the prominent early kamajor initiator, died in September 1996, allegedly after being tortured by soldiers; his death led to a conflagration in which eighty people died (Muana 1997, 96). The ongoing mass recruitment and initiation of kamajors expanded the reach of the force and generated military successes the army itself had not. In late 1996 and early 1997, the kamajors hit the RUF headquarters at Zagoda and killed RUF commander Mohammed "Zino" Tarrawallie, a major military achievement (see Abdullah 1998, 228).[3] In some sectors, the tensions grew so fierce that the army's chief of staff, Brigadier Hassan Conteh, gave "shoot to kill" orders to the military to be executed against kamajors.

The faction of the armed forces that announced its control of the government over the Sierra Leone Broadcasting Service radio transmission on the morning of 25 May 1997 listed the changing relationship between the central government and the militias among its reasons for intervening. Led by Johnny Paul Koroma, the Armed Forces Revolutionary Council claimed that SLPP support of the kamajors was an effort to fan tribal animosities in Sierra Leone by concentrating all power in the hands of Mendes and antagonizing other ethnic groups. The AFRC announced that the SLPP was funneling a greater share of funds and materiel support to the militias than to the country's army. The coup, they claimed, would right the balance and restore the military's sole claim to the legitimate exercise of violence. To do so, the kamajors would be outlawed immediately: "We are all one; the war is over. As I am talking now, as the spokesman now, all Kamajors are to be disbanded forthwith. No more Kamajors, no more civil defense forces as from now. We are the National Army. We have to fight for this country through the support of you, the nation."[4] For the nine months it was in power the AFRC's mode of rule was quintessentially "necropolitical," to use Achille Mbembe's term. The junta practiced a form of governance in which "the political, under the guise of war, of resistance, or of the fight against terror, [made] the murder of the enemy its primary and absolute objective" (Mbembe 2003, 12; see also Höller 2002). The enemy here was not simply the SLPP party or the militia it had come to rely on, but the civilian populace of Sierra Leone as a whole. Summary executions, the amputations of civilians' limbs, and virtually unchecked predation collapsed rule into retaliation. The junta leaders blamed everyone for their marginalization, and once in power they created a paranoid regime that made few real efforts to govern. The regime's purpose was its own protection and enrichment. There were no avenues of appeal to the decisions made on the ground by ill-disciplined soldiers and their partners in the RUF. Videos from the period record young officers, many of them evidently drunk, enforcing "the law" through hasty tribunals and immediate firing squad executions. The AFRC created a state of perpetual emergency and martial law that showed little sign of becoming a functional polity if allowed to continue.

The New Political Imaginary

Perversely, it was the SLPP's exile from power, the junta's outrageous claims on sovereign authority, and the ban on the kamajors that most shifted the nature of the kamajor militia. It did so by giving the kamajors a narrow political focus. From the moment of the coup, the kamajors were redefined by the categories of the state. The nascent movement had, until 1997, constituted itself through opposition to the threats facing rural communities. The kamajors' early manifestations were not tied to a specific political project. It was instead a community of the sort that Giorgio Agamben has called "whatever singularities" (1993, 85–87), a loose collective not defined by the categories of the state. Even the ties of many of its leading members to the SLPP opposition prior to the election did not unify the movement. There were too many working parts and too many divergent interests for the defense forces to cohere at this stage. By contrast during the junta period the militia defined itself in opposition to those who perverted the functions of a legitimate national government, and its "project" became one of seizing the state. "We fight for democracy" and "the defense of life and property" became the militia's dominant slogans, mantras that were repeated by fighters and were encoded in the militia's propaganda efforts. The identity of kamajor combatants was discursively tied to capturing the institutions of Sierra Leone's constitutional democracy. The movement's non- or antistate character was now defined specifically by the need to recreate the state rather than simply defend against it. Along with other, smaller pro-government militia forces, the kamajors were rechristened the Civil Defence Force, a name meant to place the movement within a genealogy of state-sanctioned outsourcing of security for the protection of democratic institutions: "Civil Defence Force" was thought by militia leaders to sound militant enough to reflect the group's armed campaign, while still evoking a democratic constitutional order (rather than a revolutionary or millenarian project).

The militia's efforts during the junta period graphically illustrate the complexities of politics in the postcolonial African state. It signifies the aporia in which postcolonial African subjects often find themselves: caught between thoroughly "criminalized" states (Bayart, Ellis, and Hibou 1999) and the recognition that a functioning national government is required for stability. The CDF's slogans and the rhetoric of CDF combatants reveal the desire for an ideal democratic state, a popular imaginary of a political system that could guarantee the rights and security of citizenship. As Patrick Bond points out, the state, despite its "admittedly rancid and repressive" nature in Africa today, appears to many African activists as the most likely source of protection against the otherwise unchecked ravages of the global marketplace (Bond 2006, 155). Faced with a regime like the AFRC and RUF junta, for which violent profiteering was so nakedly its sole purpose, the political fantasy of a well-functioning, democratic polity was salient indeed. The CDF responded to the necropolitics of the junta with a vague but powerful narrative of fighting for the ideal government that might replace it.

At the same time, CDF combatants' stated goals make clear the practical limits of that political fantasy. The winner-takes-all system of electoral politics in Sierra Leone, as in so much of sub-Saharan Africa, makes it virtually impossible to disaggregate the ruling party from the abstract or impartial institutions of the state (see Reno 1995; see also Southall, Simutanyi, and Daniel 2006). Opposing a blatantly unconstitutional and repressive government of military and rebels, rank-and-file CDF fighters conflated the SLPP party with a democratic ideal. In fighting for the elected SLPP government—the first in Sierra Leone to be internationally recognized as such since Siaka Stevens came to power—the kamajors turned CDF saw themselves as fighting not only for the party but for the institutions of a sovereign democratic state. The two were inseparable at that moment. It was impossible for most CDF fighters to imagine how it could be otherwise, to conceive of a state that was structured differently. Later, when the SLPP had been restored to power, the conflation of the party with the political fantasy of ideal government would be challenged repeatedly. But with the SLPP forced out of power and sitting in exile, it was possible for youth affiliated with the CDF to live for—and fight for—a political project that was both material *and* idealistic.

The upshot, however, was that the political imaginary of the CDF movement was organized according to the categories of the state. Whatever experiments or unforeseen consequences might have come from the grassroots mobilization of the kamajors were curtailed by the AFRC coup because the militia took its sole new task to be the recapture of the Sierra Leonean capital and hence the state (and, subsequently, the overthrow of Charles Taylor in Liberia). What had begun as a decentralized community defense effort, as a creative war machine, was in the end captured by the logic of the state. Its revolutionary possibilities were curtailed by the fantasy of a democratic polity that could only be imagined in the form of a reinstated SLPP.

The actual restoration of the SLPP revealed the fantasy. Norman retained his post as deputy minister of defense, and Joe Demby the post of vice-president. But the preponderance of CDF fighters felt that they went unrecognized and unsupported after their integral role in reestablishing the government. The SLPP relied on the CDF's security function in the postjunta landscape and granted CDF veterans use of the Brookfields Hotel in Freetown, allocating militia members a stock of arms and a regular ration. But these benefits were funneled through SLPP stalwarts who brazenly manipulated the allotments. Norman and the CDF's new "Administrative Wing" solidified loyalties and their personal patronage networks through the appropriation of state resources. The Sierra Leone parliament's monthly financial contribution of rice and other provisions codified the militia within the security apparatus of the national government but also effectively wove it into the functional logic of a neopatrimonial postcolonial state. The vast majority of the CDF rank-and-file fighters found themselves excluded from those disbursements, or found that access to them required other favors done for CDF leaders. Membership in the force did not come automatically with any rights or rewards from the state. Fighters were forced to work the patronage networks erected by senior men in the organization, a precarious and unstable situation that guaranteed them nothing in return for their role as combatants. The social category of youth, marginalized and given short shrift by the national "gerontocracy," once again became the prevailing reality for many young men who had fought for what they imagined could be a more equitable political future.

A year after the war ended, a passing comment on the outskirts of Freetown revealed just how implausible was the CDF combatants' conflation of the fight to restore the SLPP government and the fight for an ideal democracy. Mohammed Gleh, a kamajor from the border regions of Pujehun who fought in Freetown in 1998 and 1999, was living with his family in a *pan-bodi* shack in the mountain forests overlooking the city.[5] He was a squatter making a living breaking rocks for the houses of elites and occasionally selling djamba to fighters across the border in Liberia. There were persistent rumors that the government of Sierra Leone would force squatters off the land as government ministers and business elites sought to escape the crowded urban center by relocating their own homes to the cool mountains. When I asked him about this, Mohammed argued vehemently that as a citizen of Sierra Leone, and one who had fought for the restoration of the legitimate government, he had an inalienable right to land. His squatter's rights, he claimed, were inviolable. As one of the men gathered in the small crowd turned away, I heard him mutter that killing too many people had clearly made all the kamajors crazy. If some of the CDF fighters clung to the fantasy of a truly democratic state post-AFRC, the majority of Sierra Leoneans had long since recognized the fallacy.

Even as the youth who made up the bulk of the CDF were excluded from the new dispensation, Sierra Leone's political, militia, and military leaders set out to officially enshrine the CDF within the actual institutions of governance—effectively ending any distinction between the militia and the apparatuses of the state government of Sierra Leone. In a 1999 handbook titled *Recommended Values and Standards*, prepared by the Technical Committee of the restructuring campaign, the organization refers to itself as the Republic of Sierra Leone Civil Defence Force. The name mimics that of the state army (Republic of Sierra Leone Military Force); the handbook states the purpose of the force as being to "serve any democratically elected government . . . in [a] wide range of operations from collection and collation of intelligence information, [to conduct] warfare to liberate the nation from illegal governance, to aid in peace support operations and adhere to the wish of the civil authorities" (1999, 3). For a few years, the CDF leadership continued efforts to make that institutionalization permanent. The militia's important role in the defense of the government (both in the countryside and in the capital, particularly during the 6 January 1999 invasion) and its work with ECOMOG and to a lesser extent the British military provided a backdrop against which the CDF leaders proposed a Territorial Defence Force (TDF). The TDF would be a standing militia organized at the chiefdom or district level that would stand apart from the state army but work as a supplement to it—and as a check against it. As envisioned by the CDF leadership, the TDF would provide a state income for select former CDF fighters and would make them the beneficiaries of both training and material support (including weapons) from British and United Nations donors who had taken up the challenge of reforming Sierra Leone's security sector. How seriously the idea of a TDF was entertained by those outside the CDF itself is unclear. But by the time of Norman's arrest for war crimes by the Special Court for Sierra Leone, the idea was dead.

In sum, as the CDF moved from defending rural communities to fighting to reinstate an elected government, and to protecting that government from a military that had proven itself to be uncooperative, it grew much harder to construe the force as a grassroots mobilization of society against the state. The Black December operation and the other efforts by the CDF to restore the SLPP shifted the "defensive" role of the militia from one of defending rural communities to defending the state—albeit in the form of the SLPP and a certain fantasy of democratic governance. The militia grew more predatory and more abusive toward the population it was ostensibly meant to defend (though it never approached the thoroughly paranoid, necropolitical mode of violent authority exercised by the AFRC and RUF). Equally important, the movement grew less creative. It ceased to experiment, to open up new ideas or envision new possibilities for a future in Sierra Leone. It became, in Deleuze's and Guattari's Nietzschean terms, a more reactive, less active force. As the government it sought to defend was pushed out of power, the reinstatement of the "legitimate" state—and everything that defines the postcolonial African state today—became both the *casus belli* and the raison d'etre of the movement as a whole.

The Triumph of the State

The contrast to what the CDF might have become is striking. Anticolonial movements for African independence across sub-Saharan Africa (especially those that required violent confrontation with colonial powers) created transnational networks and alliances with multifaceted relations to the states through which they passed. Negritude, Pan-Africanism, Black Zionism, African Socialism, and Marxism were all movements that both connected histories of struggles to points around Africa *and* imagined a different future and new forms of political alliance. These were movements and moments in which "struggles in other parts of the world" were not necessarily "written in an incomprehensible foreign language" (Hardt and Negri 2000, 57). That the CDF's transnational connections came almost exclusively in the form of commercial networks or forces specifically interested in the recapture of the state (and not in its reform or rethinking) underscores just how hegemonic the prevailing logic of the African state has become.

The CDF leader Hinga Norman may have expressed this best when on various occasions he articulated his vision for Sierra Leone in the wake of the overthrow of the AFRC. His vision was somewhat more nuanced than that of the rank-and-file CDF fighters. Norman told a number of audiences that his intention was to seize the capital from the junta and then institute a three-year state of martial law, overseen by himself and the CDF. Three years of extraconstitutional rule, he reasoned, was all the "international community" would tolerate before demanding the full reinstatement of the constitution.[6] Norman seemed to understand that, as William Reno puts it in his analysis of contemporary "warlord politics," statehood in some postcolonial African polities is defined principally through recognition by other states, rather than through any internal obligation to the national citizenry (Reno 1998, 5–7). Three years, Norman reasoned, was as long as he and the CDF could legitimately govern under emergency measures. The United Nations, the United States, the United Kingdom, and the World Bank would allow him three years before it demanded accountability and the complete restitution of the SLPP government. Within that three years, however, he would be free to negotiate a wide range of contracts both in Sierra Leone and outside it, contracts that would solidify his patronage network and his political hold, either through subsequent elections or as a private power broker.

This was the model of sovereign power championed by Charles Taylor in neighboring Liberia, and was the model proposed by LURD leaders when they overthrew him. Just as Norman did, LURD commanders during the push on Monrovia routinely spoke of the three-year grace period of extraconstitutional rule they expected to enjoy once Taylor was removed. A full year before they overthrew him, LURD commanders were already signing contracts with European and Lebanese businessmen for resource concessions in the post-Taylor period.

What Norman and the LURD leadership proposed was not a challenge to the existing state order so much as a practical understanding of how postcolonial states work. (Maxwell Khobe, the ECOMOG leader, apparently realized this as well; despite his assurances that Norman and the kamajors would be airlifted to Freetown for the final push against the AFRC, in the end Khobe elected not to bring significant numbers of kamajors, or Norman, to the capital.)

Yet even as the CDF was increasingly organized according to the logic of the state, it, too, bred war machines. Norman and the coterie surrounding him found themselves at odds with a faction of the movement that powerfully identified as youth, and came to define themselves less in opposition to the deposed junta and the RUF then to a gerontocratic order from which they felt excluded. This narrative of youth exclusion had always been a part of the RUF's own peculiar discourse. But as the numbers of CDF combatants grew, and as young, nonelite men began to take on greater importance as commanders and patrons (largely through battlefield successes and clever manipulation of the flow of military hardware, both of which I take up in the next chapter), many CDF fighters began to think of themselves more and more as part of a youth "rebel" movement that included the RUF and extended beyond the borders of Sierra Leone. Gangsta icons from the United States like Tupac Shakur, reggae stars like Bob Marley and Peter Tosh, and a range of African guerrilla movements like UNITA in Angola and the Sudan People's Liberation Army were all discussed by CDF fighters as fellow travelers in a war that was as much against corrupt elders as it was against the RUF or the junta. What was striking about conversations with CDF militia fighters in the wake of the SLPP restoration was the sense of disaffection so many of them felt from the SLPP leadership and the leadership of the CDF itself, and how many combatants applauded the RUF's (and even sometimes the AFRC's) initial goals for the invasion. While most combatants faulted the RUF for allowing their "revolution" to devolve into an undisciplined campaign of pillage, by the end of the war a significant number of CDF fighters referred to *themselves* as "rebels" and claimed to be in sympathy with the RUF's project of creating a different, youth-led future for Sierra Leone. That this rhetoric never generated a coherent political vision or ideology may be, as Abdullah (1998) has argued for the RUF, a product of the failure of political imaginary on the part of lumpen youth. But certainly it is noteworthy that by the end of the war the CDF had continued a legacy that stretches back decades in Sierra Leonean politics: "youth" remained one of the few salient categories of political opposition to the state.

The three plateaus of the kamajor militia movement I have described thus far (mythopoetic origins, mobilization, and institutionalization) trace an arc. In Deleuze's and Guattari's terms, these were moments of increasing capture of a war machine by the state. The fourth plateau is the endpoint of this arc. It is the moment in which that war machine is fully captured. This period saw the end of the Sierra Leone front of the war and two national elections in that country. It also saw the rise of a new front in Liberia and the overthrow of President Charles Taylor. My purpose here is to explore how all of these events, and others that concerned the young men embroiled in the Mano River War, belong to a qualitatively similar logic—the logic of contemporary capital's global empire.

The Fourth Plateau: Capital's "Axiomatics"

Hinga Norman's three-year postjunta plan never materialized, but it is emblematic of what the movement became in its final manifestation. Into its institutional, state-defined logic came a new calculus: the profitability of participating in a violent, armed faction. From 1998 onward the CDF became not only a mode of deploying male youth but of employing them. The nationalist political and social language of the CDF did not disappear. Rather, it came to incorporate a defining economic logic as well, effectively erasing the distinction between these spheres and organizing them all according to the dictates of today's global economy. This is the logic I explore in the remainder of this chapter and in the chapters that follow.

To understand the kamajors' fourth and final plateau, we return for a moment to the theoretical landscape I mapped in the introduction. The period was, and remains, defined by what Deleuze and Guattari called the "axiomatics" of the late stage of capitalism. Deleuze's and Guattari's critique of Freud and Marx in *Capitalism and Schizophrenia* is that both misunderstood the crisis that confronts the modern subject. Each finds the root of conflict in some immutable force. Sexuality and the gendered family create the conflicted interior, psychic life of the individual for Freud. Differential access to the means of production creates the exterior world of economic classes for Marx. Deleuze and Guattari challenge the foundations of both approaches. The real object of Deleuze's and Guattari's critique, however, was not Freud or Marx but the ways in which Deleuze's and Guattari's contemporaries understood the political upheavals of the late 1960s. *Capitalism and Schizophrenia* proposed an explanation more nuanced than either the psycho-dramas of Freudian commentators or the simplistic class analyses of the period's Marxists. Deleuze and Guattari did not break entirely from either one, but brought the two together.

What they propose is an analysis of "production *in general and without distinction*" (1983, 302). In contrast to Freudian psychoanalysis and Marxian class analysis, Deleuze and Guattari argue that the dualism of interior and exterior worlds, private and public lives, libidinal and political economy are simply conventions rooted in the way capital "codes" all manner of production. Capital's processes are as much about the manufacture of individual desire as the manufacture and consumption of commodities.

The implication for anthropology, particularly an anthropology of war in Africa today, is that we cannot disaggregate discrete questions of individual psychology, economic determinism, cultural logic, or political projects. For lack of a better term, we require an approach to political crisis that is more holistic. An anthropology of violence in this mode does not treat violence as a symptom. It doesn't necessarily diagnose root causes. Instead it treats violence as a form of labor and looks to see what violence produces and what it *does*. It looks to map how violence travels and asks for what it might be exchanged.

Most scholars of the Mano River War recognize this implicitly. Responding to simplistic explanations of West African conflicts that circulated in the popular media and in policy circles in the 1990s, anthropologists, historians, and political scientists struggled to account for what Yusuf Bangura called the "several logics" of violence (Bangura 2004, 24). There is now a general acknowledgment that the dynamics of this war are too complex to be thought of in exclusively economic, political, cultural, or psychological terms. Still, thinking with these spheres together is not easy. In even the most subtle analyses of the conflict there is a tendency to bifurcate the lives of combatants into interior and exterior domains. Invariably, one of these is reified, given precedence over the others and made to serve as an explanatory foundation.

David Keen, for example, has drawn on the writings of the American criminal psychologist James Gilligan (1999) to understand the wartime dynamics of the RUF. Violence committed by groups like the RUF has its political and economic dimensions, writes Keen (2005), but it also has a psychic connection to individual combatants' sense of humiliation and shame. Perpetually denigrated, marginal young men joined the rebels and were further humiliated by the failure of their rebellion and by the opprobrium of civilians. They responded by violently asserting themselves against a public that did not give them the respect they felt they deserved: "[O]ur understanding of the Sierra Leonean war," Keen writes, "is furthered by the idea of a shameless community encountering a threat of shame" (64). This is hardly a Freudian analysis of the sort that circulated through French intellectual circles in the late 1960s and early 1970s. Keen goes to some length to connect the psychic life of combatants to the supraindividual forces of the economy and politics. Nevertheless, in Keen's writing shame and humiliation are normative categories and they belong exclusively to the interior life of the persons who made up the "shameless community" of the RUF. The meaning of shame is assumed to be self-evident. What is missing are the ways in which that term might shift meaning in relation to (for example) different contexts of culture or class. Or the way it might lose meaning altogether in the modern global economy of affective labor or in the modern way of war.

Conversely, a number of Sierra Leone scholars have drawn attention to the character and make-up of the "lumpens" who constituted the RUF and much of the armed forces of the state. The contributors to two important works, a 1997 edition of the journal *African Development* and a 2004 CODESRIA book edited by Ibrahim Abdullah, offer subtle looks at youth culture and popular political imaginaries at work in Sierra Leone. Marginal urban and village youth brought into a rebel movement and a state army that could not or would not control them turned this lumpen culture into devastating practices of violence. Here again, this is not the vulgar Marxism of immutable class conflict. Scholars like Abdullah, Bangura, and Ismail Rashid are careful to trace the specific histories and cultural practices that make up what they call the lumpen demographic that fought the war. They are attentive to what was specific about the culture and psychology of marginal Sierra Leonean youth. But this approach risks reifying these lumpen youth as a class. "Lumpens" end up having a collective character that is ultimately determined by the exterior forces of the political economy. "It ought to be stressed," as Bangura puts it, "that lumpens or marginals have been well theorized in Marxist literature as constituting poor material for progressive social change. . . . [L]umpens abuse drugs and are prone to random violence in pursuit of objectives" (2004, 21, 34).[7] There is no room here for thinking about the production of individual lives or even the production of lumpenness itself. Everything is subsumed under and explained by the marginality of certain violent youth.

In truth, nothing in the experience of West Africa's young male combatants was so easily fixed. Not their class position, not their emotional or psychic relationship to violence, not their sense of their own history or their imagination of the future. Reifying either the psycho-dramas of combatants or their class character obscures critical dynamics underlying this war: the extent to which combatants were unmoored from virtually *any* certainty about themselves or their world; the extent to which all aspects of their lives were made available to forces larger than themselves; the creative potential (as well as devastation) that this deterritorialization of life itself unleashed. This is not unique to the Mano River War. It is the condition of postcoloniality for many African youth, exacerbated perhaps by wartime dynamics but not limited to them.

Put differently, and drawing on the Deleuzian framing I employ here, nothing in the lives or experiences of militia fighters was outside the possibility of exchange. This is a complex idea and it requires some investment in the language and logic of contemporary Marxism. But the upshot is a way to think about all manner of wartime dynamics—the experiences of individual combatants, the collective mobilization of armed groups, the political and economic projects of elites—as part of the same broad and infinitely transformative play of forces.

Deleuze's and Guattari's corrective to Freudian and Marxian analyses of crisis in the modern moment was to focus on what they called capital's "axiomatic." They suggest that according to capital's particular organizational logic all aspects of the social world are rendered abstract and made into equivalent exchange values. Capital's "cash nexus" allows for the exchange and combination of a virtually unlimited range of practices, beliefs, images, and material objects as though all were commodities, the values of which are tied to their circulation. They refused to disaggregate interior and exterior spheres. Nothing, they argued, operates outside the logic of capital's modes of accumulation and exchange.

In Marxian terms, this is the condition of life under the real subsumption of labor. The real subsumption of labor is the point at which labor power no longer needs to be harnessed for the production of capital's surpluses, but organizes itself toward that end. As Marx wrote in the *Grundrisse*, the real subsumption of labor is the moment "the product ceases to be the product of isolated direct labor, and the combination of social activity appears, rather, as the producer" ([1857] 1973, 709; see also Hardt 1995, 38). Put simply, any aspect of the lived world can be productive of capital's form of value. For Marx, capitalism in an earlier moment was characterized by the "formal" subsumption of labor—a contest to harness the productive capacity of a people according to the logic of the production of exchange value. The labors that characterize noncapitalist social organization are co-opted by means overt and unseen for the production of surpluses as defined by the capitalist mode of accumulation.[8] Under formal subsumption there remains a space outside, a sphere of "nonwork" or purely social relations. Labor formally subsumed means there are still spaces of leisure, play, reproduction, ritual, or imagination that are completely outside the calculus of capital. There are political projects not mediated by capital's forms of value. By contrast, capital achieves the *real* subsumption of labor when the space of nonwork disappears, when there seem to be no relations not organized according to the exchange-value-producing regimen, when there is no outside to capital. Subsumption is real when all relations—"social subjectivities, sociality, and society itself" (Hardt and Negri 1994, 7)—seem extensions of the logic of capital. It is at this moment that we enter postmodernity.

Production without limits is how Deleuze and Guattari characterize the processes of production under the real subsumption of labor, and nowhere is it more clearly evident than in the warscape of the West African postcolony. Violence itself enters the networks of circulation and exchange. According to capital's logic of surplus production it becomes interchangeable with diamonds and cash, its value translated into political subjectivity and masculine identity. More than simply a tool or a strategy, violence is itself a commodity, circulating through networks of commerce and exchange.[9] So too are the bodies, the imaginaries, and the very futures of those performing that violence. They become integral to a new regulatory logic at work in the African postcolony.

The New Economy

Restoring the SLPP government in 1998 did not end the war in Sierra Leone. Fighting between remnants of the AFRC, RUF, CDF, and ECOMOG continued in the countryside. As they had throughout the war, ambushes and attacks on villages took place more frequently than pitched battles between forces, with the notable exception of the major rebel assault on Freetown on 6 January 1999. The Freetown invasion set off an extremely brutal month of fighting in the capital. The eastern sector of the city was hit especially hard, while a combined ECOMOG and CDF force dug in among the western neighborhoods. Since the overthrow of the AFRC junta, kamajors and other CDF forces, as noted, had been barracked at the downtown Brookfields Hotel, and during the invasion personnel from the hotel operated under the direction of ECOMOG commanders as well as under their own internal command.

Though integral to the defense of the city and the eventual routing of the AFRC and RUF forces, CDF activities during the 6 January invasion contributed to a growing popular ambivalence about the movement, both domestically and internationally. Kamajors looted deserted houses as AFRC and RUF forces abandoned their positions, the militia displayed the severed heads of supposed rebels and collaborators outside its Brookfields Hotel barracks, and CDF combatants working with Captain Evil Spirit of ECOMOG at the Aberdeen Bridge participated in highly visible, systematic extrajudicial executions (Human Rights Watch 1999, 43). Such intense violence was of mounting concern, as was the militia's increasingly blatant profit taking.

It is important to note that for the most part, CDF fighters saw themselves as participants in a just cause, aware of the boundaries between legitimate and illegitimate violence and appropriation. A CDF commander I spoke with in the aftermath of the fighting listed the goods his men had looted during the 6 January offensive: motorcycles from UNICEF, computers from various United Nations offices, beer and rum from the national brewery, chickens from farms on the outskirts of town. "We ate well then," he said. "In war, you eat very well." In recounting this story the commander was careful to qualify these as legitimate appropriations for a national defense force. These were items either essential to the task of defending the nation (alcohol, food, transportation) or goods intended for the citizenry of Sierra Leone anyway (the United Nations material). Looting was simply a more efficient mode of distribution than the corrupt and bloated United Nations bureaucracy. By contrast, and unlike the AFRC and RUF, this commander maintained that the CDF had left the property of civilians untouched. "I'm proud we never looted the center of the city. We could have destroyed Freetown, but in the center of the city, no one touched a thing."[10] Like the militia movement itself, the conversation wove together otherwise disparate discourses on violence, citizenship, and economic security in the postcolony. Here was a young man narrating a story that was at once about the war and about postcolonial subjectivity, at least for male youth. One eats well in war. The traffic in violence makes the distribution of goods—goods that belong to "the people"—more efficient. And the CDF's quasi-state violence actually served to protect the security of noncombatants against the failings and machinations of other state and nonstate forces. When Janet Roitman writes of banditry in the Chad Basin that "violent appropriation is a modality not only of social mobility but also of social welfare, being intrinsic to the nexus of relationships that provides and ensures economic security" (2006, 258), she could well be writing of the Mano River region in the decade following the SLPP restoration. Still evaluating themselves in contrast to the rebels and state army—and increasingly to their own leadership—CDF fighters did not for the most part see themselves as oppositional to the noncombatant population. Yet young men's ability to exchange violence (including withholding it) had become key to their participation as subjects in the new postmodern West African landscape. Wartime conditions made this glaringly obvious, but as we will see it was a condition that lasted beyond the war don don declaration of January 2002.

If this was how combatants saw themselves, it was not a vision of male youth embraced by many noncombatant civilians. The new economy of violence was a growing source of concern. It was unquestionably instrumental in staving off rebel advances, but was itself increasingly predatory. The city swirled with stories of armed robberies and attacks were blamed on the CDF almost as much as on the AFRC and RUF. CDF "missions" now included attacks on business rivals of the movement's leaders and sponsors, often under the guise of rooting out collaborators. Upcountry, especially in the south and east, the CDF presence was most visible on the country's road network and it was here that most civilians encountered the kamajors. Kamajors in the towns and villages near major roads set up roadblocks, searched vehicles, and taxed drivers or passengers. In the summer of 2000, the southern route between Freetown, Bo, and Kenema was completely under the control of the kamajors, while the more direct northern route was subject to attacks by the West Side Boys and the RUF. Traveling the southern route in a minivan crammed with market women and students, I counted forty-five kamajor checkpoints

10. The kamajor checkpoint at the Mabang Bridge on the southern road to Bo, August 2000.

(along with three from other security services) in the ninety-mile stretch between the towns of Songo and Bo. At every checkpoint save one the driver paid a tax of five hundred to a thousand leones, and at many of these roadblocks the passengers were searched and individually taxed as well. These taxes were portrayed by the militia fighters as an extension of the community support that had sustained them throughout the war and as a form of salary for their labors providing security. "War effort" taxes were similarly collected in markets or other public places policed by the kamajors, often pre-empting the authority of governing bodies like the town council to collect taxes or place surcharges on economic activity.[11] But maintaining security in the aftermath of the 1998 SLPP restoration was not simply an opportunity to loot or profiteer. It was work for the men who participated in the CDF. A form of work with no outside, a life's work. The performance of violence had become a trade and the foundation of an identity. The discourses that circulated among combatants were still those of "defending life and property," of fighting for democracy, and of accepting the responsibilities of manhood.

This suggests an alternative to the much-discussed and by now tired "greed versus grievance" debate about African warfare.[12] Combatants performing the work of this war were no more greedy than other laborers in the postmodern global economy, and their work was inextricably tied to their understandings of the rights and political responsibilities of citizens and of men. What they were producing at highway checkpoints was both a livelihood and themselves.

What the CDF in its last iteration seems to represent, in other words, is a "collapsing" economy of values. Collapsing in the sense of an erasure of distinctions between value regimens. Discourses of manhood and citizenship, ethnic nationalism, and national citizenship all became subject to evaluation on the same scale, a scale of tradable commodities and interchangeability with violence, cash, and debt. Desperate poverty, the disruptions of life processes throughout communities, and the exigencies of war led to a new mode of evaluating relationships (and persons) on a monetarized scale (Mbembe 2006). This put CDF fighters at odds with a number of other "regulatory regimes," including not only the United Nations, international NGOs, and international judicial bodies but also a great deal of the noncombatant populace in Sierra Leone. Many of those institutions generate discourses and normative visions of combatants as either political subjects (revolutionaries, rebels, or insurgents), economic agents (greedy or impoverished), or social actors (tribalists or nativists). Very few seem willing to consider combatants as all of these simultaneously—or more accurately, to recognize that these are no longer separate domains. For the young men who participated in the movement there was no easy separation in how they evaluated themselves as "fiscal subjects" (Roitman 2005, 31) versus other forms of participation in the world—participation as national citizens, as men, as members of an ethnic group.

Media reports from the late 1990s to the end of the war, and much of the record generated by the SCSL and the TRC, have tended to miss this. They treat the CDF synonymously with the RUF and AFRC—one more of the indistinguishably violent factions in a civil war without logic or rules. Such narratives overlook the documentation of human rights observers, which consistently catalogue significantly fewer abuses committed by the pro-government forces than by the army or the rebels (see, for example, Human Rights Watch 1998, 1999, 2003; Physicians for Human Rights 2000). They have also occluded any political evaluation of the actions of the movement, giving no weight to the defense of the capital and an elected government versus the efforts of the AFRC and RUF forces to sack the city and reinstate the junta. But perhaps most important, they ignore the extent to which the CDF exemplified a mode of young male subjectivity (and participation) that was becoming generalized across the region and extended beyond the official end of the conflict. Joining the CDF and putting one's body and its capacity for violence into circulation as a tradable commodity had become the grounds for economic, political, and social being. This is more than simply a "local" understanding of international discourses. It was, rather, an emergent form of participation in the global economy, a form that made the CDF a dangerous ally.

The organization seemed to recognize in the wake of the 1999 fighting that its relationship with the civilian populace was deteriorating. The internal report from September 2000 calls June 1999 the low point in relations between the CDF and civilians (RSLCDF 2000), though relations worsened further still as the force set up increasingly extortionate roadblocks and checkpoints around the country. A series of high-profile incidents brought the militia unwanted attention, including the hijacking of a truck carrying soldiers' pay to the east, allegedly orchestrated by Allieu Kundewa, and skirmishes over control of diamond digging sites. Equally troubling to many Sierra Leoneans were pronouncements by the SLPP about its vision of the CDF and its future. In late January 1999, James Jonas, a key government minister, was reportedly seeking assistance from London in arming and training a territorial defense unit three times the size of the national army (Bundu 2001, 109). In a national address in February, President Kabbah made clear that the SLPP government considered the CDF and ECOMOG—an irregular militia and a foreign interventionary force—to be the true defenders of the state.

For ECOMOG at least, that security mandate was terminated with the signing of the peace accord in Lomé, Togo, in July. The controversial agreement opened the way for a United Nations peacekeeping force and for the disarmament of the various fighting factions. An exceedingly corrupt and ineffective disarmament program (DDR) did not stop the CDF from conducting massive recruiting and initiation drives, nor did it dismantle the highway checkpoints. And on 8 May 2000, the peace agreement fell apart. Foday Sankoh's bodyguards fired into a crowd of demonstrators outside the RUF leader's Freetown residence, killing at least twenty people. Despite Sankoh's almost immediate arrest and a British intervention force sent to secure the capital, disarmament proceedings were suspended for a year and hostilities continued between the RUF, CDF, and remnants of the AFRC.

The 8 May incident stimulated a mass remobilization of kamajors around the country. As was true throughout the war, it is impossible to accurately assess the number of forces in the kamajor movement or the CDF overall. *Africa Confidential* put the figure of "pro-government forces" at 11,500 in June of 2000, while the CDF leadership routinely claimed that it commanded 99,000 fighters. In his TRC testimony, President Kabbah asserted that the pro-government forces numbered 86,000 at the end of the war. In part what makes assessing the numbers so difficult is that the end of disarmament and the remobilizations of 8 May led to a massive "top-up" operation on the part of initiators.

These ritual reinitiations, which borrowed the local terminology for adding money to a cellular telephone account ("topping-up"), were intended to bring new combatants into the militia and to renew the bulletproof status of previously initiated kamajors. Initiations in this period constituted a significant departure from the operational structure of the movement to that point and it glaringly illustrates the militia's new economy. In what was recognized as a moneymaking scheme for initiators, various kemohs began conducting mass initiations for anyone willing to pay for them (as opposed to working with local chiefs and other elites to identify and sponsor initiates). Sheik Walid Kallon at Bandajuma Sowah described in naked detail his need to turn protective medicines into a business enterprise in the absence of government "encouragement" for his services. The kamajor High Priest Allieu Kundewa created a series of new kamajor units with ever more expensive initiations and minimal screening of recruits. Newly designed rituals were developed that relieved the initiate of any need to observe behavioral restrictions to maintain his bulletproof status. Initiators charged more for them than for "traditional" initiation ceremonies which came with prescriptions on sex, drug use, or looting.

The CDF's September 2000 restructuring report blamed the high cost of initiation for the increasingly exorbitant tariffs charged by combatants at checkpoints along the southern highway. The central tenet of kamajor identity, the thing that guaranteed a fighter his bulletproof status and made him a Mende male—initiation—had become quite pricey and demanded ever greater financial investment. With no alternative but to continue this war-related effort, CDF fighters extorted more and more funds from passengers on the country's roads.

In some cases, CDF units further alienated local communities with their broad definition of "security." Titus Dauw, a kamajor at the Bo CDF headquarters, explained to me in mid-2000 that it fell upon the kamajors to do such "security jobs" as combating thieves and punishing people "guilty of involvement in social vices." The absence of a robust police force in most rural areas meant that citizens took their complaints about neighbors to local CDF commanders. These in turn arbitrated matters much as the police force in Sierra Leone does—by taxing the parties they deemed guilty or by working on behalf of those willing to pay for justice.

Even as the ranks of the CDF swelled over the summer of 2000, and it broadened its own understanding of its role, the CDF's claims to a security mandate became increasingly implausible. The United Nations peacekeeping deployment was expanded (eventually reaching seventeen thousand troops, the largest in United Nations history at that point). A small number of British troops remained in the country to begin training the new Sierra Leone Army and to unofficially help stave off another coup or RUF invasion. The DDR program was reinstated, and though it had only limited success in demobilizing the CDF it did mark the end of official government reliance on the force for security.

However, it was not until the "official" end of the war and the disarmament campaign on 18 January 2002 that the end came for the CDF as well. Its demise was made more painful and complex by exacerbating tensions between rank-and-file combatants and the CDF leadership. Many kamajors complained that Hinga Norman and others with the CDF Administrative Wing were hoarding the contributions of donors and distributing them only through their personal patronage networks. Eddie Massallay and other key figures, especially those associated with Pujehun and the eastern regions, led a restructuring campaign which was at least partly an effort to break Norman's hold on the movement. Kamajor fighters confronted a postconflict landscape they did not understand, in which economic security was tied to mastery over the bureaucratic maze of NGOs and development institutions. The small wartime spaces of exception that militia members had carved for themselves disappeared, and the boundaries between licit and illicit production were redrawn by forces over which most combatants had little influence or control. Illiterate or rural CDF members in particular were surrounded by a world of vast "relief effort" wealth (manifest in the form of new Toyota Land Cruisers and cellphones), but little sense of how that world was accessed.

A Sierra Leonean fighter who joined the Special Forces in Sierra Leone and then LURD in Liberia described the bafflement many young men experienced when, in the wake of the Taylor overthrow, he found himself stranded and destitute in Monrovia. "I am not supposed to be here," he said.

> [I was] thinking that I would be someplace else. That I would be proud for serving my country. But nothing like that. [I thought I would] get more money. [*Question: From where?*] From the international world! The international community! I suspected they would pay me for the good job I have done. For overthrowing Charles Taylor. I was in Special Forces. I take myself as a mercenary. My mission was accomplished, so I expected I would be paid [by the United Nations] because of my good job. To re-install peace in Africa as a whole. Because I can say that because when peace comes to Liberia, it will be in all of Africa. It was not an easy task to get rid of Charles Taylor. It was not an easy task.

The case of Mama Munda is also illustrative. Mama Munda, as noted earlier the only recognized female kamajor, found herself at the end of the war in Bo with her handful of remaining Kasela War Council fighters. During the Bo disarmament proceedings her men were largely shut out by other CDF leaders in the fierce competition to enroll fighters for benefits, and shunned by those like Norman who could command government resources. Mama Munda learned of a plan by the wife of M. S. Dumbuya, a Sierra Leone Defense Force official and the head of a Temne militia, to start a CDF Wives, Widows, and Orphans NGO and apply for international funding. This was widely seen as a canny move to attract foreign cash; it was clear to most Sierra Leoneans that there would be development assistance available in the aftermath of the war for programs focusing on women and children, and much less for programs that concentrated on young, ex-combatant men. Mama Munda complained bitterly that as the sole female kamajor only she had a right to head such an organization. Mama Munda, who is illiterate, then attempted to start her own Wives, Widows, and Orphans organization, expecting that it, too, would produce foreign donors. Dumbuya proved much more adept at maneuvering the complexities of international bureaucracy, and her organization received at least one substantial foreign grant; Mama Munda, on the other hand, was limited to generating meager funds locally by charging a fee to be officially registered in her as-yet-unfunded organization.

The regime of "production in general and without distinction" that these examples illustrate is one in which it is impossible to disaggregate the meanings of security, profit, citizenship, gender, and generation. Fighters collapsed any distinction between what it meant to be a man from what it meant to make a living from what it meant to be a postcolonial, postwar citizen. The logic of "looting" during the 6 January invasion was not economic as opposed to social or political. It was all of these at once. The ability to generate revenue through a postwar NGO was tied to questions of gender identity and the rights to compensation for the defense of the nation. For a time in the last days of the Sierra Leone front of the war, CDF fighters had some control over those processes. They could at least envision some lines of flight, ways to experiment in creating an alternative future. With the war don don declaration they were overtaken by an altogether different, more mystified sociopolitical landscape dominated by NGOs and elite patronage networks from which they were largely excluded. Some responded by moving across the border and joining LURD or one of the other Liberia factions. Others remained in the city, becoming part of the rapidly expanding urban fabric. Most moved between each of these and many other spaces as opportunities arose. Many found themselves in the complex world of West Africa's resource-extraction industry, most notably the diamond trade.

"The Heart of the Matter": The Diamond Connection

Diamonds may be, as one investigative report on the trade puts it, "the heart of the matter" (Smillie, Gberie, and Hazelton 2000). It is too simplistic to say that the war was "about" diamonds, but there can be no question that the wartime trade in gems and other natural resources fueled the conflict and largely funded it. But like every other aspect of the kamajor movement, the diamond connection—its meaning, its mechanics, and its significance—changed over time. I conclude this chapter with a brief examination of how the CDF connection to that trade exemplified the complex overlapping logics that characterized the militia's final plateau.

11. Mining operation on the border between Sierra Leone and Liberia, 2005.

Most of the analysis and commentary on the diamond connection to the Mano River War has focused on the RUF and Charles Taylor. The argument that this was a war motivated solely by greed generally takes Taylor and his associates as the case example. This is true not only of economists such as Paul Collier but also of military analysts who see in West Africa a harbinger of future "resource wars" and proliferating "dark networks" that build strength through illicit trade (see, for example, Renzi 2006).

The CDF's relationship to the diamond trade is more complicated. It is also more illustrative of the future relationship between mobilizations of young men, violence, and the resource-extraction industries of postcolonial space. CDF fighters were not motivated to take up arms by the lure of diamond profits, nor did they (in this last plateau of the movement's trajectory) simply funnel the proceeds of the trade into a war chest that allowed them to continue to fight. Rather, the mines represented one more space of possibility. In it they could solidify patronage networks or escape them. As on the battlefield, violence in the mines could be exchanged for other commodities. And the diamond fields represented a discursive field in which combatants worked out new possibilities for what it meant to be a man and to be a citizen. CDF men in the diamond pits of the southeast created a laboring self, exploiting and responding to the conditions created by violence and war.

Like the Sierra Leone Armed Forces under the APC, NPRC, and SLPP, like the RUF, and like even ECOMOG, the CDF units operating in the diamondiferous regions of the east functioned as digging crews as well as a security force. Writing in 1999 the anthropologist Caspar Fithen argued that the diamond fields around Kenema and Zimmi in the southeast were relatively underexploited historically in comparison to those further north such as Tongo and Kono. Rural Mende elites hoping to profit from the diamond trade were largely cut off from the Tongo and Kono fields by the volatility of the region and by the rapaciousness with which those mines were exploited. To develop the more secure but underdeveloped and undercapitalized southern mines, he writes, figures like Joe Demby and Kemoh Brima Bangura needed a trustworthy labor force willing to operate on a "dig now, pay later" basis. They found them, or made them, in the kamajors. Unable to make large capital infusions into insecure digging projects, entrepreneurs drew on a kamajor labor force capable of defending their plots and willing to dig as part of a Mende nationalist project—and, crucially, without a daily wage (see Fithen 1999, 243). The ethnicized patronage networks that were raising an irregular army were simultaneously raising a labor force. In both instances they used a certain "cultural capital" to mobilize youth and to insist on fidelity.

In the postjunta period the work undertaken by this pool of CDF youth became harder to justify in relation to an ongoing war effort and was less dependent on rural cultural capital. The fruits of earlier diamond mining by kamajors and CDF units lay in trading diamonds for weapons from ECOMOG officers or raising cash for the war effort through sale to international buyers. From mid-1998 onward it was less clear how the traffic in diamonds contributed to the movement as a whole. The rhetoric of mining as part of a nationalist project or a war effort gave way to the language of work and the obligations of patronage relations tempered by war and the war economy. The militia bore less resemblance to any preceding form of hunting society or Mende ethnic project than it did to Executive Outcomes and other corporate partners of mining and security interests (see Reno 2003, 61). Tellingly, during an interview at CDF headquarters in Kenema a highly placed kamajor told me that he considered the movement at that time (mid-2000) to be a "security firm." Established Lebanese diamond dealers in the region contracted CDF units to protect their concessions and often to dig the pits. Younger Lebanese men willing to take risks forged alliances with their cohort of young CDF fighters. Larger numbers of international freelance buyers braved the Sierra Leone warscape and made deals with local CDF commanders for secure access to plots. The trade in the late days of the war and its immediate aftermath was more volatile at all levels. Control over the pits was violently contested and conditions in the mines precarious, making an always dangerous industry even more so. Youth who made themselves into big men through wartime activities commanded crews and controlled parts of the trade from which they were previously excluded. As they had throughout the war, these figures unmoored the conventions from which they had previously been excluded.

This new configuration of forces, however, continued to draw on all the multiple discourses of the kamajor movement: protecting the nation, defending civilians, exercising the rights and responsibilities of manhood, marshalling occult technologies. Two Greek buyers making their first trip to Sierra Leone in 2000 told me that they had been directed to local

CDF offices to find the small-scale digging projects they sought, and that they had been threatened with kamajor retaliation if they attempted to work outside CDF channels. This "retaliation," they said, would be both physical and occult—kamajor-mined diamonds, they were told, would turn to dust if the miners disapproved of the price they were offered.

The multiple discursive registers—social, political, and economic—that were embodied in this new relationship of the militia to the diamond trade, this sense of a mixed mining and security operation, are evident in the narrative of a CDF commander operating on the border between Sierra Leone and Liberia just after the junta was overthrown. Ibrahim Tucker was a regional commander close to Eddie Massalley. The junior son of a ruling family in the south who had established himself largely through his CDF efforts, Tucker oversaw a large swath of territory around the Mano River. As such, his responsibilities included guarding against a cross-border attack from Charles Taylor's forces or the RUF, providing security in the region's towns and villages, and overseeing the mining of diamonds in fields near Zimmi. He describes here an incident in which a South African company arranged with Taylor to mine diamonds in the river. At this point the war was ongoing, so Taylor was (at least in theory) more than simply a rival businessman. In fact, Tucker was involved in the budding movement to start LURD and overthrow Taylor, so he could hardly be said to be dispassionate about the Liberian government. Yet he leaves open the very real possibility of a mutually beneficial alliance with the Taylor government. Nothing is foreclosed. As with most of his youth cohort, Tucker kept open the infinite play of possibilities and linkages, knowing that any of them might prove profitable and that any one of these links had interchangeable social, political, and economic valences. The "fact" of the war does not preclude a business arrangement, and that arrangement is in turn cast in the language of both patronage politics and youth development. Tucker slips easily between spheres, discussing Taylor, himself, CDF fighters, and the nation in terms that aggregate what would seem incompatible (or at least separable) domains of politics, economy, and sociality:

> They [the South Africans] came as a company through Taylor. They decided to work in the Mano River. They went there unbeknownst to us. They did not tell us. And the river is for both Sierra Leone and Liberia. And according to the map of that river, the diamond deposit was on our side in the river. One day, they went with their equipment and started mining. My

platoon commander at that time went and reported that issue to me, that the South Africans had brought their equipment and they are mining in the water. And the deposit was on our side. I told him to warn them that they should move from that place. He warned them, advised them by talking to them that they should move. They did not take him serious. He went to me for the second time. He told me that he has talked to the people but the people did not take him serious. I sent him with my operations commander. "Go with the platoon commander and see if this report is true. If it is true, call the guys and tell them not to mine in that territorial water. If they refuse, give them a warning shot. If they refuse [again], fire at them." They tried to talk to them; they did not take it. They gave warning shots; they did not take it. I told them they should fire at them. So they folded up their equipment and they got back. The operation was stopped right there.

I sent a message by telling people across [the river] from Sierra Leone to Liberia, that if South Africans want to mine on this side it should be through agreement between the Sierra Leonean and Liberian governments, not only the Liberian government.

I was defending that particular place because it's my right. It should be in the knowledge of the authorities. If that arrangement would have been done officially and genuinely, maybe it would have been better for all of us, both Liberia and Sierra Leone. But if I stay at that particular border, as an authority, taking no particular action, then my own higher authority will accuse me that maybe I am in a deal with them. But it's not true.

[If they went through the proper channels], I would welcome them. I would like those people to work in our territory. Reasons? One: Sierra Leone should benefit from our resources. Two: For the youth to have employment. Am I right to say so? You may have all type of resources in your land, but if you do not mind maybe you will not get the benefit. It should only be in the proper manner, that's all. To benefit the indigenous [people].

[*Question: Who are the proper authorities?*] In the first place, I have at that time Eddie Massalley.[13] I would go to Eddie Massalley and then Eddie Massalley and myself would go to Hinga Norman. Maybe at that level I may not be there now. From that level Hinga Norman will either invite the minister of mines or pass through the president to invite the minister of mines. It was easier at that time because of the war. If you want to develop some company now [after the war], there is a procedure. The difference at that time, you come with your company, maybe you only pay your tax to the government. But now everything is restricted. Law and order.

12. LURD fighters at the Lofa County town of Voinjama, 2002.

Tucker's vision of the possibilities represented by a foreign mining interest and the proper channels through which it should do business seem jarringly at odds with the all-against-all, anarchic portrait that is generally painted of West African warfare. But it is remarkably consistent with the portrait of war as a violent mode of participating in today's global economy. The work of war in his narrative had become just that: work. An ongoing war is not an impediment to making business arrangements with one's enemies, provided these arrangements are done properly. This is not simply a cynical market logic—it is still cast at least partly as a project of postcolonial citizenship, working for the benefit of the nation, and as a project of both personal right and collective advancement. All underwritten by violence.

A 2009 *New York Times* article on the mobilization of diasporic Somali youth to fight in the Horn of Africa illustrates just how generalizable—and how easily misunderstood—the CDF example might be. After detailing the mostly economically and socially marginal lives of a group of young Somali men in the Twin Cities in the United States, the article describes the Ethiopian invasion of Somalia in 2006, an event that galvanized some of these youth to return to Somalia and join the Shabaab militia: "If the Ethiopians were seen as infidel invaders, an insurgent group known as the Shabaab—'youth' in Arabic—was emerging as 'freedom fighters.' In its online propaganda, the Shabaab conflated nationalist sentiments with religious ideology, following a tactic honed by Al Qaeda."[14] What the article effectively pinpoints is the overlap between these youths' economic exclusion, "nationalist sentiment," and "religious ideology" (as well as a certain gendered insecurity, a point the author alludes to but does not fully explore). These forces are effectively interchangeable. Access to cash, pursuit of a nationalist project, religious obligation and fulfillment—none of these is the "real" catalyst that facilitates the mobilization of these youth. The dividing line between them is effectively erased, as it was for CDF fighters mining diamonds and laboring at the frontline or at roadside checkpoints. There is no easy separation of spheres. The article's mistake, however, is to propose that this erasure is "a tactic honed by Al Qaeda." The impression is of a deliberate strategy of confusion on the part of faction leaders, duping gullible young men into misrecognizing their "real" situation. What we learn if we take seriously the lessons of the Mano River War is that mobilizations of young men such as that described in the article reflect not so much a carefully crafted tactical campaign as the postmodern, postcolonial condition. For the young men who enter these networks, this is not simply propaganda. It is life arranged according to contemporary capital's global axiomatics.

II BUILDING THE BARRACKS

chapter 4

BIG MEN, SMALL BOYS

GENERAL JOE STOOD INSIDE the Bo town soccer stadium facing an angry mob of youth on the other side of the wall. He ordered the Guinean peacekeepers to throw open the gates. Then, like Moses in a red tracksuit and straw sun hat, he waded into the sea of sweating bodies, parting it with kicks, curses, and punches. Several hundred young men, many of them armed, arranged themselves into three orderly lines while Joe shoved and threatened. It was an incredible display. Even more remarkable was that as he corralled these CDF militiamen, Joe simultaneously singled out those he knew or those with whom he had previously made deals. The chosen ones he pushed to the head of the lines, reminding them as he did that they must come see him after the disarmament proceedings ended. While the United Nations peacekeepers and military observers, journalists, and other CDF commanders looked on, Joe used his body, reputation, wit, and bravado to order the universe according to the peculiar dictates of patronage politics in today's postcolony.

In this chapter I explore one meaning of a contemporary African militia through the stories of two persons associated with the CDF. The biographies of General Joe Nunie and Mohammed Maada Gleh are very different. But together they illustrate important nuances about a key dynamic within the CDF and a central tenet of postcolonial militarism more generally: how the patron-client relationships that dominate social, political, and economic life in the region organized relations of power and authority within the movement.

Contrary to common perceptions of the CDF, existing relationships were not replaced by a military command-and-control structure when the CDF emerged in the middle 1990s. The CDF was never an army in the conventional sense. Relationships between those with authority in the organization and those without it were never dictated by a purely military logic. At the same time, the CDF was not simply the mobilization of existing social institutions. As I explored in chapter 2, a long-standing fascination with West African secret societies led some observers to assume that the CDF was simply a Poro mobilization. A related theory argues that the CDF should be seen as one component in a war understood to be an intergenerational struggle between big men and small boys, the playing out on new, more violent terrain of an age-old conflict between male youth and their elders for the limited resources available to men in the West African postcolony. While this is true to a point, such framing misses a great deal of nuance when it comes to how the CDF (and later LURD) actually functioned.

Each of these misreadings obscures some of the larger lessons that we might take from the CDF about how relations of authority become "deployable" in the region's conflict zones. Contemporary militias like these represent neither the absence of social control (the military model) nor the simple retooling of existing institutions (the big man–small boy or

13. General Joe after calming CDF fighters at the Bo disarmament center, 2001.

Poro explanations). Instead they need to be seen as the militarization of much more complex and poorly understood logics of patronage, wealth, and value.

The biographical narratives I take up below will be more meaningful when read against a general set of observations regarding the logic of patronage in this part of West Africa. And so I begin with the ways in which patronage has tended to figure in the literature on both the CDF and the region more generally.

The Logic of Patronage

In 2005 the prosecution in the CDF trial at the Special Court for Sierra Leone submitted a report prepared by the British military expert witness, Colonel Richard Iron (see chapter 3). In his report and then his subsequent testimony Iron argued that war is defined by the suspension of normal sociality. This breach produces two possible results: anarchic, chaotic violence or the erection (intentional or organic) of military structures organized under a uniquely military chain of command. "Military organization," Iron writes, "therefore exists in any conflict waged between recognized groups; otherwise it is simply a state of aimless violence" (2005, B2.1).[1]

Certainly the CDF did not operate in a state of aimless violence. But, contrary to Iron's claim, neither was it a military organization. "Sociality" did not cease to exist in the Mano River War any more than it does in any conflict (see Richards 2005a). Instead the CDF's principal framing logic was one that pervades many spheres of social, political, and economic life in the Mano River region: relations of patronage. What patronage means in practical terms is that social networks based on debt obligations, social standing, and position are crucial to everything from employment opportunities to ritual initiations to individual identity. This was no less true of the CDF than of other facets of social life in the region. Subjectivity (in and out of wartime) must be understood as a web of relations. "People here," writes Charles Piot, referring to West Africa generally, "do not 'have' relations; they 'are' relations" (Piot 1999, 18; see also M. Jackson 1998, 3).

Patron-client dynamics name this web of relations as relations that are, to borrow Jane Guyer's term, "ranked" (2004, 68–82). The being of an individual is measured vis-à-vis others—comparatively, but also cumulatively. That measure may be taken on a variety of scales: money, heritage (royalty or slave, ruling house or stranger), age grades, ethnicity, conspicuous consumption of commodities, gifts or favors exchanged. Whatever the scale, to a large degree West African social worlds are defined by exchanges and alliances among unequal partners—among clients and patrons.

At least since the colonial period (and, according to Guyer 2004, 27–47, long before) a host of value regimes seem to operate simultaneously and often in competition. Ethnicity, family connections, monetary accumulation, spending, religious or political office, each of these threads helps constitute relations of patronage and clientalism in multiplex ways. But central to all of these are relations of debt and the obligations that bind those who owe and those who are owed into some form of community. "To survive in such a dangerous world," writes Bruce Berman in an overview of patronage politics across sub-Saharan Africa, "requires both support and protection, which is precisely what patrons and clients are supposed to provide for each other, cemented by ties of kinship and ethnicity, and the reason why wealth is invested in developing and maintaining social networks" (1998, 338; see also Bayart 1993, 218–27). Patronage organizes the web of relations by weaving people into the fabric of obligation and responsibility to others. Anthropologists' long-standing interest in West African measures of "wealth in people" (Bledsoe 1980; Guyer 1995) is essentially an interest in how value is locally construed and how power and profit accumulate within this web. In specifically male gendered terms, it is an interest in how some become big men and others remain small boys.

In Mende the concept of patronage has historically been expressed in terms such as "standing for" others (to "stand for them" or "be for them," *numui lo va*). As the anthropologist Mariane Ferme writes in her ethnography of Mende social practices, "The crucial point, then, was that everyone must be accounted for by someone else—that everyone must be linked in a relationship of patronage or clientship" (2001b, 106). The person who stands for someone else assumes responsibility for his or her behavior within a community and provides for his or her basic needs; acts, in other words, as a patron. In return, a patron can expect the performance of favors and control a client's labor. A patron can stake claim to a share of the wealth that a dependent or client might accumulate, and a patron is defined by some level of obligatory respect, support, and privilege. This is at least the abstract ideal, whether it is ever fully realized as such.

Across the African continent youth is often defined by its place within this patronage system. Amidst the state's legal definition of the boundary between childhood and adulthood and the age norms defined by global NGOs and the United Nations is a more amorphous definition of youth as those who have no formally recognized dependents of their own. The dividing line between youth and adulthood is often one that overlaps that between patron and client. While no adult is ever free of clientalist obligations to someone, an adult claims a sphere of dependents that is not yet available to youth regardless of their age. And increasingly, it seems, crossing the line between youth and adulthood is an impossible challenge for young men.[2] The life events that mark the transition and that cultivate dependents—formal marriage, initiation, establishing a farm or business—are prohibitively expensive.

In a study of child soldiers on both sides of the border between Sierra Leone and Liberia, William Murphy (2003) charts how this logic of patronage worked even at the level of the youngest combatants. The child soldiers of this war, he writes, "illustrate a broader principle of youth clientalism in Africa (and elsewhere): the production of dependency on patronage when local and national structures fail to provide for the social and economic needs of youth" (62). An "ideology of dependency" (75) that characterizes social life in this region meant that young people for whom the vicissitudes of the war disrupted kin relations and other expected pathways of security and well-being looked for patronage elsewhere. For child combatants, that "elsewhere" was the various militias. Commanders in these movements could parlay the profits of war into ever-expanding spheres of patronage influence, and youth whose survival depended on securing themselves in a web of relations did so by serving as militarized clients.

The Military Imaginary

The Iron report to the Special Court missed the CDF's patronage dynamics because it drew on a perhaps understandable, but nonetheless unfortunate, surface reading of the militia's own terminology. "Commander" and other terms of rank were common enough throughout the movement's history, as they were among the rebels and in the various Liberian factions. But even when the CDF employed terms like "commander," terms that imply a military organization, these indicated patron-client relationships rather than military rank. For a supposed military organization, the CDF had an overwhelming number of "commanders"—and a concomitant paucity of privates or other nonofficer ranks. A number of persons claimed the title of "battalion commander," "company commander," or "platoon commander," but these titles were not used systematically and did not automatically correspond to a list of duties or a fixed number of subordinates. More often than not they were issued as rewards. Changes in rank did not necessarily signify a change in command. This suggests more than simply that the CDF "was just not a very good [military organization]," as the Iron report puts it (2005, A1). It illustrates, rather, that CDF hierarchies were rooted in a less bureaucratic and more personalistic set of understandings about authority and responsibility. A former kamajor put the relationship in the explicitly patrimonial terms common to patronage relations by drawing a familial connection between commanders and their dependents: "The same way I give [orders] to my son, I can give them to [my fighters]." Another made an even more dramatic paternalistic analogy: "All of the men you see around, they all look at me as a model. They look at me as if God is looking down at me, and they are just waiting for him to deliver."

As a patron, a "commander" would be responsible for his "clients" in ways not defined by military necessity or protocol. In addition to providing food, shelter, weapons, and ammunition, a patron-commander would be a resource in family emergencies or an arbiter for disputes among equals. He would be expected to stand for those beneath him in cases where allegations were made by local authorities or others within the movement. In return, a patron-commander's dependents would be expected to offer security for the "big man," share a portion of whatever wealth they might accumulate, and tend to his needs as necessary.

There are two simple illustrations of the primacy of patronage within the CDF as opposed to a purely military command. First is the fact that so many "commanders" and other titled people within the CDF had no military experience whatsoever, but had been important or respected community members prior to the war. Their patron status and their networks of dependence (their "wealth in people") simply continued from peacetime into wartime. This was certainly the case with the majority of members of the Base Zero War Council, few if any of whom had a military background. In his testimony before the Special Court, for example, Samuel Hinga Norman notes that Alhaji Daramy Rogers "could be a useful member [of the War Council] at Base Zero" because he was "an Alhaji and a politician."[3] In the same vein, Brima Jolu Kenneh Sei in Panguma, one of the key figures in efforts to retake Tongo during the junta period, was voted a commander by the chiefs and town council because he was section chief of one of Panguma's seven sections and therefore considered an "upstanding citizen." Prior to this, he had no military background or training. This was also true of Moinina Fofana (the eventual CDF director of war), who had no military experience but had achieved a degree of status as a local businessman and benefactor for internally displaced persons.

There were no fixed definitions attached to specific ranks that codified the duties, obligations or spheres of command for specific positions. Terms like "adjutant," "platoon commander," or "battalion commander" could mean different things in different parts of the organization or at different times in its history. Most important, it could mean different things based on who held the position. This is exactly the opposite of how such titles work in a strictly military organization, where rank implies fixed roles regardless of the people who fill them. Instead, most combatants understood the use of these titles as a way to map patronage networks.

Take the term "adjutant." This was a relatively common title that Eddie Massalley, the commander in Pujehun, gave to combatants with a small number of clients and to persons who could read and write and were therefore useful organizers. "Adjutant" is indeed a rank in a number of professional militaries, with various duties depending on the service in question. Yet when asked what duties an adjutant was intended to perform, one of Massalley's former "adjutants" said he had no idea what the term meant or what duties it implied. Massalley, he said, used to give out titles liberally and named a number of combatants as his adjutants. Nevertheless, because Massalley had given it to him, "Adjutant" became a nickname by which everyone at Bo Waterside knew him and by which everyone knew that he was close to Massalley.

Also illustrative of the primacy of patronage was the relative frequency with which captured RUF combatants were integrated into the CDF and established long-term, trusting ties with their new CDF commanders. A relatively large percentage of CDF fighters were former RUF combatants who switched sides, either voluntarily or when captured by the CDF. To be accepted within the CDF, a former RUF fighter required someone to stand for him—to vouch for him as a person worthy of joining the society and as someone for whom the new patron would be responsible. Describing a situation in which he stood for a captured RUF combatant, C.O. Death, a commander in Bo, explained how to this day a former RUF fighter he captured and brought into the CDF comes to visit him and pays him respect as a social elder: "He is always my boy. He's just like my junior brother now. After I did that for him, his family took me to be part of them." The upshot of the primacy of the patronage network is that, for most combatants, the person of most import was their immediate patron, rather than persons who might be of superior (military) rank but to whom they had little if any direct connection.

In short, the social logics that predated the war remained salient for the CDF during the war. Rather than a military organization, the CDF is better thought of as the militarization of that dominant logic, or the militarization of a particular network of social relations. The organization did not simply come into being out of the necessity of controlling the violence around it and in the absence of other social structures. Instead it emerged from a conjunction of patronage demands and opportunities reconstituted by the contingencies of the Sierra Leone warscape.

The Variability of Patronage

If Iron's "military organization or chaos" hypothesis is refuted by the ethnographic evidence that pervasive patron-client relations gave these militias their meaning, it is nevertheless possible to go to the opposite extreme. There is a risk in reifying patronage as a social institution. As Mary Moran (2006) has argued, it is tempting to read too narrowly the mechanics of the big man–small boy relationship, or what has been called West Africa's mode of gerontocratic rule. Read in this narrow sense, events such as the Mano River War are explained as an effort by male youth to seize some kind of authority from elders who have otherwise denied it to them completely by abusing the relationship between patron and client. This is war construed as an act of generational revenge or patricide.

There are two problems here. First, such framings tend to generalize for the entire region a social dynamic that is most pronounced among the Mande ethnic groups of northwest Liberia and eastern Sierra Leone. Generational conflict may be a recurring theme across the region, but as Moran's own fieldwork in southeast Liberia suggests, communities without a Poro tradition or with non-Mande style age grades can be characterized by very different kinds of negotiations between generations and across gender lines. The idea that social institutions meant to govern relationships between men of varying seniority somehow failed, resulting in a brutal civil war, risks overlooking the many subtle locally specific ways in which youth and elders interact and negotiate power more peacefully.

Even more important is the great deal of variation and nuance found in the overlapping discourses that impact relations between generations and between clients and patrons even within Mande communities: discourses shaped by ideas of cosmopolitanism and rural tradition, by human rights rhetoric and that of democracy, by new religious movements, and by the labor of violence. Discussions of patronage in Africa in general tend to gloss over the fact that these positions are inherently unstable in relation to one another; as Berman puts it, "big men and small boys are also potential rivals who can turn and devour the other" (1998, 338; see also Barber 2007, 114). Some markers of status are harder to challenge or actualize than others. But patron and client relationships are not immutable. "[A]ll men are striving to increase their *bona* [the Liberian Gola term for a sphere of dependents] in order to improve their wealth and power in the world," writes Warren d'Azevedo in an ethnography of western Liberian kinship, "but all men are also striving to attach themselves to a *bona* of some more powerful person" (1962, 513, also cited in Murphy 2003, 75).

For example, the fact that the CDF's "military" titles did not correspond to designated community roles and did not imply a fixed set of responsibilities also made them subject to a great deal of manipulation. Combatants often referred to "419" claims (after the Nigerian Internet banking scams), a process whereby fighters would claim a certain rank or title for themselves in the hopes of speaking the claim into reality. Titles in these cases were used to express an aspiration rather than an actual position. As I explore in what follows, Gen. Joe was widely said to have nominated himself to be a CDF general. His "rank" became a reality because no one dared challenge him and he was able to cultivate clients by spreading around the spoils of war.

At the same time, for many young people, the war offered a way to bypass the existing pathways by which one ideally established patronage networks of one's own. Young men who were referred to as "commanders" at various levels claimed to have achieved that rank as a result of distinguishing themselves through their hard work, bravery, and trustworthiness. These are persons who successfully challenged the standard routes by which young men achieved status (paying one's dues to a patron until reaching a certain age, marital status, or inheritance worthy of a "big man") by finding an alternative: attracting clients by establishing effectiveness on the battlefront. Because the patronage system which dominated the CDF overlapped so extensively with the patronage networks that operated prior to the CDF, this often meant that young commanders acted independently of more senior men if by doing so they could establish the means by which to secure clients of their own.

Consider again the case of Brima Sei at Panguma. A relatively junior person, Musa Junisa, established himself as the commander at Panguma, ahead of Brima Sei, by securing ammunition from CDF patrons at two locations, Base One and Base Zero. When the junta took power in 1997, kamajors at Panguma had enough weapons but not enough artillery to fight the AFRC and RUF there and at the important diamond mining center of Tongo. Musa Junisa and a few other fighters traveled secretly to Gendema, where they were given approximately a dozen rocket-propelled grenades by CDF leaders there. They then proceeded to Base Zero, where a separate clique of CDF big men gave them cartridges for AK-47s and G3 rifles. Returning to Panguma, Junisa displaced Brima Sei as commander in part through his ability to control this ammunition and therefore create a network of dependents. From February 1998 his new authority allowed him to claim the title of director of operations of the Eastern Region—a title bestowed on him by the leadership at Base Zero, to whom Musa Junisa was now in debt.

The provision of weapons as a means by which to garner and maintain support was fairly common in the CDF. Important Mende political figures such as Daramay Rogers, George Jambawai, and Albert Nallo all traveled to CDF-held areas and dispensed weapons and ammunition. These activities should not be seen simply as carrying out the duties attached to rank; rather, they were efforts to obtain clients and establish patronage relationships in a highly competitive and diffuse field. Where a supply officer of a certain rank in the British military may be charged with distributing supplies, within the CDF a person would as likely be considered an "officer" (a person of importance or rank) by first having demonstrated his ability to procure and distribute supplies.

What these examples suggest is that patronage is unstable in a more complex sense as well. Big men and small boys can always potentially displace one another—"devour the other" in Berman's terms. But even the very criterion for evaluating power and authority is subject to negotiation. "Conversion" between regimes of value has always been an area of contestation in Africa (Guyer 2004). Procuring arms for distribution to clients, attracting followers through battlefield heroics, or spreading the spoils of war—there is no fixed way to evaluate how these actions should translate into prestige or new ways of "ranking" patrons and clients. These are matters of negotiation. The upshot: while the logic of patronage runs through the story of the Mano River War, it was never a singular story.

Until now, anyway. In an essay on postcolonial politics, Achille Mbembe argues that the money economy as it works in Africa has generated what he called "a new *economy of persons*" that is "based on purely market and object-like relationships" (2006, 304). I return to this idea in the conclusion to this chapter, but raise it here to position the stories that follow in relation to the larger project of the book. What we see in these narratives are the vicissitudes and nuances of postcolonial patronage. But we also see in them how patronage itself is becoming enmeshed in a more singular logic of global capital and the state.

Mohammed Maada Gleh

Mohammed breaks rocks.

It is "work" only in that it fills his days and demands much of his slender body. Smashing stone into gravel with a small hammer is one of the tasks Mohammed performs for the right to remain a squatter, a caretaker of someone else's land. What money Mohammed has comes in other unreliable and hard-won ways: hustling on the streets of Freetown, performing odd jobs for mechanics or welders, or, his most lucrative activity these days, running djamba to the Liberian border. My own visits to Freetown are sporadic and unannounced, but when they happen they bring an infusion of rice and cash.

The fruit of Mohammed's labor is an unfinished concrete box, slowly

14. Mohammed Maada Gleh, 2003.

evolving into the retirement home of a doctor living in the United States. Mohammed, his family, and the slow alchemy of transforming stone to gravel to concrete are the only protection the doctor has against others occupying his land. Legal land titles are a fragile guarantee against theft in Sierra Leone. More reliable are the bodies and, if necessary, the violence of young men.

Many wealthy residents of this crowded West African city have relocated to the hills to escape the noise, the pollution, and the crush of displaced victims of the long war. With them have come squatter caretakers like Mohammed. Four years ago Mohammed, Adama, and their baby, Struggle, were among the first to settle here when they put up a small *pan-bodi*, a corrugated metal shack. They are pioneers of a sort. When the houses are finished they will move on, further into the forest at the outer margins of the urban landscape or back to equally marginal spaces in the heart of the city.

Mohammed's is a rich and difficult story for me to tell. It is literally difficult: Mohammed has narrated the events of his life differently over the years. What I know (or think I know) of it comes from piecing together shreds and narrative patches that do not always cohere. My relationship with him began in the ruins of the downtown Brookfields Hotel, where Mohammed lived with hundreds of fighters and their dependents providing security for a government that mistrusted its own military and feared an incursion from rebels in the hills. What Mohammed has told me of the early war years is often conveyed in allusions or generalities. Like many Mende narratives, his stories are sequenced by theme or purpose rather than chronology. His speech also reflects the many border zones of his life. He slips without warning between the Mende dialect of the southeast and a thickly accented Liberian English; between the basic Krio of traders in Freetown or Kenema and the rough Krio slang of marginal urban youth. He can be wildly animated one minute and stop mid-sentence the next, or trail off into a mumble made rough by years of cigarettes and djamba. Though he knows that I circulate his image and his stories, I have never recorded a conversation with Mohammed and rarely write notes in his presence. Writing his words takes too much of the energy I need just to hear them, and he is uncomfortable with a microphone. In every sense, his voice is difficult to capture.

Mohammed's story is a challenge for more profound—and more personal—reasons. Mohammed and I are the same age. We are both fathers, and have celebrated together the births of our children. But where years, parenting, and profession have marked my own transition into adulthood, Mohammed lives and is defined by a different life calculus. He remains a "youth" in the eyes of the Sierra Leonean state and by the social measures in this West African postcolony. It is a label with political and economic valences. It means that according to the logic of patronage that demarcates his social field, he has few recognized dependents of his own. It means that he has never formally married, lacking the resources to stage a wedding and to provide Adama's family with the requisite gifts and honors. And it means that he is beholden to others for his basic necessities. In return for the meager graces he receives from older, wealthier men and women, his labors are largely at their disposal. He can be called up as needed for work on the plantations or the mines, on the battlefields or in timber camps across the region—all of them dangerous locations that make the divide between war and peace obsolete. When politicians and the political parties that back them need young men to campaign (often by attacking supporters of rival parties), Mohammed and other youth will be called upon to play their part. I know Mohammed too well to think of him as typical of anything. At the same time, the seemingly inescapable trap of youth in which Mohammed finds himself resonates with the biographies of many young men in contemporary Sierra Leone.

Mohammed was not easy to locate after he moved up into these hills.

I lost track of him, Adama, and Struggle when the last kamajor fighters were evicted from the Brookfields Hotel in mid-2002. By the end of the next year I had heard only rumors: that he had gone to Liberia as a mercenary, that he was again selling djamba on the border, that he remained in the city living with the family of a friend. It was only recently that I understood that this invisibility at the far reaches of the city was both circumstantial and strategic—a point to which I will return. But on the summer evening that I first saw him there after a year out of touch, he seemed a young man determined to shape his own future.

Like other former kamajors, Mohammed claimed that if necessary he was prepared to hold the land he occupied by force. "God wanted peace in this land," he said, the city and sea stretching beneath him, "so he sent the kamajors." The reward, promised by the state and backed by God, is that every citizen of Sierra Leone now has a right to land. That Mohammed could speak of violently defending the territory guaranteed him as a citizen while serving as no more than a caretaker for an absentee landowner exemplified the contradictory logic of postcolonial patronage.

In the abstract, the webs of patronage to which Mohammed and other rural Mende male youth are beholden chart a relatively smooth life path. Young men achieve adulthood through a series of events that mark their progression: the various stages of initiation into men's secret societies like the Poro; a formal marriage; establishment of a farm and a household. These are achievements facilitated by one's elders, to whom youth owe debts of respect and labor. Over time, people transition from clients to patrons in their own right, providing for those younger than themselves and expanding their own client networks as a mark of social status and age. The city offers a parallel track. Children and youth labor in the home or a family business for patrons who provide them with schooling, room, and board. Rural families not uncommonly send children for fosterage to extended family or former neighbors living and prospering in the city (see Bledsoe 1990; Gale 2008). Rural, urban, or a combination of the two, these relationships are intended to instill in young people the knowledge to function as adults and the resources to put such knowledge into practice. Of course, one never escapes the logic of patronage, and there are always those to whom one is beholden. Nevertheless, a life well lived is said to be one that progresses from youth to adulthood, from the preponderance of one's troubles being those of a client to being those of a patron.

The abstract, however, is a fantasy in contemporary Sierra Leone. There are those who question whether there ever has been an ideal past in which elders possessed both the material riches and the goodwill to meet all of the demands placed on them by their superiors and by the young. Certainly by now the financial capacity is gone for all but a few elites. Successive economic crises have swept West Africa for decades. The long-serving president of Sierra Leone, Siaka Stevens, put the national economy in peril by using state coffers to fund his own patronage network. Structural adjustment measures further strained the resources of Sierra Leoneans across the board, and the end of Cold War machinations by the superpowers meant a deepening of the economic crisis. The war and a thriving black market in diamonds and timber have made instability the only marker of normalcy. The result for many young people is that adulthood appears as a status foreclosed by a greedy gerontocracy and a perpetual state of economic distress. Conversely, the agency that youth ascribe to adulthood is rarely experienced as such; senior people find themselves constrained by the demands of their dependents and by those with greater wealth or political authority.

Mohammed spent the first five years of the war as a noncombatant trading djamba from the forests to the villages along the Liberia border. The military coup left him stranded in the town of Kenema. When he eventually made his way back to his village, he was taken prisoner by the local kamajors, who labeled him an RUF collaborator for having been so long in enemy territory. Mohammed escaped and crossed the Liberia border where he was captured again by a kamajor contingent. This time he was sentenced to death for drug smuggling and collaboration.

From this point Mohammed's story is one of the perverse logic by which patronage functioned during the war. For some young people the disruptions of the war presented escape routes from highly exploitative relations with their elders. Young men with military experience or the bravado to make their names through violence could attract clients of their own. The combatants who surrounded them relied on the protection of these commanders and the food, medicines, and weapons they could accumulate or take by force. In return young rank-and-file combatants gave their loyalty, their muscle, and the goods they might procure at the battlefront to their new commanders. For some who were smart and lucky, this was an opportunity to break the perceived stranglehold their elders maintained on wealth, prestige, and—ultimately—

adult manhood. Theirs may have been a rebellion against the patronage system, but it was hardly a revolution. At best a few young men managed to accelerate their own climb in stature and bypass years of efforts to cultivate clients of their own. They most often replicated the very relationships they sought to escape. The rhetoric of a more equitable social future that pervaded all the factions did not necessarily make those young men who profited from the war more benevolent patrons than those they supplanted. Moreover, such successes were generally fleeting and dangerous. In the end, the majority experienced the war simply as an intensification of violent instabilities of patronage rather than a qualitative shift in their nature.

Mohammed's death sentence was commuted when a local commander, C.O. Bobby, intervened and agreed to stand for him. Though Mohammed had never met C.O. Bobby before, the man claimed Mohammed was a distant relative for whom he would accept responsibility. It was an intervention that spared Mohammed's life, but also bound him to Bobby as his patron and as his commander. Along with the other members of Bobby's unit, Mohammed began weapons and tactical training. He was initiated into the kamajors.

Over the next year, Mohammed fought with C.O. Bobby and his unit across the east of Sierra Leone. He spent the majority of his time on the Liberia border, ostensibly to guard against an invasion by Liberian president Charles Taylor. In practice he helped Bobby and other commanders run small-time diamond mining operations, trading rough stones with Lebanese merchants and the occasional South African buyer.

When C.O. Bobby was wounded at the battlefront, Mohammed went with him to Freetown for treatment at the capital city's Connaught Hospital. With Bobby having no family in the city, it fell to Mohammed to provide for his patron's needs during his recovery. It was during this period of Bobby's convalescence that Mohammed met his next patron, a young man named Junior who was barely older than Mohammed himself.

Most young combatants had no real chance of becoming commanders in their own right. Instead the war offered them two spaces of possibility. It allowed some to violently react against their social landscape, taking vengeance on the real or symbolic persons and structures they saw as the agents of their marginalization. In its successive waves of attacks across the country, for example, the RUF committed a number of high-profile atrocities against chiefs and chiefdom elders and spectacularly destructive raids on schools, churches, and universities. The war also presented some young men with opportunities for mobility between patrons. As they were deployed around the country, units of male youth encountered one another on the battlefield as enemies or allies or sometimes both. Captured, coerced, or persuaded, combatants unwilling or unable to return home commonly served in multiple units during the course of their careers as fighters. The result was an often dizzyingly complex web of alliances and betrayals that never mapped easily along ethnic, sectarian, or even family lines. Over and over, the stories I was told by combatants and ex-combatants underscored that for most young people, opportunities arose from the most unlikely quarters—but even the most reliable relationships were never guaranteed.

Junior was a well-regarded figure within the CDF. The son of a wealthy businessman in Monrovia, Junior was known for recruiting fighters from the forested border between Liberia and Sierra Leone. Though he was a patron in his own right, he was also widely regarded as a youth leader frequently at odds with the CDF leadership over their corruption and lack of regard for rank-and-file combatants. It was one such rift that landed Junior in the hospital; an assassination attempt by an elder in the CDF had failed to kill him, but he required emergency surgery and a six-month recovery.

Mohammed's shift in allegiance from C.O. Bobby to Junior was relatively amicable. C.O. Bobby's wounds meant that he could not lead his unit to the battlefront any longer, and his ability to provide for his "boys" was therefore severely compromised. Bobby planned to return to his village outside Kenema and the uncertain prospects of earning a living in rural, wartime Sierra Leone. Unprepared to move back to his own village, Mohammed began to assist in caring for Junior, whose future promised to be one of continued engagement in the war. Junior saw to it that Mohammed had a weapon when he went to the battlefront and enough food when he came back. Mohammed, in turn, fought when Junior needed him to fight. He surrendered to Junior what spoils he captured at the front and gave him a cut of what monies he might find through small-time hustles, odd jobs, or favorable trades. Perhaps most importantly, it was Junior who facilitated Mohammed's continued stay in the city by allowing him to barrack in the ruins of the Brookfields Hotel.

Jah Kingdom was the name for the space under the swimming pool at Brookfields.[4] The defunct utility room was the site of a small bar where CDF fighters could buy rum, marijuana, and cigarettes from King, a Nigerian mercenary and petty trader. Mohammed and Adama lived in one of the shower stalls of the former men's locker room.

Around the time the war "officially" ended in January 2002, Mohammed and Adama moved. The girlfriend of another Jah Kingdom resident picked a fight with Adama. Despite Adama's eight-month pregnancy, the woman kicked her in the stomach, an act against which Mohammed felt King and the other men present should have intervened. I arrived at Jah Kingdom in time to see Mohammed and Adama stuffing the last of their belongings into a duffel bag. Following them up from below the pool and toward the front gate of the hotel, I prepared to see them off for good. Instead they entered Block C, one of the large complexes of guest rooms. Dragging their bags to the top floor, Mohammed stopped at a room sealed with a small padlock. With a knife he pried off the latch and pushed open the door. While Adama spread their bedroll on the floor, Mohammed explained that if the previous occupants had intended to return, they would have put a stronger lock on the door. Apparently he was right. Mohammed, Adama, Struggle, and a few friends who moved in with them were still there when United Nations peacekeepers arrived to evict everyone from the hotel eight months later.

For Mohammed, leaving his home in Jah Kingdom could not have meant leaving the city of Freetown. If the war promised young men with gumption the possibility of reconfiguring their patronage ties and escaping the perceived injustices meted out by a greedy gerontocracy, in the postwar period that promise lies in the city itself. The sheer number of people offers the hope of new patronage networks on a scale unthinkable in rural communities. But the city is also a qualitatively different space of possibility. When the war ended there were scores of international NGOs operating in Sierra Leone, the majority in Freetown. The streets were choked with white Toyota Land Cruisers, every one embodying the promise of steady employment, training, even sexual liaisons that could lead in unforeseeable directions. The city offered the infrastructure and knowledge base to gamble on the "DV," the lottery give-away of United States visas that signified overseas employment and possibilities for lucrative business and marriage arrangements. Like other West African cities, Freetown now hosts a slew of charismatic churches and evangelical pastors who promise phenomenal prosperity in this life through prayer and tithing. Freetown is a place of enormous risk, but it is simultaneously a space of enormous (though mysterious) possibility.[5]

Ironically, of all the possible futures the city embodies, one of the most difficult and most desirable is a return to the village. Like many ex-combatants Mohammed fantasized about returning to his village as a big man, able to "sit down" on his family farm. This imagined future pictured Mohammed employing village youth to work his land. It enrolled him in the deliberations of the community's elder men and it gave him the opportunity for a formal marriage and the recognition of his children. Mohammed had taken steps to make this a possibility before the last RUF invasion of Freetown. Having accumulated some cash during the fighting, Mohammed sent money back to the village for local boys to clear a small plot. For a brief moment the plot made tangible Mohammed's future livelihood and the privilege and responsibilities of adulthood. The Freetown invasion and the decision to barrack the CDF at the Brookfields Hotel, however, kept Mohammed in the city. Well before he returned to the village the forest reclaimed his small farm.

When I talked with Mohammed outside his pan bodi house, he explained that ex-combatants who came to Freetown to protect the government were abandoned there without support. The cost of living even the most rudimentary urban life meant that he now had little in the way of cash or goods. And returning to the village empty-handed is unthinkable. At best the village people would gloat and mock, saying that only a fool would go to war and to the city and come home empty-handed. At worst they would be suspicious and offended, convinced that war and urban living had indeed been profitable but that their prodigal son was too greedy to share his gains. As one of Mohammed's friends put it: "Your own mother will welcome you back because she's your mother. [But] if you choose not to do farm work, you leave the village and go to the city and you are not successful, you go back, people will laugh at you. But leaving to go and fight without coming back with anything, that will even make it worse."

This was a common story, and it has meant a proliferation of young men who cultivate the city itself for their subsistence. To *dreg* in the parlance of Freetown's urban youth is to hustle, moving from point to point around the city and across the boundaries of legality. It evokes getting by through the collection of debts, the provision of favors, outsmarting or outrunning others for what one needs—a beg, borrow, or steal existence that is the fate of ex-combatants from all factions. To be a "dreg man" is to be on the move and on the lookout for new patrons and more profitable liaisons. But it is also to look for profitable opportunities beyond those relationships—opportunities to live off the fat of the urban land as an independent young person and eventually find the resources and wherewithal to become a patron in one's own right and to live as an adult or a *kpako* (big person).

As a result, for many people one of the most frustrating and worrisome aspects of the end of the war is the failure of young male combatants like Mohammed to leave Freetown and cities such as Bo, Kenema, and Makeni and return to their villages. Every neighborhood in Freetown is dotted with *potes*, the wooden stalls where young men gather to smoke djamba, drink, and talk. These social spaces for the urban poor became highly politicized at various moments in the country's history. It was in the potes that the language of revolution circulated in the waning days of the Stevens regime and from which the RUF's early leaders emerged. In the first years of the war the national army inflated its troop levels by conscripting underemployed and untrained urban youth from spaces like the potes, resulting in an escalation of atrocities committed by uniformed soldiers. Talk in the potes today is of corruption in the government and of the suffering of black men around the globe, as expressed in reggae and hip hop. Reservoirs of young men languishing in the city suggest that the labor pool of violence remains a real and constant threat. For other inhabitants of the city, these young men appear too readily available for use by elites-turned-warlords or disaffected politicians.

Sitting on the hillside over Freetown in late 2003, Mohammed tensed when I mentioned Junior's name. I had spoken to Junior only the day before, and knew that he planned to return briefly to Freetown from neighboring Liberia. Now an important figure in the rebel forces that had just overthrown Liberian president Charles Taylor, Junior was living in Monrovia along with many of his fighters. As the Liberia war drew to a close, each of the factions was making its final push for territory, loot, and position.

I asked Mohammed, not for the first time, why he hadn't followed Junior across the border to fight. Many of his closest friends from the Brookfields Hotel did exactly that, and a few profited handsomely from it. Mohammed's answer was what I expected: he was tired of war; his small family needed him in Freetown; he didn't trust the men going to

Liberia—they were not his people. These were answers I had heard before, and I didn't disbelieve them. Yet they were more ambiguous than they appear. His implied exercise of agency in this matter masked a more complex and even dangerous set of circumstances.

Mohammed had been similarly resolute when I spoke to him the previous year about campaigning for the Sierra Leone People's Party in the national election. After the betrayals and false promises the SLPP elite made to the nation's youth, Mohammed said, there was simply no way he would vote for the party, let alone campaign on its behalf. And yet like other ex-combatants barracked at the Brookfields Hotel, when campaign season started Mohammed was among the hundreds of young people who took to the streets for the SLPP. Whatever his personal feelings about the political landscape in Sierra Leone, Mohammed was economically, socially, and politically unable to say no when asked to join the election rallies.

"If he sees me, he will go," Junior told me when I mentioned that Mohammed said he was tired of fighting. "He knows I will protect him and create opportunities for him. If he sees me, he will go." According to Junior, once he and Mohammed reconnected in Freetown, it would only be a matter of working out the logistics and Mohammed would join the rebels across the border.

As it happened, Junior did not see Mohammed on that trip. Whatever else it may have offered him, the city provided Mohammed with a certain invisibility. His shack at the urban margins was an economic necessity, but it also enabled Mohammed to avoid seeing (or being seen by) those he might wish to avoid. Though I found Mohammed myself, it took days to do so. Junior's brief visits to Freetown to collect supplies and call up his men were insufficient to track Mohammed when the latter was determined to use the complex topography of the urban landscape to hide from an obligation he otherwise could not avoid. Patronage networks are central to every facet of existence in this part of West Africa, but there are always spaces of resistance or creative manipulation. For Mohammed and for others, that space of possibility and invisibility was a decidedly urban space. Mohammed's village on the Liberia border promised no such obscurity. Junior or his people would easily find him there. The city is often contrasted to the village as a site of opportunity versus lack of it, but for Mohammed and other young people the reverse can also be true: the city can stave off "opportunities" they hope will pass by.

By late 2006 the hillside surrounding Mohammed's, Adama's, and

Struggle's small house had become more crowded. Some of the large homes that had sprouted a few years before were complete. The land had been more clearly demarcated into plots and the scale of activity—in particular the hard labor of smashing stone—had escalated. The hillside now felt less like an urban outpost and more like an industrial zone, although its marginality to the city center remained pronounced. The rutted mud pathway which connected the tarred road into town with the expanding community in the hills was no better than it had been three years before, but it extended further into the bush and now carried heavy vehicles loaded with gravel, charcoal, and timber. At the junction, the pote where Mohammed spent much of his time seemed to be constantly packed with young men.

Mohammed's small pan bodi was itself more crowded. Mohammed and Adama had a second son, Daniel, and Adama was pregnant with their third child. The pan-bodi was no longer a simple one-room lean-to but had expanded. Its zinc and wood construction was subdivided into two rooms and its walls fortified into something closer to solid.

Knowing that I would be traveling east the next day to rendezvous with Junior, I asked Mohammed if they had been in touch. He had not, but in contrast to our earlier conversations about his former patron, Mohammed was interested in the details of our meeting and insisted that I let Junior know where he was. The living, he had heard, was easier in Monrovia than it was in Freetown. The large United Nations peacekeeping force that was guarding the peace in Liberia meant there must be jobs, and the rumor (which I knew to be false) was that there was electricity even for the poor in the Liberian capital.

Reconnecting with Junior at that moment was an uncertain proposition. Though his fortunes have waned considerably since the end of the fighting, Junior was still surrounded by a large number of ex-combatants. His capacity to help them, however, was stretched thin. What's more, he was playing a dangerous role in Sierra Leone's national political dramas. Junior was courted by two parties, each interested in his ability to deliver the youth vote and young men for campaigning. Becoming one of Junior's "boys" again could well mean returning to violence as the campaign season began or being seen as a political enemy should Junior ally with the losing side. At the same time, the doctor's house would eventually be finished and he would no longer need Mohammed to guard his plot or break his rocks. The limited autonomy offered by an absentee patron and life in Freetown had not brought the wherewithal for Mohammed to become an "adult" on his own. Yet moving closer to Junior seemed an uncertain course for transcending the boundaries of youth and its obligations.

General Joe Nunie

Three days into the disarmament proceedings at Bo, Joe Nunie had lost none of his enthusiasm for the back and forth of the negotiations. His sparring partner was usually Major Rhodes, a New Zealander working with the United Nations. He preferred Rhodes to the Kenyan officer Apondi, who was much less willing to ignore those moments when Joe undercounted piles of ammunition or overcounted the number of fighters he let through the disarmament center gates. Both Rhodes and Apondi were military advisors to the Disarmament, Demobilization, and Reintegration Program and both had the same orders and had read the same protocols for conducting the disarmament. But they had very different styles for dealing with Joe and other CDF leaders, and in the complex drama of the DDR campaign, style mattered.

So did humor. When Rhodes stopped two children from entering the adult disarmament center, despite their claims to be in their early twenties, Joe simply shrugged and said: "Here in Africa, we don't grow much."[6] When a young man approached the United Nations observers with a peppershaker and claimed it was a hand grenade, Joe laughed as he argued the young man's case. "Sierra Leone," he declared, "is now a much safer country!"

But for the most part what Joe did was bargain. As successive waves of young men were brought to the table where the United Nations monitors evaluated their weapons, Joe acted as their advocate and intermediary. The protocols of the DDR process were straightforward. To enter the DDR center, a combatant was required to present a weapon, a large amount of ammunition, or himself as part of a team of fighters operating a "group weapon." He needed to demonstrate that he had been a fighter in one of the factions, either through some knowledge of the weapon he held, a faction identification card, or the word of his commanders or comrades. In practice these stipulations left a great deal of room for interpretation and negotiation. Joe negotiated and interpreted for the CDF. No one appointed Joe to this position and the UN did not require it. But no one stopped Joe from making himself indispensable.

The problem that many young men attempting to enter the DDR process had was that few possessed weapons of their own. The CDF had received some government support over the years, but many of its weapons were on loan from ECOMOG or seized from the rebels. There were fewer firearms than there were men who could justifiably claim to be combatants. Generally what weapons the CDF had were controlled by commanders and shared among combatants as needed. As a result, few young men could independently enter the proceedings. To secure a weapon or a stash of ammunition for disarmament they needed the assistance of the commanders and big men within the CDF. Men like Joe Nunie. And so for these youth, the process of enrolling in the DDR campaign often began days earlier when they went to see Joe or other commanders and haggled for support. Disarmament came with benefits: a cash payout for one's weapon, a small bundle of household commodities (soap, shower slippers, bucket), and a place in the jobs training program meant to give combatants a useful postconflict skill. The leadership of the militia traded weapons for a percentage of the cash payout that ranged from a third to 100 percent. Most took half. Low-ranking commanders of smaller units might have four or five firearms to dispense. Men like Joe had access to vastly more.

In addition to the deals he struck before the DDR Program began, Joe had an effective system for profiting on site. Every morning he entered the DDR center grounds in a sagging sedan so loaded with ammunition that its rear fender scraped the rutted road. Young men who turned up at the Bo DDR center from other villages or towns, men who had made no previous deals to enter the proceedings, would go see Joe or bargain with him if they made it to the front of the line. Joe would then turn to the United Nations personnel and negotiate the number of rounds of ammunition it would take to enter the militiaman into the DDR process. When they agreed on a figure, Joe signaled a young man standing by the car to bring the specified number of rounds to the table. Joe took note of the stranger's name and in Mende ordered him to come to his house when the day's DDR proceeding was done.

Joe's dealing typified patronage dynamics at the microlevel. His was on-the-fly deal making replicated day after day on multiple scales. For many of the youth who participated in the Mano River War, it was exactly this kind of gerontocratic system that they claimed to be fighting against. The manifesto produced by the Revolutionary United Front of Sierra Leone (RUF/SL) to justify its rebellion begins with a declaration that it was a corrupt patronage system against which they had launched their attacks: "We can no longer leave the destiny of our country in the hands of a generation of crooked politicians and military adventurists. . . . It is our right and duty to change the present political system in the name of national salvation and liberation" (1995). By the end of the war, rank-and-file CDF combatants openly claimed that the CDF leadership was stealing the rewards of the pro-government effort and that they, the CDF youth, were much in sympathy with their quondam enemy the RUF and its original motives for war.

And, as Mohammed's story illustrates, the war did offer the opportunity to shift their patronage networks in unconventional or otherwise unavailable ways. For a handful it opened new paths of cultivating clients of their own through battlefield opportunities, access to weapons, or the spoils of looting. But the idealism of the early RUF pronouncements and the hope of many CDF recruits notwithstanding, the militarization of youth in the region did nothing to fundamentally alter the logic of power as a logic of patronage. Here, at the war's end, young men found themselves caught in a dramaturgy of patronage even at the literal last step into a postconflict future.

Over the course of his career Gen. Joe was remarkably successful at working that logic to his advantage. Joe was originally a member of Siaka Stevens's Special Security Division, the SSD. The SSD was technically an element of the police force, though in practice it answered directly to Stevens and constituted a private paramilitary specially trained in Cuba.[7] As a member, Joe Nunie was known to have extensive security training and to be a vicious APC partisan. Even so, he was invited in 1998 to participate in the CDF's efforts to reinstate the SLPP. The man who brought him into the CDF was Albert Nallo, at that point the CDF's director of operations in the south and like Joe a native of the village of Kpetewoma Lugbu not far from Bo. Despite Joe's reputation as an APC man, Nallo brought him into the CDF as a trusted lieutenant with military experience and a ruthless willingness to hold power for himself and his allies. Whatever Joe's national political affiliation in the past, Nallo apparently assumed that Joe could be counted on as a fellow big man of the village, a rural instance of what Jean-François Bayart called the reciprocal assimilation of elites (1993, 150–79). For Nunie, the benefits of joining the CDF were obvious: the junta was clearly doomed, the SLPP would be reinstated or—even better—the CDF would itself seize power. Either way, allying with the CDF was clearly a winning strategy.

Joe Nunie's recruitment to the CDF is illustrative of the ways in which the movement was changing. In contrast to the earlier plateaus of the kamajors, Nunie was not chosen by community leaders to participate in the defense of the chiefdom or town. Instead he exemplified the opportunism of a smart social operator working the dynamics of patronage. Joe was a member of a rural elite for whom the CDF, by the time he joined it, represented little more than a new vehicle for an old operation of authority and profit. The organization was fast becoming the de facto national army for the party in power and appeared to be replacing the Poro as the locus of male authority. CDF fighters were becoming the labor pool of mining operations in the southeast and the CDF commanders increasingly found themselves with unprecedented access to the wealth of rural communities.

According to his 2006 testimony before the Special Court, Albert Nallo tasked Joe Nunie with coordinating the major offensives of the CDF in the region. Even more important, he was to stand for those whom Albert Nallo sent up from Base Zero. Nallo could not personally oversee the activities of the men he sent to Kpetewoma, so he needed someone with authority to represent his boys before the community and to control them on Nallo's behalf. Nunie asserted: "My work was so small, but it was big enough. What I used to do, all the commanders that used to come from Base Zero, they would have to sit by my foot at Kpetewoma. . . . It's like a stranger, when you come to any town, you have to sit by somebody's feet before you contact any other big man. So when they came to the village, they had to sit by my feet before they could contact any other person."[8] As it happened, Nallo had less ability to control Joe Nunie than he might have expected. Nunie allegedly began to expand his own local authority by deploying the young men under his control for his private business interests. During his own testimony before the Special Court, Nallo described how he eventually tried to intercede after complaints that Nunie and the CDF fighters he controlled were preying on Kpetewoma. By that time, however, Nunie had cultivated more highly placed patrons than Nallo, patrons on whom he could call for protection against sanction within the CDF.

Q. [PROSECUTION]: Are you familiar with a person called Joe Nunie, N-U-N-I-E?

A. [ALBERT NALLO]: Yes, My Lord.

Q.: Was he a Kamajor?

A.: He was a Kamajor.

PRESIDING JUDGE: Joe Who?

THE WITNESS [NALLO]: Joe Nunie. General Joe Nunie.

PRESIDING JUDGE: Was he a real general?

THE WITNESS: He was not a real general. General to do bad.

. . .

Q. [PROSECUTION]: Was Joe Nunie operating in Kpetewoma during the war?

A.: Yes, My Lord.

Q.: Did you have any dealings with him?

A.: Yes, My Lord.

Q.: What were the dealings that you had with General Joe Nunie?

A.: Joe Nunie used to extort people for money.

Q.: Did you try and do anything about that?

A.: Yes, My Lord.

PRESIDING JUDGE: He used to take money from people. How did he use to take the money from people?

THE WITNESS [NALLO]: They were business people. He would meet them, attack them and then take away their money. That was how he operated. . . . He went to the farm houses and then take [*sic*] chickens, poultry, people's poultry.

Q. [PROSECUTION]: Did you do anything about that?

A.: Yes, My Lord.

Q.: What did you do?

A.: I called him and said, "Joe Nunie, Lugbu is my home town." I did not call him General. I did not call him General. I said, "Kpetewoma Lugbu is my home. This is the place I was born. The people here are my people. You know that I'm your leader here as director of operations. You have been here. You are doing a lot of bad to the people here. You have no good record." So I held him and tied him [arrested him].

Q.: Did you report his activities to anyone?

A.: Yes, My Lord. I reported the matter to Chief Hinga Norman. Chief Norman didn't do anything. What I did by tying the Kamajor was the wrong thing and he reprimanded me for that.[9]

Joe's activities were profitable enough that CDF fighters working under other commanders defected to Nunie's unit, submitting themselves to his control in return for security and a share of the spoils in his version of the war. It could be ugly work. One former CDF fighter who spent time with Nunie described how he ordered a female captive, an RUF fighter captured near Tongo, impaled slowly on a long stake. "That C.O. Joe Nunie," the combatant said, "is an educated man, a good fighter, and a good commander. But he's wicked."[10] A second fighter who worked with Gen. Joe in Bo claimed to have left him after an incident in which Nunie killed one of his friends by spraying him with acid. In his unit, this fighter said, there was a boy they used to call Kasange (the Mende term for a burial shroud). The boy started fighting with Nunie as a ten-year-old, and went on to become a forward fighter with LURD before he lost a leg in Liberia. "Anyone who grows up with Joe Nunie in the bush," he concluded, "is going to be a hard man."

My own early encounters with Gen. Joe were brief but impressive. We met first in Bo in 2000 when the city was still very much a CDF stronghold. Joe pulled his battered Land Rover up to the stand of a mechanic friend of mine, a cadre of his fighters piled in the back. Though the boys who hung out at the stand joked with Joe while they welded his muffler, they were tense and uncertain around him, and visibly relieved when he left. When we met a year later at the Bo DDR center, Joe seemed to regard me as many in the CDF leadership did: warily, a journalist who could tell their personal stories and the stories of the CDF (a useful mode of praise singing) but nevertheless a stranger and an ambiguous presence over whom they had less control than they would like.[11]

I formally interviewed Joe only once. He was terse and vague, unwilling to talk about his past with the APC. What I learned from and about Joe I learned through watching him. If we take seriously Victor Turner's famous metaphor of life as social drama, Joe was an exquisite performer who understood the aesthetics of performing power.

These performances exemplified some of the particularities or microprocesses that are often occluded in discussions of postcolonial patronage. Too often we overlook the incredible creativity and experimentation that mark successful "social navigation" (Vigh 2006) according to the logic of relationships of patrons and clients. Joe made power real by claiming a certain authority and realizing it through action, wit, style, and bravado. The presiding judge's question "Was he a real general?" goes to the complicated heart of the CDF and the flexibility that belies abstract discussions of the politics of patronage. "General Joe" was a name that Nunie assigned himself and essentially made come true.[12] No one challenged his right to be a CDF "general," and so he was. He had the wherewithal to draw men to him and the support of patrons who would give him free reign. If he wanted to claim the title of general in the CDF no one was prepared to stop him. By doing so he further claimed a stake on power that was never successfully challenged.

As I mentioned earlier, when combatants referred to the everyday scams that one pulled to get by as "419" schemes, they referenced the Nigerian confidence tricks that circulate around the World Wide Web. Like the offers to split vast sums of money in return for assistance with bank details, combatants recognized that profitability could be tied to how well one worked a lie or half-truth. Style mattered, and a tale well told could often make a fiction real. One could accumulate power by deploying the signifiers of power whether there was originally anything to back up the boast or not (see Apter 1999 on 419 as a social and political strategy in Nigeria). Joe had mastered this performative mode. He makes clear that the aesthetics of how one performs one's authority is critical to cultivating relationships of patronage (see Mbembe 1992).

Joe also exemplified how important violence could be to the logic of patronage. Certainly he traded on a willingness to deploy violence to make his own version of the 419 scheme a reality. His was a mode of dramatic display that might have been sanctioned differently at other moments but is increasingly common in the contemporary postcolony. This physical performance of violence was a strategy effective for young men (or those like Nunie who were associated with youth politics despite being middle-aged) when other avenues for social advancement had been shut off. When a young man at the Bo DDR center threw a grenade into the crowd in an effort to disrupt the proceedings (the grenade failed, causing what amounted to only a minor disturbance), he was hauled before Joe. Joe gave him two hard slaps on the head. The boy melted, pissing on himself and sobbing, obviously terrified that Joe would kill him on the spot. When Joe waded through the mob of fighters outside the gate and ordered them neatly into rows, he similarly performed his power in ways that confirmed his already fearsome reputation among the kamajors at Bo. Joe's reputation for brutality, periodically demonstrated in ways large and small, was integral to the claims he made for authority. There is a common trope that runs through the region about the relationship between power and violence: those who can effectively deploy violence are very often the only ones who can effectively control it in others. This was the truth that lay at the seemingly paradoxical election of Charles Taylor to the Liberian presidency in 1997; by brutally ravaging the country, Taylor proved that he alone had the authority to overcome the violence of others and (potentially) bring peace to the country (see Moran 2006, 101–23; see also Ellis 1999; Hoffman 2006). This same demonstrable control of violence led some Liberians, including former LURD fighters instrumental in Taylor's overthrow, to muse by 2005 that the crime rate in Monrovia was so bad that they wished Taylor would return. One ex-combatant asked: "Who do we need to steer this country?" Answering his own question, he went on: "We don't need a weak man. You need someone who can say, 'I want this cleaned up!' They can't even listen to the international community if they say 'human rights.' You'll never get development like that. Taylor was the right president for Liberians."

On a more modest scale, Joe Nunie ruled his fiefdom through a similar spectacular display. He was marked as a big man by the violence he could summon and effectively deploy. When Joe's former fighter described him as "an educated man, a good fighter, and a good commander," the final observation—"but he's wicked"—is only partly an indictment; that "wickedness" was the quality that made possible the other three.

On 9 August 2007, five years after the war ended, Joe Nunie was in the streets putting that phenomenology of power to work once again for the SLPP. At a rally in advance of the national elections, Nunie marched with a group of former kamajors now calling themselves Bundaya or Bundayillah (roughly "one family") a nascent political body of SLPP affiliated ex-combatant youth. Nunie marched in an SLPP-green trench coat, heavy boots, dark wraparound sunglasses, and his wartime "controller," the occult protection that he used to repel enemy bullets. In contrast to the suits, Mao shirts, or gowns that marked party bosses, town and chiefdom authorities, or men made big through business, Nunie signified power that was claimed and secured through violence and the performances of the body. Other notables drove the march route in luxury cars or SUVs. Joe walked, surrounded by young men screaming as they paraded across Bo: "We are the kamajors!" Where other big men displayed their power of mastery over the national bureaucracy, transnational business, or even the occult, Joe displayed his mastery of the power inherent in youth violence. When describing the chaotic and at times confrontational march through town, Joe told me: "When we move, you know it is a powerful move."

When the war officially ended Gen. Joe became the chairman of the Bo District chapter of the Motor Drivers and General Transport Workers Union. The union included a large number of former combatants, many of whom began earning a living driving motorbike taxis in Bo and smaller towns around the country. Just as he had as a CDF commander, Joe organized the labor of his charges and protected them for a portion of their pay. As the 2007 national elections approached, each of the three political parties courted the leaders of the various wartime factions in an effort to recruit thug laborers for the violent work of campaigning (see Christensen and Utas 2008). These former commanders could still draw together the bodies needed for violent work, this time the work of electioneering. Some did so informally, others through the organizations they formed in the aftermath of the war—"development" cooperatives or NGOs that repackaged kamajor units for the new landscape of a postwar political economy. As election season drew near, Nunie brought

15. General Joe Nunie (left) and other leaders of Bundayillah, Bo, 2007.

together his former CDF charges and union members and together with other mid-level CDF figures formed Bundayillah.

On the night of the SLPP rally, I sat with Joe in the parlor of a small guesthouse. Bundayillah, he claimed, was a development organization. Its sole purpose was to advocate for ex-combatant youth and secure a livelihood for them as veterans of the war. After careful consideration, and despite the neglect the kamajors had experienced at the hands of the national government, Bundayillah had decided to align itself with the SLPP. The party in return awarded Joe and his organization with a road-building contract, and Joe was certain that when the SLPP won the election there would be additional contracts to follow. The SLPP had betrayed them in the past by failing to adequately compensate the CDF for the work it did on behalf of the country, Joe said, but Solomon Berewa, the SLPP presidential candidate, understood that. He would do right by the youth of Bundayillah, and they in turn would campaign for the party and defend it if need be. Bundayillah, he said, was an organization for the development of the country and the development of Sierra Leonean youth. It was a not a military force. But he added to this an ominous coda: "We need them [the ex-combatant youth]. That's why we are organizing them. That is why we formed this organization. We may need them at any time. We are not going to leave them out. We are a standby force. We are not expecting any problem. But if the SLPP had had a higher vote, they [the APC] would have tried something. That's why we are a standing force. We work with the police, with the army. We are a standby force." Shortly after that, Joe Nunie said his good-byes and walked outside to his waiting motorbike. It was painted SLPP green, and on the mudflap was a roughly painted version of the party's palm leaf symbol. On the front was a makeshift sign, tellingly fastened with thin wires that could be easily removed: "Donated by the SLPP."

The nature of the kamajors and the CDF movement changed over time. What began as a disparate collective of mobilizations, a war machine community of resistance, grew into a more institutionalized, state-like sodality. This presented individual combatants and commanders with a variety of limits and opportunities that shifted through the course of the war and beyond. At some moments militia members experimented with new possibilities, bluffed or bullied their way into profitable new arrangements. At others they were confounded by the seemingly immutable logic of gerontocratic power in a corrupt, criminal state.

The stories here chart that progression. Though Mohammed and Gen. Joe were both associated with the marginal, youth politics that was integral to the Mano River War, they maneuvered from very different positions: Mohammed as a true outsider, Gen. Joe as a big man, albeit one whose base of power was the village, the much-despised security forces, and his own imposing presence. By the end of the war Mohammed and Gen. Joe mapped a narrowing landscape of possibilities for such men. Their room for maneuver, experiment, even revolution shrank as the militia became ensconced in a more rigid, formalized logic. Of course the possibilities of creating other futures never disappeared entirely. The state, as Deleuze and Guattari put it, is always breeding new war machines. But whereas in the early days of the movement the war opened up new possibilities for a range of persons, by its end it was those already in positions of power who could make the most productive use of the habitus of war.

Mbembe's description of a "new economy of persons" (2006, 304; see also 2003, 33) in the postcolony today is apropos here. This new regime of value is one in which the strange circulation of money—its scarcity in most instances, its overabundance in others, and the mystifying routes by which it travels and accumulates—are making all relationships between postcolonial subjects "purely market and object-like." Specifically, it is the inability to effectively manage debts, the heart of the relations of patron and client, that has foreclosed alternative ways of being-with-others and being-in-the-world: "The widespread drying up of liquidities, followed by their progressive concentration along certain pathways whose conditions of access have become ever more draconian, has resulted in a brutal contraction of the number of people capable of passing debts on to others—capable, that is, of submitting others to obligations which they are compelled to pay off in an appropriate manner. The nature of debt itself has changed, with the 'protection debt' becoming the ultimate signifier of kin relations, be they real or fictive" (2006, 304). Mohammed found himself trapped in this new economy of persons. His relationships of patronage were increasingly relations of "protection debt." He submitted himself to the authority of successive commanders in relations that, while often described in familial terms, were harshly utilitarian. They were predicated on a patron's ability to provide the material basic for life. They were less about sociality than survival. Mohammed faced little prospect of escaping these webs of relations by becoming an adult or a patron himself. His avenues of escape were limited to disap-

16. Former CDF Special Forces fighter Hassan Jalloh with the Bundayillah contingent marching for the SLPP, Bo, 2007. (Photograph by John Hoffman)

pearance into the fabric of an ever-expanding city or submitting himself to a patron made more powerful by war. Dregging represented one form of debt maintenance that denies sociability. It allowed for a subsistence living but it offered no alternative vision of the future. It is debt oriented exclusively toward survival, not debt organized around the making of a community (see Piot 1999, 52–75).

Mohammed's inability to return to the village suggests a similar predicament. By describing the shame of returning empty-handed from the battlefield and predicting that he would be greeted with scorn, Mohammed named a condition in which he as a subject represented no productive or positive potential. He was someone in whom no one in his natal community was prepared to invest. His value was purely a market value. With no liquidity after a decade of war he was a person of no worth.

Those for whom men like Mohammed did remain valuable were those like Joe Nunie. Nunie emerged at the end of the war as a powerful patron because he controlled violence and the bodies of those who could perform it. These were people for whom rank-and-file combatants, and young men more generally, represented a labor pool capable of being deployed for all manner of work—much of it violent, unregulated, and unrewarded. As I take up in the chapters that follow, this is the new reality for many young men in the aftermath of the Mano River War.

chapter 5

THE BARRACKS

July 2005: Monrovia, Liberia

THE SQUARE BLOCK between Benson, Centre, and Lynch streets in downtown Monrovia is the laboratory of the future of urban West Africa. The Liberian Defense Ministry building sits at the north end of the block, a nondescript, decrepit concrete box. At the south end lies the Palm Grove Cemetery. Crammed between is the stuffing of Monrovia's urban fabric: wooden kiosks, concrete shops, and zinc-covered houses squeezed end to end around crowded and impossibly shaped yards.

From his third-floor office, Joe Wylie, the deputy minister of defense for administration in the national transitional government of Liberia (NTGL), could look out on the barricades that close Benson Street to traffic. Only his Jeep Grand Cherokee and the imported SUVs of other ministers are allowed through by the Nigerian peacekeepers who secure the city. The morning I visited him, Joe's desk bore the universal trappings of an upper-level bureaucrat: flat-screen desktop computer, remote control for the wall unit air conditioner, Joe's two cell phones and his palm pilot. As various civilian and military personnel came to him with requests or documents, Joe briefed me on the security situation in the country, on his personal affairs since last we met, and on his plans to ask the NTGL budget office for five thousand dollars cash for a plane ticket to the United States and a rental car so he could visit the Pentagon.

A week later, I sat a few hundred feet from Joe's office in a metal hovel in the Alcatraz ghetto. Like any of the city's ghettos (as they are called in Liberian English),[1] Alcatraz was a collection of makeshift dwellings inhabited mostly by underemployed young men. In the yard, a collection of youth played checkers, talked, and smoked cigarettes or marijuana. Inside a mostly bare room, I spoke with ex-combatants Abdul, Lansana, and George about life in the army of former Liberian warlord-turned-president Charles Taylor, about their interest in mining diamonds, and about the ongoing war in neighboring Côte d'Ivoire. All three said they were tired of war and uninterested in recruitment for the Ivorian conflict. If they could find patrons, each would go to Greenville and the Sapo Forest Reserve, where it was rumored a large deposit of diamonds had recently been discovered.

There is without question a dystopic narrative in both the parallels and the contrasts of these two encounters. It is a narrative of crumbling infrastructure and failed governance, of the twin crises of neoliberalism and neopatrimonialism. It is a narrative of the "worlding" of African cities (Simone 2001), in which urban Africa becomes a staging post for opportunities beyond its own borders. Joe Wylie and the youth in Alcatraz fought on opposite sides of the war, yet none found it noteworthy that they now all hustled on the same city block for opportunities to escape the city they once sought to control. It seemed just one more development in the absurd trajectory of the city of Monrovia and those who live there.

African cities have always presented a challenge to the anthropology of Africa. As Sally Falk Moore recounts in her history of Africanist anthropology (1994), it was southern Africa's mass urbanization that disrupted the functionalist and salvage narratives of much classic British social anthropology. More recently, writers such as AbdouMaliq Simone (2001, 2002, 2004), Fassil Demissie (2007), Filip de Boeck and Marie-Françoise Plissart (2005), and Achille Mbembe and Sarah Nuttall (2004) have again examined urban spaces as crucial fields for the "project of defamiliarization" of postcolonial metanarratives; in this case, metanarratives of a continent in collapse (Mbembe and Nuttall 2004, 352). In contrast to the view of the African city as a negative space measured by its deviance from an abstract, properly functioning norm, recent works on the city privilege the creation of new types of urbanity through experimentation and creative bricolage.

Disrupting the imaginings of the African-city-as-failure is difficult enough when the city from which one writes is Johannesburg, Dakar, Kinshasa, or Nairobi. It becomes an even greater challenge when the city in question is Luanda or Mogadishu, Kigali or Kisangani. These are cities in which the forces that "overpopulate" the African urban setting—people, wealth, poverty, occult forces, uncertainty, death (Simone

2001, 17)—include the literal forces of rebel movements, military insurrections, and militia mobilizations. Must we "write the world" differently (to paraphrase Mbembe and Nuttall) if the African metropolis from which we write is Freetown or Monrovia and not Johannesburg or Dakar? Although violence may be integral to the fabric of any African postcolonial metropole, do cities so thoroughly defined by overt warfare represent a different urban architecture altogether?

After a decade and a half of the Mano River War, Freetown and Monrovia epitomized the African urban landscape as urban warscape. The populations of both cities swelled with refugees and internally displaced persons from throughout the region, placing enormous pressure on already fractured infrastructures. Direct military incursions into both capitals radically impacted the shape and future of these cities, and the post-conflict period has seen very little improvement in basic services.

Nevertheless, on the basis of the configuration of space, bodies, subjects, and violence within specific locations in Freetown and Monrovia, I suggest that these cities are best understood not in terms of destruction but as zones of excessive production. Like any space of capitalist production, the crucial element is the organization of labor. Inspired by Agamben's writing on the camp as the *nomos*, or organizing principle, of modernity, I suggest that the nomos of West Africa's postmodernity is the barracks. The barracks concentrates bodies (particularly male bodies) and subjects into formations that can be deployed quickly and efficiently to any corner of the empire.[2] The men may be called up at any moment as laborers on the battlefield, workers on the plantation, or diggers in the mine. The barracks organizes male sociality itself around the exercise of violence and circulates that violence within an exchange economy. In this chapter I trace these movements through two specific sites, Freetown's Brookfields Hotel and the Duala neighborhood of Monrovia. What we see from Brookfields and Duala is the same view we see from Joe Wylie's window and the checkers table at Alcatraz: a city and its populace reorganized and reorganizing itself to service the united functions of a resource-extraction economy and war.

Charles Taylor and the National Patriotic Front of Liberia had reached Monrovia by late 1990. Fighting between various NPFL factions, government forces, and ECOMOG damaged the city even further. The relative calm following Taylor's election in 1997 allowed for the resumption of limited city services, but the three "world wars" (the local name for the three major attacks by LURD forces on Monrovia) once again wreaked havoc on both the physical urban environment and on the everyday existence of its inhabitants.

Freetown fared little better during its phases of the war. Although the residents of Sierra Leone's capital city were famously ignorant of what was happening in the early period of the conflict, by 1995 fighting reached the Freetown environs. The 1997 coup d'etat led to massive devastation as junta forces pillaged the city and ECOMOG first bombarded the city from air and sea and then (together with Sierra Leonean irregulars) fought a brutal urban ground war to reclaim the capital. The city was rocked by additional bouts of urban warfare, notably the 6 January 1999 invasion and the 8 May 2000 "incident" in which the RUF leader Foday Sankoh's fighters opened fire in the city.

Beyond the overt destruction inflicted on the urban landscape, the city figured prominently in other ways in the conflict. For example, it was the bolstering of the Sierra Leone Army's ranks with untrained urban youth that is largely responsible for the "sobel" phenomenon, the predations of soldiers on local populations, and the collaboration between soldiers and rebels to profiteer from the black market trade in diamonds. Underemployed urban youth made up the majority of the fighting forces on all sides. Many of these untrained young men were drawn from Monrovia's ghettoes and the potes of Freetown. Although it is frequently described as a "bush war," the Mano River conflict could be said to have both made the city and been made by it.

It is increasingly clear that the conceptual opposition of war and peace in postcolonial Africa is both unfixed and unhelpful. Too often, as Paul Richards notes, "war is foregrounded as a 'thing in itself' and not . . . one social project among many competing social projects" (2005a, 3). In the previous chapter I argued that the Mano River War was not the suspension of the "normal" functioning of relations of debt and patronage. Here I make a parallel argument about the city itself. The Mano River

War was as much a logical extension of the way the city works as it was a disruption to it.

Such an approach shifts the burden of understanding the dynamics of postcolonial warscapes from an exclusive focus on what is destroyed. It seeks simultaneously to understand what is being produced. Anthropologists engaged in the study of violence have long been interested in its productive capacity. What concerns me here is the extent to which the specific mode of production of this African war zone is increasingly indistinguishable from the mode of production of the postcolonial city itself. Simone suggests something similar when he writes that in African cities today, the logic of accumulation and expenditure is so pervasive, so thoroughly mystified, and so thoroughly connected to a world economy that it generates its own social reality:

> In many respects . . . the operations of the global economy make it nearly impossible for many Africans to continue functioning "inside" their cities. A seemingly arbitrary circulation of the unknown has penetrated these cities. What makes people rich or poor, what accounts for loss and gain, and "working assessments" of the identities of who is doing what to whom are viewed as more uncertain. As the "insides" of African cities are more differentially linked to proliferating networks of accumulation and circulation operating at also increasingly differentiated scales, this uncertainty is "materialized." In other words, it takes the forms of specific bodies and identities, in which parts of bodies, as well as part-objects, specific locations, and built environments, are seen to embody particular forces of well-being and success. (2001, 17)

The result of this regime of production is the complete reconfiguration of the city and of those who live there. Life within that space is a process of constructing fragmented and often contradictory selves; it is an experience of being subjected to arbitrary, uncertain, and unpredictable forms of discipline, which may demand life itself (Mbembe 2003; Mbembe and Roitman 1995). Within the city are multiple invisible cities, or what Simone calls the "product and practice" of making reality from incoherent assemblages of divergent and contradictory forces (2002, 28–29; see also de Boeck and Plissart 2005, 243–44).

This is the space of a new Pentecostalism that blurs the boundaries between tithing and pyramid schemes, wealth in this world and salvation in the next. It is a space of the virtual production of Internet 419 schemes and what Sierra Leonean combatants came to call "419ing": boasting of high military rank with enough conviction that someone would believe it and thereby make it real. It is a space in which being a refugee or displaced person under the care of multinational corporate NGOs can be the most stable occupation and the only one that guarantees access to basic services once performed by the state, at least until the war ends or the contract runs out or a change in government of a distant European country leads to a shift in foreign aid priorities.

This is a form of urban organization in which movement is necessary for survival, both physical and social. The Krio term *dreg*, used to describe the everyday processes of getting by, envokes this emphasis on profitable movement when it refers not only to the "hustle" of life at the margins but also to the act of moving about the city to get one's business done. As a former LURD fighter put it, "In Monrovia, only the strong survive. Monrovia is not for a lazy man."

The city as a machine of production of this type is not the modernist archetype of the city as rationalized instrument. "Urbanization conventionally denotes a thickening of fields, an assemblage of increasingly heterogeneous elements into more complicated collectives," writes Simone. But in these African urban centers "the accelerated, extended, and intensified intersection of bodies, landscapes, objects, and technologies defer[s] calcification of institutional ensembles or fixed territories of belonging" (2004, 408; see also Njami 2001, 72). The city itself fails to solidify. The postconflict city fails to rebuild. The urban infrastructure is constructed from a more diffuse array of relationships between people, markets of exchange, occult imaginings, and temporary alliances and enmities. Movement replaces identification as the locus of production and political participation.

Partha Chatterjee's distinction between the citizenry and the population group is instructive here. For most world cities, he suggests, the calculus of residency is not one of a "homogenous" citizenry able by rights to place demands on city or state governments through appeal to the city's public institutions. Rather, the city comprises heterogeneous populations to be managed. Governments reach accommodation with population blocks based on a cost–benefit analysis. Services are provided here, compacts can be negotiated there, all in an effort to keep populations in check, deploy them when possible, and contain their inevitable potential for disruption (Chatterjee 2004). Such accommodations certainly characterize many African postcolonial urban zones—although the governing structures with which these heterogeneous political populations reach accommodation are less likely to be the functioning government of the city or the state than multinational corporations, warlords, or NGOs. As I take up in greater detail below, what is key to these strategic alliances is the population's capacity for violence.

Building the Barracks

The philosopher Giorgio Agamben suggests that the camp stands as the nomos of modernity. Auschwitz, he argues, is the logical extension of the spatialization of biopolitics and represents the modern form of sovereignty (1998). The camp is the instantiation of the point at which the state of emergency becomes the norm—the moment when the police, rather than the law, are allowed to decide fundamental matters of life and death without review or fear of sanction. It is the moment when what Agamben calls "the care of the nation's biological life" (175) becomes a political task.

The camp is therefore above all an institution with the capacity to effectively police and manage its borders and internal functions—indeed, this is its primary purpose. It is a machine for the processes of classification, containment, and if necessary efficient extermination. Yet its efficacy relies on a very particular, hegemonic configuration of the modern institution.[3] What we find in West African urban centers, however, is not the perfection of the modernist institution as manifested in the asylum, factory, clinic, school, or prison. Unlike these institutions, movement rather than classification of identities is the key productive capacity in the West African postcolony.

I therefore find the barracks a more fitting spatial model for the nomos of Africa's postmodernity. In a very literal sense the importance of the barracks is evident as we look around contemporary, cosmopolitan Africa. The barracks has become a complete social space. In addition to its security functions, in cities from Freetown to Monrovia to Brazzaville barracks are becoming important economic and social locations, as security service offers one of the few stable sources of income and as a wage earner's dependents crowd these structures. They are becoming important locations for political life as well, as the question of whether the armed forces remain barracked is increasingly the determining factor in the success or failure of any transition in government.

Yet the barracks is not simply becoming more important as a site on the urban landscape. It is becoming the model of that landscape itself. Unlike the camp's logic of classification of bodies and subjects, the barracks represents a shift in emphasis to the body's capacity for overconsumption and violence. To participate in the various overlapping economies of West African postcolonial urban life is increasingly to work out a technique for the strategic performance of violence and its exchangeability with other tasks. The barracks, literally and figuratively, is the spatial arrangement by which violence is alternately contained and deployed. It historically represented the point of intersection of violence, sovereignty, and economy. The barracks guaranteed the colonial project's entwined motives of resource extraction and political rule. Its reservoir of legitimate violence was the most powerful tool in building the neopatrimonial postcolonial African state. And in the new age of empire, the barracks has become not only the engine of a dramatically expanded service and production economy but also the police force for securing the neoliberal market.

The movement of bodies into and out of the barracks, and the relationship between that movement and the deployment or restraint of violence, is its organizing principle. The barracks is designed for rapid assembly and rapid deployment. At its most effective, the barracks makes the speed of movement a weapon. And as is becoming increasingly evident as private security contractors become more visible on the world stage, efficiency of the nexus of violence and movement is also the locus of the barrack's form of profit (see Virilio and Lotringer 1997).

For example, the process of disarming combatants through the DDR campaign ended Sierra Leone's war, but it replicated in many ways the habitus out of which the war developed. For ex-combatants at the Bo DDR center, the small cash payment and the promise of some level of skills training presented the only viable economic opportunity available, and it was predicated entirely on the ability to pass physically into the DDR center's space. The young men who gathered for days outside the gates with their weapons knew that there were a limited number of slots in the disarmament centers and that only the proven capacity for violence (the possession of a weapon, withstanding the riot conditions at the gate) would earn them entry into the process. Some who managed to break through the heavy United Nations security cordon were allowed to stay, whereas others were violently evicted, illustrating the extent to which strategies of economic accumulation, and therefore social standing and political influence, were predicated on which physical spaces could be crossed and how violence facilitated that crossing.

The same dynamic was at work in a perverse way in the amputee camps. Most of the estimated twenty thousand victims of the RUF's apparently random attacks on civilians, in which they used machetes to amputate the limbs of noncombatants, died. Of the few thousand who managed to survive, many ended up in camps in Freetown. The largest of these, the Aberdeen Road camp, became a required stop for visiting journalists, NGO workers, and dignitaries. No single space became more synonymous with the horrors of the war in Sierra Leone. Consequently, no space received more assistance than this camp. Relief organizations and charitable donors targeted the camp for funding projects or brought cash donations, and it soon became clear that being one of the war's most tragic victims had ironically become one of the few guaranteed means of generating an income. The population of the camp swelled as destitute extended family members showed up in the capital to live with their mutilated relations. Despite the fact that a number of organizations not only donated artificial limbs to residents of the camp but also showed them how to cheaply and effectively manufacture their own, almost no one within the camp chose to use them. Instead, the amputees developed a mode of narrating and displaying their violations prominently.

Here, it was not the body's capacity to inflict violence that opened the door into economic life but a related willingness to make constantly visible the evidence of past violence. The effectiveness of this strategy was largely predicated on the easy localizability of these bodies in one place. A variation, but a consistent one, on the barracks logic of the postmodern postcolony.

If the barracks is becoming the nomos of West African postmodernity it would seem to mark a departure from the enclave production in resource-extraction economies emphasized in some of the recent literatures on the state in Africa (see, for example, Ferguson 2006, 194–210; Reno 2001; Watts 2004). Ferguson, for instance, argues that the "Angola model" of resource extraction has generated a network of enclave spaces in which some form of state order appears intact, albeit on an "as needed" basis and largely by outsourcing the functions of the state to pri-

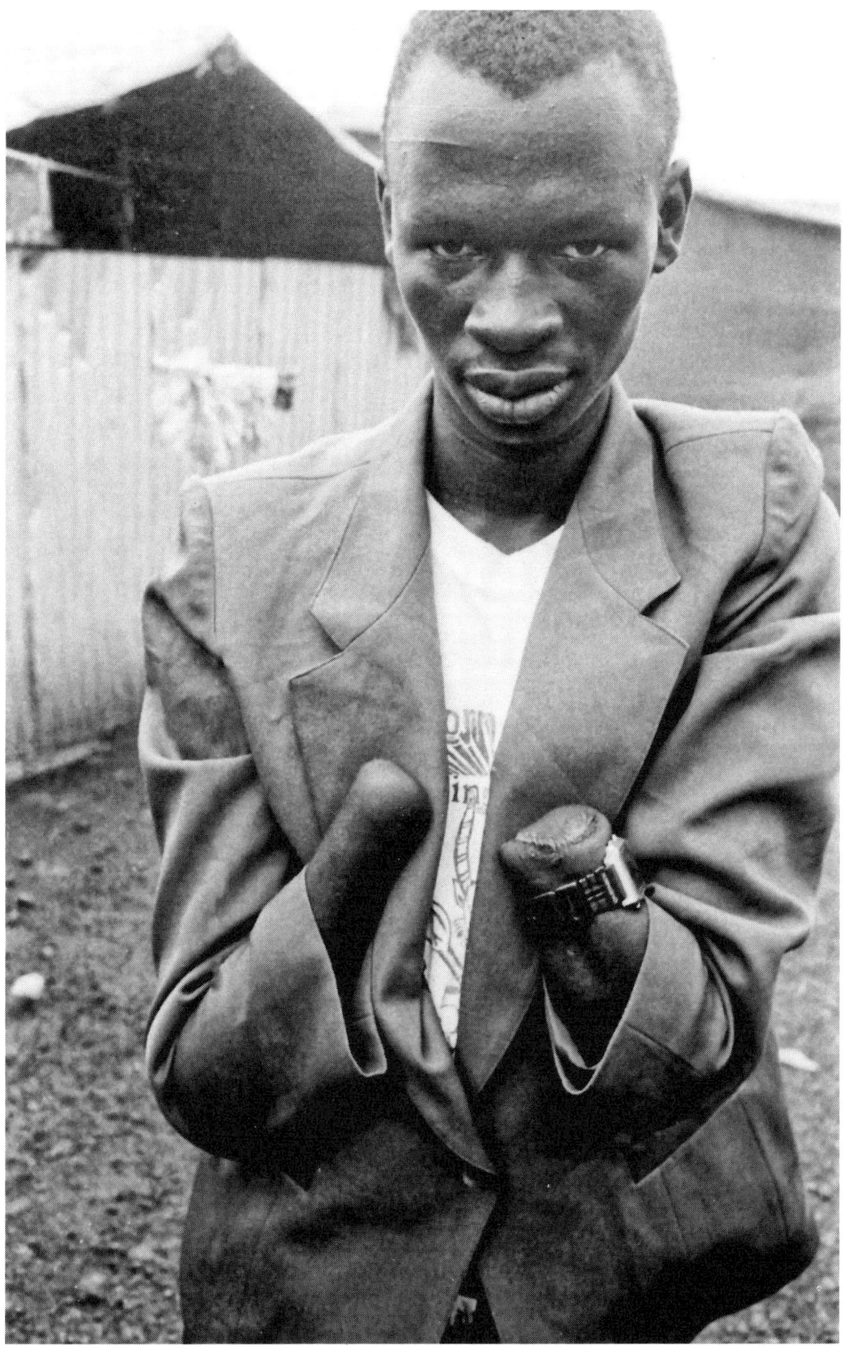

17. At the Aberdeen Road amputee camp, Freetown, Sierra Leone, 2000.

vate contractors. Such spaces are dependent on the smoke screen of state sovereignty in order to legitimate what happens inside these enclaves to the outside world.

Of course, the just-in-time production of security for mining and other ventures in the Angola model is exactly what took place in Sierra Leone during the war years. The spatial metaphor of the enclave as a zone of selective state sovereignty, however, is less applicable there in part because alluvial diamond production is very different from the capital-intensive oil-extraction industry that animates the Angola case. What is required for surface mining in this region is large numbers of laborers with minimal skills and tools. The critical factor is the movement of that labor, the ability to effectively deploy the bodies of young men, at least temporarily. Thus unlike in the metaphor of the enclave, with its implication of a segregated, defined, and defensible space, what matters in the mining economy of the Mano River region is flexibility of movement through multiple spaces. What is required is the barracks' ability to allow for the temporary colonization of space and then, when necessary, the rapid redeployment of bodies to another location.[4]

The barracks also represents a somewhat different political geography from the one envisioned by Mbembe's necropolitics. As I argued in the introduction, the Mano River War was never fundamentally about "relations of enmity" (Mbembe 2003, 16), or the strict classification of bodies and subjects into those who could be killed and those who are allowed to live (the notable exception being actions of the AFRC and RUF junta). This, Mbembe argues, is the essence of postcolonial necropolitics. With it comes a certain mode of sovereignty that he, following Eyal Weizman (2002), calls "vertical sovereignty." The colonial model of space organized into zones of occupation ("territorial fragmentation") (Mbembe 2003, 27) is made more complex in today's postcolony. The separation of the "settlers' town" from the "Negro village" that Frantz Fanon ([1961] 2005, 39) describes at the heart of the colonial project is today a more intricate fabric of enclave spaces, throughways, subterranean passages, and airspace. The goal is still to classify and to contain. But in the new geography of the necropolitical these various territories do not sit side by side; they overlap and overlook one another and shift boundaries at hyperspeed. "Under conditions of vertical sovereignty and splintering colonial occupation," Mbembe writes, "communities are separated across a y-axis" (2003, 29).

The case on which Weizman draws is the conflict between Palestinians and Israelis, and for that purpose it makes a great deal of sense. Mbembe, however, extrapolates from this a more universal postcolonial reality. From his discussion of the territorial fragmentation of vertical sovereignty he moves into an exegesis on late modernity's war machines and enclave economies. But while the barracks spaces of the Mano River region represent a kind of territorial fragmentation, they organize space differently. They do not map a distinction between "friend" and "enemy" or "settler" and "native." They do not create enclaves, the borders of which must be policed and the residents of which must be carefully classified. Instead they represent points of assembly. Various identities may be important to how those spaces function—refugee, combatant, citizen, and so on—but those identities are fluid and fungible. What is more important is the orientation of these barracks spaces toward an elsewhere: the resettlement of refugees, the transit of laborers to the mine or the battlefield. Efficient movement, not isolation, gives the barracks its meaning.

I turn now to two more extensive examinations of West African barracks spaces. In the first, Freetown's Brookfields Hotel, I am particularly interested in what Simone has identified as the way postcolonial African cities "operate as a platform to engage in processes and territories elsewhere" (2001, 18). In other words, my concern here is with the process of deterritorialization, or how the barracks organizes immediately and effectively deployable laborers—whatever the particular task may be, and wherever within the reach of the empire they may be needed.

In the case of the Duala neighborhood of Monrovia, I focus on the corollary processes of assembly (or reterritorialization). For the barracks city to deploy laboring bodies for work on the battlefields and resource-extraction industries of West Africa, it must also be able to effectively assemble them. This is relatively straightforward in a space such as the Brookfields Hotel that housed hundreds of combatants. But even in less literal barracks spaces, the rapid call-up of laborer-warriors is written into the very logic of life in the city.

Freetown's Brookfields Hotel

Located in the Brookfields neighborhood of downtown Freetown, the Brookfields Hotel has approximately 150 rooms spread over eight two-story and three-story buildings. Before the war the hotel boasted a swimming pool, a well-regarded bar, and a decent restaurant. It was a favored hangout for both local elites and international tourists. Brookfields was also the site of the government's hotel and tourism training school, through which the state was working to expand an increasingly important sector of its economy.

The hotel was first used as a barracks by the forces of the RUF in 1997. When the junta was driven out of town and the SLPP government restored to power, the CDF took over the hotel as its own barracks. The CDF remained until August 2002, eight months after the official end of the war and four years from when it first took control of Freetown.

Until their forced removal, several hundred male combatants lived or temporarily resided at the hotel along with their dependents. The latter included wives, girlfriends, children, friends, and extended family. Most residents were young, a majority under thirty years old. Individual rooms were nominally assigned to specific combatants, although in practice the population of the hotel was highly transient. The infrastructure was in poor condition. Although there was surprisingly reliable electric current, there was no running water and the septic system had long since overflowed. None of the rooms contained their original furnishings, and many had been burned out or at least partially destroyed. On average, each of the rooms housed four to six people, who often slept in shifts throughout the day and night.

The hotel was more than the backdrop against which the story of the kamajors unfolded. It seemed to exemplify, rather, what Allen Feldman describes as the way in which "bodily, spatial, and violent practices" form a "unified language of material signification" (1991, 1). The form of the hotel (a generic modernist structure designed for mass temporary housing), its location in the city (at the edge of downtown, sandwiched between the mountains and the city's heart), even its past connection to the world economy (absentee Chinese owners and a history of elite and foreign patronage)—none of these were incidental to the role that the space played in shaping the urban front of the war. Together they made it possible for the hotel to concentrate the labor force of a violent economy into a single space and orient it toward deployment throughout the city, the country, and the region as necessary.

During the later war years, Brookfields was the largest single space in which kamajor combatants gathered anywhere in the country. From the restoration of the SLPP government in 1998 until the kamajors were evacuated in mid-2002, the occupation of the hotel was posited as insurance against both a renewed rebel incursion into the city and a second coup by the state's armed forces. It housed frontline troops and commanders temporarily in the capital for meetings with the organizational leadership. Units waiting for redeployment elsewhere in the country frequently cycled through Brookfields. The hotel hosted the vanguard forces meant to protect the leadership and served as the base of the Special Forces, the most professionalized contingent within the militia. The compound was a weapons cache, a meeting spot, and a housing unit for wounded combatants unable or unwilling to return to families or homes outside the capital.

As the war drew to a close and combatants were less frequently sent from Brookfields to front lines throughout Sierra Leone, the hotel became the major transit point for combatants moving into Liberia with the LURD forces. Two operatives, one a midlevel commander in the Special Forces and the other the wife of a prominent LURD supporter, recruited combatants to join the new movement in its effort to overthrow Charles Taylor. Recruits living at the hotel or traveling there from outside came to the hotel room of one of the two operatives. They received a small cash payout for travel expenses and instructions on how to take the ferry from Freetown to Conakry, Guinea, and then how to proceed by land to the LURD rear base at Macenta on the border between Guinea and Liberia. Among combatants and ex-combatants this underground railroad was an open secret. Fighters throughout the country knew to make the trek to Freetown and Brookfields and whom to ask for once they arrived. Many lodged at the hotel while waiting for arrangements to be made for their transport. In a sign of the extent to which becoming a "regional warrior" (Human Rights Watch 2005) represented a vocation rather than a sectarian affiliation, at least some of those who passed through Brookfields en route to Liberia were former AFRC junta soldiers and occasionally former RUF rebels (the ostensible opponents of the hotel's occupants).

These deployments to the region's frontline spaces were at least in part dependent on the infrastructure, physical and bureaucratic, of the capital city. CDF leader Sam Hinga Norman's position as deputy minister of defense in the SLPP government meant that the organization was a quasi-state organ of governance. The regular provisioning of the CDF from funds allocated by the legislature also forged an important link between the capital and the militia. The movement of combatants across international borders required that combatants, few of whom possessed passports, be issued government identification cards and travel documents. Recruitment required the relative anonymity of a chaotic urban environment and the various registers of "invisibility" that make it possible for marginal youth to circulate and congregate without attracting the gaze of the police, the military, or international peacekeepers.

Similarly, when the disarmament campaign was instituted to collect weapons and register combatants for benefits and future jobs training, rather than deploying DDR personnel to the bush the program relied on local commanders to assemble their troops in urban centers, often for extended periods while the slow and haphazard process of registration was carried out. In Freetown, Brookfields provided a site within the

18. On the city street, 2003.

city in which all of these activities could be coordinated. Combatants without financial or relational resources could sustain themselves at the hotel while awaiting the next stage in their deployment. The most common sight at the hotel throughout 2001 was groups of young men sitting idly on the steaming asphalt of the parking lot, waiting for news of the DDR. Few were willing to leave the city, or even the hotel, for fear of missing out when the trucks arrived to carry the young men to regional training centers that would help them (at least in theory) earn a postconflict livelihood. No one could say for sure when that day would come. Rumors spread through the hotel that tomorrow or *nehkst tumara* (Krio, "next tomorrow," or the day after tomorrow) the trucks would come, and for a few days the parking lot would be even more crowded than usual.

Other rumors, whispered rumors, kept some of the men waiting on the walls around the parking lot or playing checkers beneath the shade tree at the lot's edge. These were rumors about Liberia and the possibilities of joining LURD forces—rumors of a new transit route opening up at the Mano River Bridge, a route that would offer easy access to Monrovia and the potential wealth that might come from full-scale war in Liberia's capital city. One needed the city to make these futures possible: the city's networks of bureaucratic recognition, the city's locus of transnational institutions such as the United Nations, and the city's aggregation of rumor and information. By the late stages of the war there was a marked shift in the divide between city and bush that characterized the war's earliest days, when residents of the capital were largely unaware of and uninterested in the encroaching fighting. By the latter stages of the conflict, the city and its functions were critical to this "bush war."

The city as the living heart of the warscape was also a matter of architecture. Simon Njami has argued (2001) that what is distinctive about the contemporary African city is that it is not "solid" in the same manner as a Paris or New York. The meaning of the city is not in its "geometry": "It's no longer a question here of a physical city, with its street names, its signs, but of an intangible phenomenon" (72). Spaces and structures are subject to continuous appropriation for new purposes, reinscribed both physically and socially. The Mano River region's urban spaces were continuously redesigned throughout the war: vast modernist projects like the national stadium at the heart of Freetown, one of Siaka Stevens's nation-building projects, became a squalid refugee camp multiple times and the scene of horrific public killings. The urban beaches of both Freetown and Monrovia were made famous for their periodic "beach parties," the group executions of deposed government ministers. When the RUF launched the 6 January 1999 invasion it first smuggled weapons into the city and buried them in the city's graveyards. When the invasion began the RUF corralled residents of the east end of the city and forced them to march down the major thoroughfares, an effective human shield against counterattack by ECOMOG. Urban spaces designed to facilitate the massing of people were not simply the backdrop of much of what took place in this conflict but were its conditions of possibility—the hotel turned barracks, the stadium turned camp, the bridge turned checkpoint.

Within the city, the concentration of kamajor combatants into a single, fortified space (or, to return to Chatterjee's formulation, their constitution as a political populace) made it a zone of legal exception with which the state had reached an ambiguous, and ambivalent, accommodation. No one paid rent for residence at Brookfields and the city's provision of electricity was free of charge. The kamajors were barracked at Brookfields to protect the city, yet they were widely understood in Freetown to simultaneously represent its greatest threat. Residents of Freetown, and even government officials, spoke of the hotel and its occupants as the most likely flash point for violence in the capital.

For the Sierra Leone police and military forces the hotel was largely a no-go area. This was illustrated to me by a midlevel commander living at Brookfields. Sitting with him on the low wall bordering the parking lot, I mentioned that I had been invited to visit another commander at a guesthouse up the road. This commander suggested that I be careful. This could, he said, be a "black money" scheme, a trap under which I would be arrested by the police or the Criminal Investigations Division (CID) for attempted counterfeiting and forced to bribe my way out of jail. Or it could be an ambush, with thugs waiting to rob me (or worse). Meet anyone you want on the hotel grounds, he suggested, but be careful anywhere else in the city. The police and CID are corrupt, but they do not dare enter the hotel.

The hotel, therefore, seemed to occupy a double status beyond the reach of the law. It was safer to those inside because the police dared not enter, more lawless and threatening to those outside for the same reason. As if to underscore the point, there was a rumor among former Sierra Leone Army personnel that soldiers who entered the hotel grounds were being eaten by the kamajors, a discourse that seemed to underscore the complex relation of the kamajors as the state's surrogate organ of violence to the conventional state apparatus for controlling and exercising violence. Cannibalism, as Rosalind Shaw has argued (2001), is a recurrent regional trope through which analyses of legitimate and illegitimate power are voiced.

As a reservoir of extralegitimate violence, Brookfields simultaneously constructed and threatened the state. The bodies and weapons contained at the hotel safeguarded the SLPP from both the rebels and the army, but they were left largely unsupervised and underprovisioned. As a result they guaranteed the stability of the state but undermined the security of the city as militia fighters forcefully seized what they needed from the surrounding residents. A makeshift jail erected in the ruins of the reception area held a succession of Freetownians accused of various crimes. Many of these detainees were released after paying a fine to Cobra, the former SLA soldier turned kamajor policeman, or Duwai, the commander of the forces quartered at the hotel. While occasionally condemned by government leaders, such extralegal violence was necessary for the protection of the wartime state. It allowed the party to maintain a loyal force at minimal cost, and the kamajors perpetuated the crisis environment that allowed for their own quasi-legal profiteering.

But even those leaders who bridged the gap between leadership of the militia and elite status within government found themselves only partly in control of the violence contained at the hotel. Public office holders on a number of occasions deployed kamajor combatants in their security capacity to generate private resources. These deployments frequently exceeded their intended purpose and generated excessively violent encounters.

For example, Borbor Sau, who was responsible for driving one of the four-wheel-drive pickup trucks the kamajors used during attacks, liked to tell the story of an "operation" in the eastern part of the city. Hinga Norman ordered a group of kamajors to clear out a house that he claimed was being used by rebel collaborators, although it was well known that Norman was involved in a business dispute with the owner of the residence. As the militiamen herded people from the building, a crowd of local residents gathered and threw stones at the kamajors, creating enough of a confrontation that a contingent of Nigerian peacekeepers was deployed to secure the area. The crowd grew increasingly hostile toward the militiamen, challenging the Nigerians to arrest or engage the young men militarily. As the confrontation appeared headed for disastrous climax for the outnumbered fighters, Borbor Sau facilitated the kamajors' escape by driving his pickup truck into the crowd and running it back and forth through the assembled bodies. "We damaged a lot of people that day," he concluded, grinning.

Borbor Sau's narrative underscores the extent to which the postcolonial African state is constituted by the uncertain legitimacy of its organs of violence and by the way it organizes that violence. The very presence of the kamajors in the city was predicated on the inability of the state to trust its own military. Yet as a surrogate organ of violence, it erased the distinction between the public security functions of a state army and the private accumulation efforts of its commanders. The militia could be deployed as efficiently against the residents of the city as in their defense—always with the potential for excess. This was graphically symbolized by the severed heads that periodically appeared mounted on poles around the hotel. Outside of the capacity of their own bodies or the intervention of an exterior force (such as the ECOMOG troops), the residents of the city had no recourse or appeal against the activities of a military institution able to claim the mantel of the state regardless of its actual functioning.

A single space within the hotel compound illustrates the import of the barrack's organization of violence to the capital. Jah Kingdom, the utility rooms, bathrooms, and storage areas beneath the Brookfields Hotel's swimming pool where King, the Nigerian expatriate fighter, operated a small bar and kamajors and their dependents lived in the shower stalls, was a warren of small rooms covered in graffiti and posters. Young men and a handful of women spent large portions of their days and nights playing checkers, listening to music, smoking cigarettes and djamba, or sleeping on straw mats. Jah Kingdom was rumored to be at the center of an extensive drug ring and the city's network of armed criminal gangs. King was known as a central figure in the organization of ex-combatants in armed attacks on the growing numbers of NGO offices and living quarters. Despite its reputation as a criminal haven, however, the occupants of Jah Kingdom were among those chosen for training by British military advisors for the new Sierra Leone armed forces, an amalgamation of fighters from each of the warring factions. Periodically a British military Land Rover pulled into the parking lot to collect trainees or drop them off. Greeting the others in the parking lot or saying good-bye, the Jah Kingdom kamajors would make the trek through the reception hall and

19. King's room at Jah Kingdom, Freetown, 2001.

past the makeshift mosque and medical clinic, then disappear into the equally obscured spaces of Jah Kingdom and the new training center of the Sierra Leone armed forces.

Jah Kingdom also provided young men to canvass and rally on behalf of the SLPP before the 2002 elections—a deployment of youth in what often became quite violent political contests (see Ferme 1999). As election season neared, power brokers within the SLPP who had not frequented the hotel in years began to drive their tinted-windowed sedans and SUVs into the Brookfields parking lot. Through an open window they chatted with some of the more senior commanders or found their way to the rooms of some of the bigger men in Block C. Cigarettes, marijuana, beer, and rum—"motivations" in the vernacular—plus plates of rice and occasionally cash for transportation, these were the price of drawing large crowds on rally day. Though combatants complained bitterly about the SLPP and the party's treatment of the CDF and though many vowed that they would never vote for the SLPP again, at rally time there were very few who refused to join the campaigns as they marched through the streets.

In August 2002, a Nigerian contingent of the United Nations peace-

20. Graffiti at the Brookfields Hotel, Freetown, 2003.

keeping force made good on a long-standing threat to move the remaining CDF fighters from the hotel. For months before that day the fighters who could leave the hotel had done so. Those who still occupied the rooms were the most desperate. They threatened to burn the hotel down if forced to leave, or to violently stake their claim on the buildings and defend their position. As it happened, the eviction was relatively peaceful. When the Nigerian troop carriers pulled into the parking lot, the young men slipped out the back of the hotel compound and into the city streets. A few boarded a government bus that was to drive them out of the city and upcountry to Kenema or Bo. After nearly five years of occupation, the barracks at Brookfields disappeared and, apart from the graffiti and trash, there was no evidence that the kamajors had ever been there.

On a visit to Freetown in late 2003, I stopped by the Brookfields Hotel once again. The CDF combatants had been evacuated, and ironically the Truth and Reconciliation Commission (TRC) sponsored by the United Nations had set up shop in Block A. In the very same room in which I had stayed with Borbor Sau and a half dozen other combatants, I spoke with an investigator in charge of coordinating the testimony of CDF "perpetrators" of abuse. File drawers inside the room contained narratives of the war's violence taken across the country. Like any TRC, its intended purpose was to offer testimonies told purely in the interest of national healing. Yet even under the TRC the hotel was a site inscribed by the logic of violence and its strategic, profitable deployment. As the investigator explained, the TRC was having a difficult time convincing CDF combatants to testify. Among the kamajors' chief concerns, he said, was the fact that in exchange for narrating their stories of violence, they would not be paid.[5]

Duala, Monrovia

The Duala neighborhood on the western edge of Monrovia straddles the main route toward the Sierra Leone border. Duala was occupied by LURD forces during each of the three "world wars" and was the target of reprisals by Taylor's militias when the first two attacks failed. It is a densely packed neighborhood, sloppy with mud in the rainy season and thick with dust in the dry.

Johnson Yard lies just off the main road, a well-thrown stone away from the Duala market and the taxi ranks for upcountry transport. The half dozen buildings surrounding a central courtyard are all owned by the Johnson family and rented to a mix of Mandingo, Grebo, Vai, and Mende families and single men. Mohammed rented rooms in two of the buildings. His two wives and two children occupied some of the space, as did two unmarried youths who had fought under Mohammed when he was a commander in the CDF and later in LURD. One of Mohammed's wives shared quarters with a well-known female LURD combatant and her boyfriend, a veteran of Charles Taylor's "Small Boys' Unit" bodyguards. Behind Johnson Yard stood a small ghetto, frequented mostly by members of Taylor's militias. As in so many other contexts, the factionalism that divided combatants during the war made no difference to where and how individuals inhabited the city, even this early in the postconflict period.

Like the Brookfields Hotel, Johnson Yard was a site for the "material signification" of laboring bodies in an economy of fungible violence, resource extraction, and the machinery of the United Nations and global NGOs. Here, too, the logic of assembly, containment, and deployment was one of putting violence and other labors of the body into circulation.

On most days, Mohammed received a steady stream of visitors. The majority were young men who had served under him in the CDF or LURD and who were now living in Monrovia. They came to Mohammed regularly to beg small favors, offer patronage payments, or pass along greetings and news of the city or of Sierra Leone, and often simply stopped to check in. Sitting on his front verandah Mohammed invited his visitors to join him for a plate of rice at lunch, interrupting their conversations to take cell phone calls or to attend to the business of being a patriarch to a large and complex family. Some of these youth lingered for hours, joining in the free flow of conversation, commenting on political topics of the day or the household activity playing out around them, sometimes teasing the children or helping with an errand or chore. An easy air of familiarity, even conviviality, belied the heaviness of many of the topics discussed.

I had seen this same cycle of visitations during the war years, when Mohammed lived at the Brookfields Hotel, and in southeastern Sierra Leone, Guinea, and Liberia when he helped rally troops for LURD. As a relative "big man" Mohammed effectively controlled the labor of these youth. When the CDF recruited Liberian veterans to recapture Freetown in 1998 and then mobilized fighters in 2001 for LURD, it assembled combatants for labor on the battlefield. These visits to Mohammed were the mechanism by which much of this recruitment took place. At other times these same youth might be "called up" for smaller operations, such as when Mohammed required the assistance of a few ex-combatants to retrieve a vehicle from someone who had not properly paid him for it. At still other times they might be needed for work in the region's mines or plantations. These visitors were a floating labor pool capable of any manner of physical work that the region—and Mohammed—could offer.

Mohammed's verandah was simply one stop in a circuit that these young men made around the city. It was an orbit that could take a day, a week, a month. The connections came in a variety of forms—kinship networks, command relations from the fighting forces, former employers, and most often a combination of all three. Each was a nodal point in a

21. On Mohammed's verandah, Duala, Monrovia, 2005.

circuit around the city that allowed young men to look for opportunities in old connections and to discover new ones in unexpected spaces in between.

During the summer of 2005 Monrovia was awash in rumors of a massive deposit of high-quality diamonds discovered outside of Greenville in Liberia's southeastern Sinoe County. Diamond diggers from the capital and across the western half of the country, many of them ex-combatants, undertook the long and relatively expensive trip east to stake a claim in the forest. Because local officials charged a digging fee per plot, rather than per digger, most went in crews. Their expenses were paid for by patrons who held rights of first refusal and a guaranteed low purchase price on any diamonds the digger might find.

Prior to the war Mohammed had spent a few months in the diamondiferous regions of western Liberia as a go-between for diamond crews and buyers in the capital. Ibrahim, one of the two ex-combatants living in his compound, was a commander on the eastern border of Sierra Leone during the war, where his men served double duty as a mining crew and border guard unit. And Ray, the other youth living at Johnson Yard, had for years been a diamond digger in the Zimmi area of Sierra Leone. Together the three men had a relatively extensive knowledge of the region's diamond economy and a desire to once again be involved.

When the Greenville rumors began to circulate, Mohammed, Ibrahim, and Ray drew up plans for their own entry into the competitive (and by all accounts highly lucrative) field. Ray would lead a crew of approximately twenty-five young men in the diamond fields in the Sapo Forest Reserve. Ibrahim would transport diamonds between Greenville and Monrovia, and Mohammed would liaise with the crew's patrons and other diamond buyers in the capital. A second former commander from Sierra Leone's CDF had reliable contacts with Eastern European buyers and had already had some success in other diamond deposits. He was willing to finance the crew's transport to Greenville and its basic provisions for the first weeks.

With the logistics of moving diamonds worked out, the simplest aspect of the project was locating and assembling a crew of laborers. On the designated morning an excess of young men gathered in the center of Johnson Yard. Well over thirty male youths had arrived not long after dawn. For hours they sat on the verandah and in the yard, waiting and chatting. Many knew one another already. Those who didn't made

22. Sacrificing for success in mining, Duala, Monrovia, 2005.

connections through mutual friends or by tracing their genealogies to a common point. The transport that had been promised to take them to Greenville had not yet arrived.

At midmorning, Ray and Ibrahim gathered the men in the parlor of Mohammed's house for a quick prayer and sacrifice for luck in mining. When it was over, everyone diving for a share of the candies piled on the sacrifice plate, the crowd of young men resumed their wait.

Mohammed and Ibrahim sent out their call for laborers through an overlapping network of social and military ties. Most of those who gathered that morning were of Sierra Leonean or mixed origins. Although Mohammed and Ibrahim knew few of the men previously, they could claim kinship ties to the majority, generally via Sierra Leonean villages of origin. Some were ex-combatants responding as word circulated among former commanders of opportunities in Greenville; in most of these cases, the connections between kinship and command were embodied in the same persons.

What was striking about the assembled youth is that most did not fit the stereotype of the dreg man, or the lumpenproletariat at the margins of the law and economy, surviving on just this sort of borderline criminal physical labor. Rather, many were secondary school children temporarily unable to pay fees or in the midst of yet another extended school holiday. They represented a kind of *population flottante* (Roitman 1998; 2005, 139–46; see also de Boeck 2002) because of their ability to quickly cross the divide between city and bush, and to profit from their mobility between spheres. They seemed also to represent a demographic fluidity: their movements undid a class and social distinction between students as citizens-in-the making, on the one hand, and lumpen manual laborers, on the other hand, working largely outside the purview and protection of the state. They typified the social dynamics of labor fully subsumed by erasing the necessity of distinct institutional identities—the student distinct from the soldier distinct from manual laborers distinct from prisoners, patients, or the insane. In the regime of production in general and without distinction (what Deleuze referred to elsewhere [1995] as the "society of control"), policing such classifications is no longer necessary. What these youth suggest is life in the city as an impossibility. There is no

23. Waiting to go to the Sapo Forest Reserve, Duala, Monrovia, 2005.

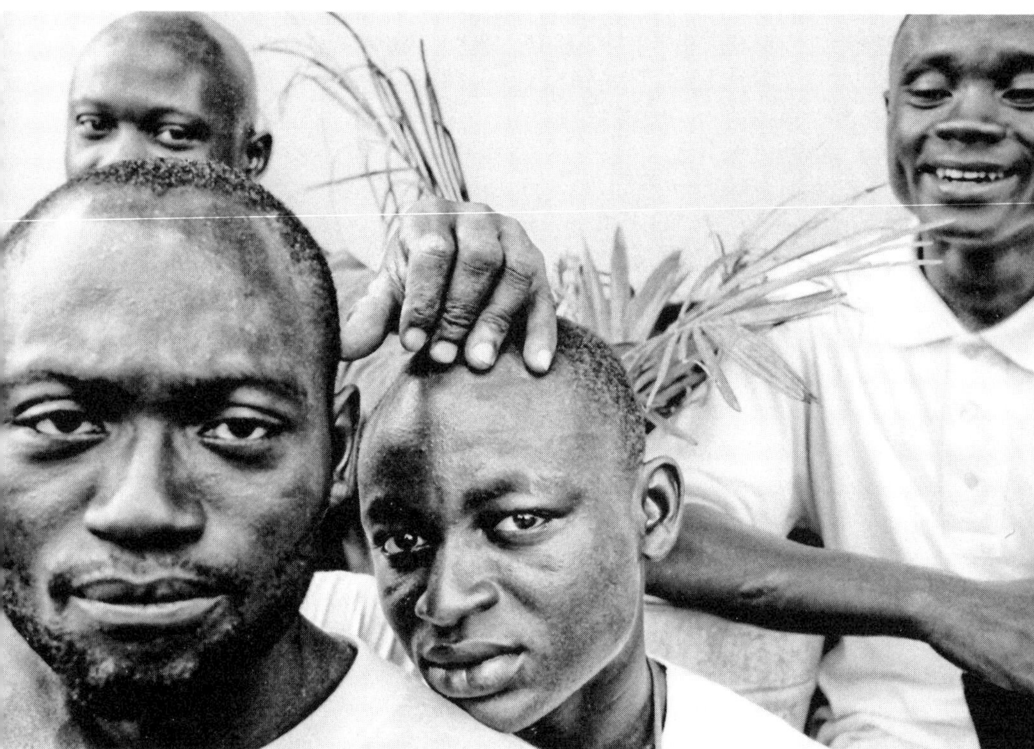

social category that signifies or guarantees stable habitation, and everyone is potentially on the market.

In the end, the mining operation never materialized. Mohammed's contact substituted his own laborers in the taxis arranged by European backers, effectively cutting Mohammed, Ray, and Ibrahim from the enterprise. As it happened, rumors of the profitability of the Greenville deposit were wildly exaggerated, and a cholera outbreak killed a number of diggers squatting in the forest.

The failure of the operation was a disappointment to Mohammed, Ray, and Ibrahim (and undoubtedly to the young men who gathered that morning), but it was not a surprise. Until fully realized, any business plan was subject to a thousand variables over which one had little control. Sabotage and betrayal were common enough elements in any venture. Rivals, even friends, are jealous and scheming. There are no limits on what one's enemies might do to thwart even the most solid plans. Of the three men, Ibrahim took the failure of the mining venture the hardest, and advocated the loudest for a search for new patrons. More than the others he was convinced that the Sapo Forest reserve was the key to a new future for all of them. For a few days he set out on his own rounds through the city, working contacts he thought might sponsor them with cash or material assistance. I walked the streets with him as we visited a succession of senior men with only a tentative connection to Ibrahim via family networks, and as he dropped in on wealthy market women whom Ibrahim knew from prior diamond deals. In one case we paid a call to the mother of a former lover who ran a small cooking stall across from the United States Embassy. The woman looked decidedly skeptical as Ibrahim laid out his Sapo plans, and she was vague in her responses to him. Ibrahim explained to me later that she had amassed a surprising amount of cash through a host of small business ventures, but she was apparently unwilling to back Ibrahim in his. A week later, he had still heard nothing from her.

When stories of the cholera outbreak began to run in the Monrovia media, Ibrahim lost none of his enthusiasm for mining. He continued to talk about assembling a crew, this time one that would be sent west to the Sierra Leone border. Ibrahim had an older brother still in a village there who could speak up for a family claim to some of the under-exploited deposits in the forest around Zimmi. All they needed was the financial backing to transport miners they could trust from the capital to the countryside, and the means to provision them for a little while. Getting the men together, Ibrahim argued to virtually anyone who would listen, would not be a problem.

As with the Brookfields Hotel, the logic of assembly here is not incidental to Johnson Yard as a physical space. Like most of Duala, Johnson Yard existed in a state of uneasy accommodation with the Liberian government and with the United Nations institutions that functionally operated the state. For example, the well-known discontent over the handling of Liberia's disarmament proceedings led to a series of mandates that prohibited large groups of LURD or other factional combatants from assembling in one place. In smaller towns such as Voinjama and Tubmanburg, this generated considerable anxiety and did serve to police the behavior of ex-combatants, at least to a degree. Young men in these towns were cautious about being seen together. The United Nations peacekeepers, especially the Pakistani contingent that controlled the western sectors, were courteous but forceful. They patrolled regularly and would intercede if they saw large collectives of young men. The local authorities were even more watchful, though for different reasons. The regulations on assembly gave them a pretext to harass young men and demand on-the-spot payments of fines for breaking the law.

In Monrovia, however, the "lines of sight" that would have made such surveillance possible were obstructed by the city itself. As the architect Rem Koolhaas has written of the West African metropolis of Lagos, a street-level view of the city is composed almost entirely of "dense foreground" (2002, 175). It is difficult if not impossible to get a long or in-depth perspective on contemporary West African cities.[6] Ex-combatants used the city to both mask and reveal themselves. Collectives of former fighters occupied abandoned or half-built structures that afforded them a kind of opaqueness; their presence there was not exactly a secret within the neighborhoods in which they were located, and they were not fully invisible. They could be located with some effort and a willingness to peer into dark and unwelcoming spaces. But they were not available to the casual observer and could maintain a plausible deniability, slipping away without leaving visible traces in an already fractured urban landscape. Many of the young men who regularly passed through Duala maintained a few locations around the city where they might sleep on any given night. The loss of any one of them would not be a disaster. During the day their hours might be spent in ghettos masked by informal settlements or the thrum of a market. Visible, but not obvious. Those who knew how could work the street in a similar way, blending with the crowds on foot when anonymity was required, collecting at certain busy intersections, taxi ranks, or trading stalls in a way that did not obviously mark these youth as conglomerates of ex-combatants—unless that is what one was searching for.

The politics of visibility generated an interesting misreading on the part of UNMIL, at least as far as Monrovia residents were concerned. On the basis of its reputation for corruption and trafficking on the black market, the Nigerian peacekeeping contingent was posted in the capital where its activities could theoretically be monitored by UNMIL authorities. That posting, however, meant unfettered access to the port and to major roadways, prime conduits for profiteering. Indeed, these activities went on as though they were invisible from the perspective of the cloistered United Nations hierarchy. Nigerian officers, many of whom had been in Liberia and Sierra Leone for years, ran an incredible array of money-making operations by cloaking themselves in the fabric of the city. Taxes could be levied on goods at port, tolls taken at urban roadblocks, diamonds and gold procured and resold from the mix of mining interests that congregated in the city. A highly visible excursion in a white United Nations Land Rover to some rural diamond office or mine would undoubtedly be noticed and remarked on. The same excursion to a crowded urban market meant deals could be done in the open with no one to watch and nothing unusual to be seen. It seemed as though the internal rhetoric of many United Nations personnel—that the international body was a neutral organization and would be perceived as such by the Liberian populace—blinded many officials to what peacekeepers on the ground were actually doing. It also made them deaf to what the citizens of Monrovia were saying: that like any other militarized party to the Mano River War, peacekeepers made their mission a profit-making enterprise. Certainly for many of Nigeria's former ECOMOG soldiers, mastery of the West African city's politics of assembly and disbursement, visibility and invisibility could be parlayed into a far more reliable income than the meager and unreliable salary of a government soldier.

When Pa Tito, a businessman originally from Grand Cape Mount County, decided to make a run for the House of Representatives in the 2005 elections, he, too, paid a visit to Mohammed at Johnson Yard. The business of campaigning in the region's elections is as much a matter of assembling the spectacles of power, including the bodies of supporters capable of violence, as it is amassing the financial resources to campaign (see Mbembe 1992; Piot 1999, 44–49). Mohammed's capacity to bring together "supporters" from the capital made him an indispensable ally. Pa Tito and Mohammed grew acquainted during the rule of the Sierra Leone junta when the kamajors amassed at the Mano River Bridge. The sleepy border town of Bo Waterside suddenly had a bustling market. Hundreds of young men needed provisions and housing. Pa Tito helped fill that need by bringing goods in from Monrovia and standing for the CDF leadership before Bo Waterside's small community leadership. When many of the same combatants returned to Bo Waterside as part of the LURD movement, Pa Tito once again helped them with provisions and lodging. The Mano River Bridge became a highly trafficked border crossing as the siege of Monrovia wore on; though officially closed at night, the border was unofficially opened from midnight to 4 a.m. to allow LURD fighters to bring looted goods back across the border into Sierra Leone. Pa Tito helped to make that traffic possible.

Pa Tito was therefore widely seen as a friend of the CDF and LURD. So when he decided to stand for the 2005 elections, there were young men who owed him favors and knew that Pa Tito would remember them once in office. As the election neared, Pa Tito began making weekly trips to Monrovia. Like the others, he came and sat on Mohammed's verandah, eating, exchanging gossip and rumors from the border, and analyzing the national political landscape and the prospects for a new government. In subtle and unsubtle ways, he made it clear to Mohammed what he needed: young men to rally for him on the appointed days, taking to the streets with Tito's party colors and his face emblazoned on their T-shirts. He needed a spectacle of force and support. Ex-combatants willing to dance, shout, and march in his name were exactly the spectacle of power his campaign required, and if there was cause for confrontation with Tito's opposition, a reserve army of violent labor would make it clear that Pa Tito had the strength to govern. Mohammed nodded his way through these conversations, and on the appointed days he duly called up men to march for Tito. When the election results were announced and it was clear that Tito had lost, Mohammed was stoic in the way he was when any of his plans to secure a hold on wealth or power failed to materialize. He was certain there would be others.

Not long before I left Monrovia in mid-2005, I had a late-night meeting with Samuel, a young Sierra Leonean man I had first met at the Brookfields Hotel in 2000. Samuel was scheduled to leave the next day for government-held territory in southern Côte d'Ivoire. After serving with LURD in Liberia, Samuel briefly crossed the Ivorian border, where he fought with the pro-government forces in that country's burgeoning civil war. Seeking out more profitable alternatives, Samuel began to run Nigerian cocaine from Monrovia through Abidjan and Man, where he purchased looted vehicles and goods from frontline commanders and sold them in Monrovia or other towns in Liberia. Samuel's story was common enough in any war zone, where fighting does not so much put an end to business as provide a cover for those willing and creative enough to exploit quasi-legitimate opportunities (Keen 2000; Nordstrom 2004). What was intriguing about Samuel's account was the flexibility of his movements and the overlap of the logic of violence and commerce. Samuel was returning to Côte d'Ivoire because the long-delayed disarmament was rumored to be starting shortly, with its promised cash payout of nine hundred U.S. dollars per combatant. Samuel was only one of many youth, some of whom had never fought in Côte d'Ivoire before, planning to race across the border in time to enroll for disarmament. As on his previous visits, Samuel planned to carry cocaine across the border. After disarmament he would take a looted vehicle waiting for him in Abidjan across Ghana and into Togo for sale in Lomè. On an earlier visit, the commander with whom he organized his vehicle sales had suggested that Samuel, who was born in Sierra Leone, apply as an Ivorian for noncombatant refugee status with the United Nations. He was among a group of "refugees" who made it as far as the last step in the registration process in Accra, Ghana, before someone recognized him as a former combatant and he was shipped back to Abidjan.

As I spoke with Samuel in the darkness at Johnson Yard, it was impossible not to map the route he followed as one of networked barracks spaces, nodal points for the assembly and subsequent deployment of bodies for all manner of labor. Battlefields, disarmament centers, refugee camps, diamond mines, timber camps, and the city itself each manifest the barracks' logic of assemblage and containment, deterritorialization, and reterritorialization.

chapter 6

THE HOTEL KAMAJOR

IN JANUARY 2002 few passengers asked to be let out at the gates of the Brookfields Hotel. The hotel compound is halfway between the Lumley Beach taxi ranks and the route's terminus at the PZ Market downtown. From the beach the small yellow cars and jitneyed minivans that are Freetown's transport fleet crawl over Signal Hill and Mountain Cut Road. Past the home of the vice-president, past the walled compounds of global NGOs, past the city's few luxury hotels. Then, as they drop into the crush of the urban center, they pass the Brookfields Hotel.

While few passengers wanted to be let down by the Brookfields, many of them wanted to talk about it. January 18 was the official end of the war and no one was certain what this meant for the pro-government militiamen who had lived at the hotel for almost four years. Newspaper features about the imminent removal of the kamajors were common, interspersed among stories about the city's rising crime rate, which also frequently referenced the hotel and its occupants. Taxi conversations about Brookfields were almost always the same: it was time, most Freetownians agreed, for the kamajors to go.

The combatants and their relations who lived in the hotel rarely rode the taxis themselves. If they needed to leave the compound they walked. Partly this was financial. Even the meager fare for a cross-town ride is exorbitant to those with nothing. But partly it was the logic of the dreg. No one who left the hotel ever had just one errand to run or one person to see. Moving around the city always meant multiple stops, planned or not. A walker could pass a thousand people on the streets. Some it might be useful to engage, some it might be better to avoid. A rider in a taxi was trapped. No way to stop a friend or relative walking by. No way to escape.

My own trips to the hotel came in a variety of forms: taxi rides, on foot, via motorcycle. Each yielded a different perspective on the hotel, its occupants, and the relation of both to the surrounding city. Walking, one engaged the petty traders and residents who populated the Brookfields neighborhood, a dense old maze at the interstices of downtown and the wealthy suburbs to the west. From the slow street-level view of a pedestrian the hotel provoked ambivalent reactions. Brookfields residents had experienced firsthand the war's sieges and occupation by the RUF and the AFRC. The pro-government forces were integral to the capital's liberation. They had likely helped deter follow-on attacks, attacks that would appear from over the hills that dropped into Brookfields on their way to the center of the city. At the same time, the residents of Brookfields were increasingly preyed upon by youth living in the hotel. A story in Freetown's *The Pool* newspaper was typical: it describes in alarmed detail how kamajors attacked a Brookfields home when the owner refused to let the militiamen in to watch the national soccer team play Nigeria. One group advanced on the house while another lay in am-

24. Borbor Sau in Block A at the Brookfields Hotel, 2001.

bush on the road, waiting for anyone who tried to flee down Jomo Kenyatta Avenue.[1]

Approaching the hotel by taxi drew less ambivalent responses, at least from the perspective of one's fellow passengers. These were mostly wealthier residents of the west end of the city, people commuting to the city center for work or errands. Though like all Freetownians they had suffered under the occupation and rebel attacks, their quadrant of the city experienced nothing like the trauma of the east. They were largely spared the events of 6 January 1999. But increasingly they were the targets of armed robberies and carjackings, a startling rise in violent crime that many attributed to the heavily armed residents of the hotel. The hypothetical role the hotel played in securing the city from the rebels was less immediate for these people than the fear of driving the beach road at night, or of waking to find that young men with military weapons had invaded their homes.

Coming and going from the Brookfields Hotel was something I did frequently in the later years of the hotel's occupation. In the summer of

25. The *Independent Observer* featuring the Brookfields Hotel kamajors, 16 October 2001.

INDEPENDENT OBSERVER

Published Daily Since 9th August 1997

Ali S. Dakhlallah of B.M. Dakhlallah at 25 ECOWAS Street in Freetown, wishes to inform customers and the general public that Egyptian rice in 25kg and 50kg bags is now on sale
Contact us on Telephone: 226558 or 226886

Tuesday 16th October 2001 — *Peace & Democracy are two sides of the same coin* — 300L

No Politics At Ahmadiyya... Teachers Resigned, Not Sacked!

Aiah E. Sam and Alpha Barrie, former teachers of the Ahmadiyya Muslim Secondary School in Freetown who were reported to have been sacked, resigned their positions at the school, according to convincing documents made available to this press yesterday.

Yesterday, the school's Principal Alhaji MP Bayoh told this press that the teachers willingly resigned from the school to pursue academic careers.

In his letter of resignation dated 10th September 2001, Aiah E. Sam said: ...

been accepted to pursue a four-year degree course in Finance Services (B.sc Hons) at the Institute of Public Administration And Management (IPAM)."

Barrie is said to have resigned his post for quite sometime now and has since been operating an institute.

Bayoh said he wondered where that reporter got his information from, adding that he was sure those teachers would be upset ...

nothing to do with the affair of Ahmadiyya. Beside, why should I sack a teacher for merely expressing his democratic right?" Bayoh questioned.

Yesterday, *The Democrat* newspaper reported that the two teachers were sacked because of political reasons on the grounds that they were not supporters of a political organization in the school known as SURKAB which was recently launched.

COUP! ...Kamajors Say No Involvement

Civil Defence Forces (CDF) Public Relations Officer, Charles Moiwo has dispelled rumours that Civil Defence Forces were planning to stage a coup to overthrow the government of President Tejan Kabbah.

During last Sunday's ***Security Talks*** programme, Moiwo described the news as lies, adding "that is the work of our detractors". He said they (Kamajors) did not take up arms because of power but to restore democracy and that "we have no intention to overthrow the government that we have fought to restore back to power in 1997".

The PRO also dispelled rumours about a planned demonstration by CDF members stationed at the Brookfields Hotel. "We were merely fighting to defend the democracy that ushered his government into power", he said.

Charles Moiwo said arrangements had now been put in place to avoid a repeat of such ugly incident and that henceforth Kamajors who were to be disarmed would now remain at their usual locations from where they would forward their list to collect their disarmament benefits.

He accused security personnel at the recent ex-combatants demonstration of beating and wounding CDF ex-fighters and said one of them was currently undergoing treatment after sustaining serious head injury

2000, and then again in 2001 and early 2002, the Brookfields Hotel was a regular feature of my research stays in Freetown. I spent nights sleeping at the hotel in the rooms occupied by friends. When I rented rooms elsewhere in the city I spent many long days on the hotel grounds. As the living quarters and main base for the CDF militia from the 1998 restoration until mid-2002, the Brookfields Hotel was an obvious choice of field site. But I also found myself captivated by its surreal environs, an atmosphere that was part rural village, part armed fraternity house.

No day at the Brookfields Hotel was typical, though I did develop a kind of research routine. Nights when I slept elsewhere in the city, I made my way to the Brookfields Hotel by midmorning. Entering the hotel I orbited a half dozen or so regular stops, places where I had friends or interesting contacts or where I knew the latest news would be available. Visits in any one of these stops might be long or short. Inevitably there were unexpected encounters along the way. Rarely on these research visits did I leave the hotel until well after dark, seen off graciously by the last person with whom I spoke.

26. Moving through the city, 2003.

This chapter charts that movement through the hotel, sometime in the January dry season of 2002. It would not be long before the kamajors who lived there were finally forced to leave.

In the Village Square

Those who entered the Brookfields Hotel from Jomo Kenyatta Avenue, the main entrance, did so by passing under a large cotton tree and through a broken double gate. There was a guardhouse but it was never occupied (at least not by guards). Still, by the time a visitor entered the gate, on foot or by car, her or his presence had been noted. The main water source for the hotel was a tap across Jomo Kenyatta, so a perpetual flow of young men, women, and children moved through the gate with dripping buckets. Under the shade tree sat hawkers eager for buyers for their T-shirts, socks, or eggs—but not so eager to enter the hotel grounds themselves. A few brave or desperate salespeople made occasional tours of the grounds, though almost always they did so in groups. One older man set up his small kiosk every day in the shade of the guardhouse where he did a brisk trade in cigarettes, rum, and painkillers. When the young men who lived at the hotel occasionally gave him a hard time, he gave as good as he got. These small acts of daily living meant that by the time visitors passed through the gates, the hotel knew someone was coming.

There was nonhuman surveillance at Brookfields as well. Kemoh Muniro, an initiator from Pujehun whose Born Naked Brigade achieved a certain notoriety during the war, lived on the ground floor of Block A. He installed over the gate a tall controller, an occult device meant to repel mortar rounds from the surrounding hillsides and to alert the kamajors in case of attack. No doubt Kemoh Muniro had planted the hotel perimeter with less visible protections as well—small bits of paper and cloth covered in koranic inscription, buried in the ground or secreted over doors or inside cracks in the walls.

And of course there were the combatants themselves. At all times groups of young men congregated around the main gate. Some sat on the low wall that bordered the parking lot. Some lounged under the large tree inside the gate, playing checkers, drinking, or talking. Others simply milled between groups. Their reason for being there was simple:

27. Petty trader in the Brookfields Hotel parking lot, 2001.

28. The front gate and controller at the Brookfields Hotel, 2001.

these were men in waiting, and if anything unusual were to happen, it was most likely to come through the front gates.

By January the population of the hotel had dwindled markedly, but several hundred people still occupied the many yellowed hotel blocks and peripheral buildings. The rumors of an impending eviction had led most of the CDF elites living at the hotel to pack their belongings and go. Charles Moiwo, the national public relations officer and a close ally to Hinga Norman, abandoned his air-conditioned room in "the Flats" around Christmas. The CDF secretary of transport, whose black Mercedes sedan was a regular feature on the hotel grounds, had not been around in weeks. The rank-and-file combatants had begun to slip out of the hotel with little fanfare. Some embarked on the surreptitious journey across the Guinean border and on to the LURD rear base at Macenta. From there they entered the mercenary circuit in the push to overthrow Charles Taylor. Others headed to the still tense eastern diamond fields of Kono and Tongo. There they took up the dangerous work of mining and negotiating the complex identity of "ex-combatant" with the former

29. Waiting on the wall of the Brookfields Hotel, 2001.

RUF boys who dug in the same open pits. The hotel was decidedly less populated than it had been earlier in the war. But it remained lively.

Anything that required an audience took place in the hotel parking lot. Surrounded on two sides by hotel blocks, on the third by a low wall and small yard, and on the fourth by the gates and Jomo Kenyatta Avenue, the open expanse of hot asphalt accommodated funerals, mass meetings, football matches, protests, and the full-time labor of waiting. The parking lot was never empty. The social architects who had reinscribed the vast modernist structure as a functioning postmodern barracks had determined that the parking lot would be the kamajors' public square.

The cease-fire and disarmament meant that very few weapons were openly displayed in the parking area. But the masculinization and the militarization of the hotel were most fully evident there in the violence

30. The Brookfields Hotel.

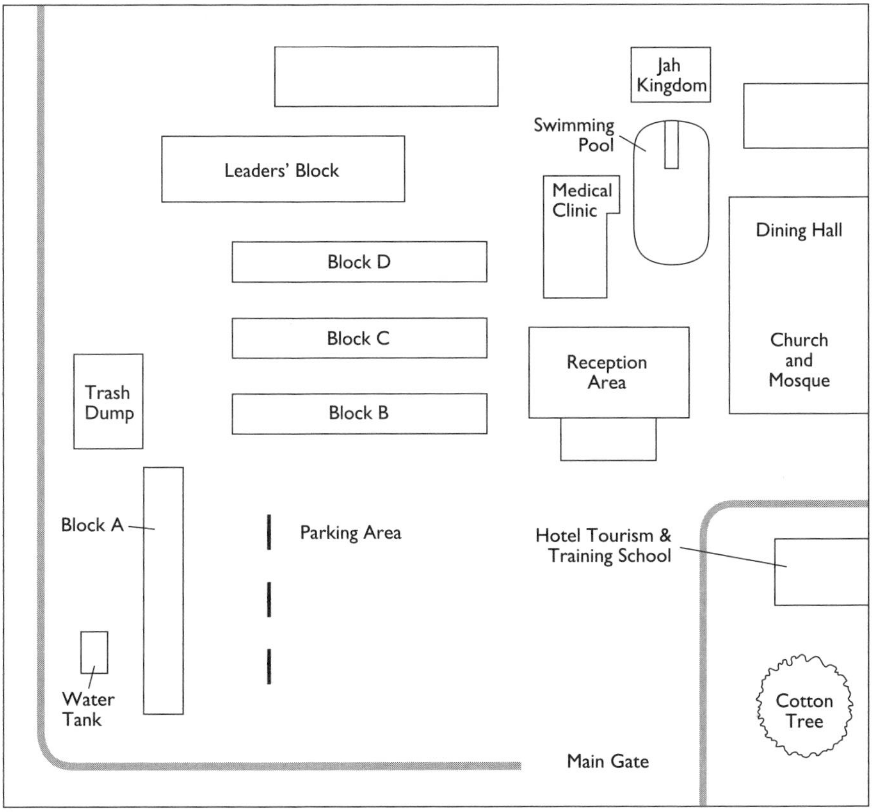

that was a perpetual part of the hotel's public life. Some of these conflicts took place in the parking lot because they required witnesses, others were created there by the collective presence of bored, edgy youth.

An example of the former: a woman suspected her kamajor boyfriend of taking a lover in another block. She stood next to the never-ending checkers game in front of Bobby Roger's room at the corner of Block A and for five solid minutes she screamed curses in Mende and Krio, aiming them in the direction of the room they shared deep in the hotel complex. The alleged transgressions occurred well away from the parking lot and the culprits were nowhere around. But this was an act of public shaming, and it was less important that her partner hear her than that everyone else did. Most of her audience pretended to ignore her. One of the checkers players tried halfheartedly to shush her, but he seemed to recognize that it was pointless and never took his eyes off the board. Like everyone else, I and a few friends sitting on a third-floor balcony pretended not to notice but took a keen, sly interest in her tirade. After a particularly cutting insult, Mohammed turned to me and whispered, "When you understand *that*, I'll award you a PhD in Mende."

Within a few days there was another fight in the parking area, this one more violent and less calculated. It elicited a very different response from the gathered crowd. Two women squabbling in a corner suddenly became a tangled mess of punches, bites, and kicks. Tripping over one another they landed in the fetid water of a small gutter beneath Block A, where onlookers encircled them. In seconds there were upward of fifty people standing around them or hanging from the balconies of Block A, egging the women on as they tore each others' clothes. The crowd chanted and cheered. One of the women broke free and ran naked and bleeding across the lot and around the corner of the building. Her adversary stood topless and cursing in the shallow mud. The crowd, primarily young men, reluctantly broke up, but for hours afterward small groups stood in the open air and recounted details of the fight, laughing. One young man spent the afternoon yelling across the lot to his friends that he had seen what he described as the loser's huge vagina, and he danced around the lot swinging his hands at his crotch in imitation.

In one corner of the lot sat an old Nissan Pajero SUV spray painted with CDF slogans, a more permanent marker of the hotel's militarization. When it worked (which those days was rare), the Pajero was driven by Borbor Sau. It had been deployed in operations around the country

31. The parking lot, seen from Block A, 2001.

and had ferried kamajors from the hotel grounds to frontline positions throughout Freetown during the overthrow of the junta and the 6 January invasion. The Pajero was on loan, at least in theory, from a once-wealthy businessman and ardent SLPP supporter to his son, a CDF commander who lived at the hotel. The Pajero was involved in all manner of "security" operations, some of them ambiguously related to the war and more closely tied to the business interests of various CDF elites. As it sat now in the parking lot, the Pajero was the source of a great deal of concern. At any given time a small gaggle of young men bent over its hood, some tinkering and others speculating as to what might happen to it and to them if the hotel was attacked. In its current state the Pajero could not be counted on to lead the counteroffensive or spirit them away.

For me, the parking area was a barometer of the mood of the hotel. I rarely entered the compound without first stopping by the low wall and finding someone there I knew. To charge into the hotel without stopping to greet the various clusters of fighters in the parking lot would have been rude in the extreme, or it would have signaled some kind of emergency. Inevitably these were illuminating encounters. If nothing particular was happening that day, the conversation would be lighter, bantering, playful. If there were rumors of new developments in the disarmament campaign, there would be more men than usual there and they would be tense. If new information was circulating about the date for eviction from the hotel there would be conversation about strategy—whether to defend the hotel or burn it down, slip away out the back or launch an assault. When my friend Gleh's son was born in the hotel, I learned about it from the boys celebrating on the wall. When Ibrahim, a combatant in Block A, died suddenly of cerebral malaria, the word circulated there first and his funeral took place in the parking lot soon afterward. One could learn a great deal about the war, about the CDF, and about the politics of life lived in common in a militarized space in this unadorned few hundred square feet.

At night the parking area was no less vibrant than during the day. At earlier moments in the war there were nights when kamajor musicians sat in the parking area and played war music on simple, handmade guitars. There was still music late into the night by January 2002, but it was the blaring music of rap and reggae from the few stereos in rooms around Block A and B. These seemed to operate on a schedule unconnected to the rhythm of night and day, which was also true of the sleep-

32. Kamajor dancing, 2001.

ing habits of many of those who lived there. The electric current at the Brookfields Hotel was surprisingly consistent in a city used to rolling blackouts, a perk that the government granted the hotel residents in return for their ostensible security function. In many rooms the balcony bulbs had been unscrewed or shot out and not replaced; some of the longer-term residents complained that the newcomers didn't realize that in the event of an attack, the lighted rooms would likely be hit first. But still the nighttime parking area was usually dimly lit by electric light and by the flicker of one working television in a room high up in Block B.

When the power did go out, the entire hotel seemed to groan at once. For a brief instant there was darkness and silence. Then a softer light spilled onto the pavement as hundreds of candles were lit across the hotel and everyone still awake moved out to the balconies for the extra illumination of the moon. I relished these moments of softer light and softer voices before the hard glare and harsh sounds made the violent edges of the hotel impossible to ignore.

The longest days I spent in the parking lot happened when I walked into the hotel grounds and found Johnny sitting on the wall. Johnny was a Guinean national who joined the CDF some time during the junta period and fought with the force all around the city. His appeal as a fighter was obvious: he was well trained, disciplined, and smart, and he had the short, powerful body of a brawler. Johnny was an expert motorcycle mechanic who had secured a postwar job with UNICEF, from whom he routinely stole bike parts to sell to me or anyone else in need of repairs. When he wasn't working, Johnny was a fixture on the parking lot wall where he drank cheap rum and told better war stories than most, his voice strangely high pitched. Johnny's wife, Baby, and his young son lived on the top floor of Block A in a room that was surprisingly comfortable. His salary provided them a modicum of luxury, and his reputation for both fierceness and charity kept them from being robbed. In the subtle interplay of forces that happened along the wall, there was a certain security for me, and I think for others, when Johnny was present. There were those to whom he deferred as required by age or rank, but even those men treated Johnny with respect. The junior boys who were on the wall day and night constantly jockeyed for position among themselves and in relation to me, working angles as we negotiated whether I would pay for their cigarettes and rum, buy rice for all those assembled, or exchange leones for their stories. Johnny effortlessly controlled these situations, brokering my purchases of food and drink in ways that seemed to satisfy everyone, or at least allowed no room for dissent. His was a small sphere of power, but an interesting one to watch: here was a man whose Guinean ancestry made him a stranger but for whom a mix of charisma, wartime exploits, and regular employment had created a measure of social prestige.

When the kamajors were evicted from the hotel, Johnny moved his family to the Liberian border. I heard from one source that he had begun a small-time mining venture, and from another that he had joined LURD. In any case, by 2005 Johnny was dead, the victim of a sudden and mysterious illness. His wife and child were stranded at Bo Waterside, where I met them again a few years later. Soon after, Baby, too, fell ill. Her death the next year left their child an orphan.

33. Baby and her son, Bo Waterside, Liberia, 2005.

MK's room

From the parking lot I entered Block A and made my way, reluctantly, to the second-floor room of MK. The journey was punctuated by brief stops: Miriam, a Temne woman who spent her days at the hotel cooking cheap cassava on an open flame, became a friend of sorts, and I often greeted her at the entrance to the building. On sunny days these were short exchanges; Miriam's cooking fire would be lit at the edges of the parking area in full view of the surrounding rooms. Seeing me speak alone with women made the kamajors with whom I worked nervous. The knowledge I was after in my research was considered male knowledge, and strangers like me could not necessarily be counted on to keep it from the dangerous hands of women.[2] On rainy days Miriam lit her fire in the hotel hallway, where I could stop for longer chats that were less surveilled. When the hotel closes, she told me, she planned to make her way to Guinea, where her father had gone earlier to find work. For now, however, she scraped together meager earnings cooking for those kamajors who could afford it. It was a precarious existence, but at least it was a familiar one.

There were other stops as well. Abdullahi lived and worked in a small crawl space underneath the first-floor stairs of Block A. One entered his domain on hands and knees. Never a fighter himself, Abdullahi moved into the hotel because he had no place else to go, and because business was good in his line of work. He sold djamba by the joint, a few cents for a finger-sized packet of marijuana and a rolling paper. His subterranean office and sleeping quarters housed in addition to him his two children and occasionally his wife. A small circle of young men sitting outside the crawl space door passed joints, and a steady stream of other young men dropped in, exchanged pleasantries and money, and then headed elsewhere around the hotel.

In a similar crawl space at the top of the stairs lived a child whose name I never learned. Most often I saw only his bedding, but on occasion he sat there, alone. When I visited the hotel a year or so after the kamajors had been removed, I peeked in the crawl space and found the boy soldier's protective necklace, a dirty knot of discolored thread with a single cowry shell in the middle.

The hallway outside MK's room was always dark, which added to the oppressive atmosphere of the place. Although I had grown close to the

34. A CDF commander and his petty trading stand at the edge of the parking area, 2001.

35. Djamba smokers, 2001.

six young men who lived together in the unfurnished room and spent nights at the hotel sleeping on the room's balcony, I rarely looked forward to actually opening the door. MK was a complicated and damaged character. My relationship with him was productive but fraught. As January wore on, he had become harder and harder to deal with. Our fighting was more frequent and more hostile as we grew at once tired of one another and more concerned at what might happen if we severed ties.

MK was a kamajor from Kenema. He was close to Eddie Massalley, one of the chief figures in the Pujehun CDF. Before the war Eddie employed MK on occasion to do odd jobs for the NGO with which Eddie worked. MK had grown up in a military barracks outside Kenema, cared for by the soldiers for whom he did favors and chores. Later MK would boast that he grew up a trained soldier, but in truth his value to Eddie Massalley was that he was smart, loyal, and tough. MK ran his own small unit of kamajors near the Liberia border, but primarily he did errands for Eddie during the war just as he had before it. When the DDR Program started, Eddie saw to it that MK got one of the coveted spots at Fourah Bay College reserved for ex-combatants. When I met him, MK was working toward a degree in geography.

MK and I were thrown together by a series of overlapping relationships. An administrator at the college was a cousin of MK's, and when he learned what I was doing he insisted that MK work as my field assistant. MK was also a client of a commander at the hotel with whom I had become a good friend. He, too, suggested that I work with MK. MK, this commander reasoned, would keep me safely within his own sphere of influence.

For a few months working with MK proved valuable. He offered a measure of protection and his room gave me a destination in the hotel. His own story of participation in the CDF and his plans for a postwar future were fascinating. We traveled together to Kenema to visit his relatives, a trip that yielded a great deal of insight into the extended kinship networks that are critical to both Mende sociality and to the CDF itself.

MK, however, was a violent and belligerent drunk. Increasingly I found that his relationships with others in the hotel were strained well before I arrived. Those we met whom he did not already know he quickly offended. More and more often he confronted me with allegations that I shamed him by not providing a cell phone, extra cash, and better clothes.

Someone in his position, working with a white stranger, needed to display the material rewards of the relationship. As long as he appeared to the world as a poor student, he was mocked at the hotel and on campus for giving away his labor, a peon client taken advantage of by his patron. MK and I had reached the point that our shouting matches were now the topic of uneasy jokes by the other kamajors who lived in MK's room. The intensifying hostility made my visits to MK's room a dreaded part of the day.

A group of us sitting on MK's balcony watched the women fighting in the parking lot below. MK and I were joined by Borbor Sau, the CDF driver, a commander named Mohammed and two of MK's other roommates: a fellow Fourah Bay student who was squatting with MK and a young man named Senasay, a cousin of MK's who was staying at Brookfields while applying for a spot at one of Freetown's universities. MK, Borbor Sau, and I drank *poyo*, the upcountry palm wine that MK favored. The small jug that MK bought on the street carried a strong taste of petrol. When we grew tired of commenting on the fight and watching the men below imitate the two women, MK and Mohammed began a conversation about initiation into the kamajor society. MK, already drunk, insisted that if I really wanted information about the kamajors I would first need to be initiated. This was a common enough refrain from kamajors I had spoken with across the country. Some made a joke of it, maintaining that true initiation for a non-Mende would be impossible, or that while other West African ethnic groups could become kamajors, whites could never really join. Others pointed with all seriousness to the rumors that white men had in fact become kamajors: men like Peter Penfold, the British commissioner in Sierra Leone and a vocal supporter of the CDF, and white South Africans with Executive Outcomes. These conversations underscored the flexibility of what CDF initiation actually meant, even to members of the society. But they also underscored the porousness of the ethnographic encounter. As I sought to frame questions and steer conversations, young men with varying degrees of knowledge developed their own ideas of what I was after and attempted to make themselves appear the holders of that treasure.

MK said flatly that to join the kamajors I would first need to kill someone. This, he argued, was a requirement of kamajor membership, a point I knew to be false. But MK was insistent. There were a number of journalists, he argued, who covered the war and had killed captives so that they could become kamajor insiders and access privileged information. There was no other way one could learn about the kamajors than to become one of them, and the price of that knowledge was murder.

Mohammed picked up the thread of the conversation, though with a humorous twist. He pretended to agree with MK and then went on to describe the many ways in which I could accomplish my task, playing up the stereotypes of the kamajor as cannibal. MK, too drunk to realize that Mohammed was subtly teasing us both, grew more and more animated as he described how the CDF dispensed with prisoners of war. This was a contentious issue later, when the CDF's reluctance to keep POWs became a possible war crime under the Special Court. But at this point it was still an openly and proudly commented-on aspect of the kamajors' mystique. Rebels were executed, they were not held.[3] Our dark banter went on until I slipped in a question about a group of CDF fighters based outside Kenema known as the Yamoto group. Yamoto were widely reputed to have cannibalized a group of RUF fighters and alleged collaborators. I had interviewed men who claimed to belong to Yamoto but had spoken with few people I trusted about what happened there. Mohammed stopped joking and changed the subject, shooting MK a look that even in his drunken state caused MK to end that line of conversation.

The balcony of MK's room offered more than a site of conversation. It afforded a privileged point of view from which to both participate in and observe the public and private life of the hotel. Situated above the parking lot it gave access to the full expanse below. Like the others who lived in Block A and Block B, one could chose to engage directly in what happened in the hotel's public square, or one could maintain a discreet but attentive distance. I was not alone as an ethnographer in doing so. Everyone living at the hotel treated the balcony as a liminal space from which they could participate in or observe the communal everyday of the barracks, at once involved and slightly removed.

The balcony also provided insights into the more mundane politics of domesticity within the movement. MK's balcony served, as it did for many of the rooms, as a de facto kitchen. Cooking fires were common on the balconies. MK, who had no wife or girlfriend, cooked for himself when he had the resources, a practice that made for running commentary among his roommates. MK hauled up his own firewood or charcoal and his water, his cups of rice, and his bags of chicken feet. Over a small flame he prepared rice and soup or thick knots of cassava root. His willingness to do "women's work" elicited a mild ribbing, though it was never pushed far enough to anger him. His roommates, all bachelors themselves, frequently shared in MK's meals.

Mohammed, whose own small family lived in Block C, was given a harder time when his girlfriend, Ophelia, showed up one evening at MK's room. Mohammed, MK, and I sat talking on the balcony. Ophelia somewhat shyly presented Mohammed with a sandwich wrapped in tissue. "He gets hungry late in the day," she explained to us before she disappeared, leaving MK and Mohammed looking shocked. Ophelia was not known for her interest in cooking or domestic chores of any kind. She was better known for her temper and her frequent fights with Mohammed in their small room. Ophelia had once been the girlfriend of an ECOMOG soldier, a casualty of the Freetown combat with the junta. Mohammed, who commanded a group of Liberian mercenaries allied to ECOMOG, met her shortly afterward at the Nigerians' headquarters. Theirs was a stormy relationship defined by wartime contingencies, a complex mix of survival calculus and desire. Mohammed's common-law

36. Struggle, born in the Brookfields Hotel, 2002.

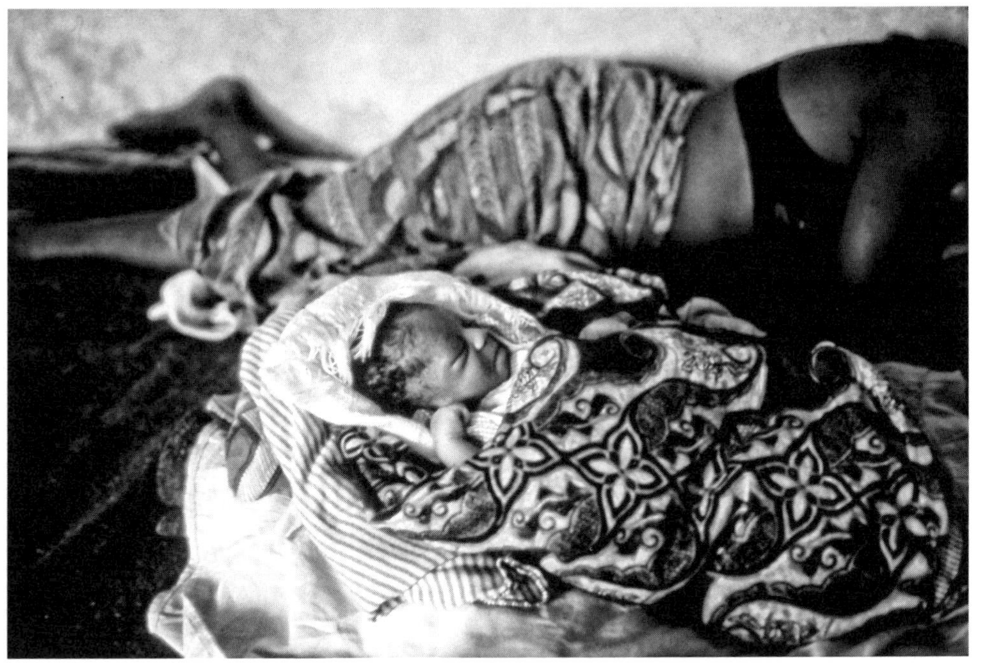

wife, Massa, was the more likely of the two women to perform domestic labor such as cooking or bringing Mohammed his food. Massa, however, had been sent to live with her family in Kenema when Mohammed joined the CDF. The Mano River War redefined all manner of relationships. For combatants such as Mohammed, it often created two kinds of "wives"—those who were intimately woven into their wartime activities, and those who were separated as much as possible from the front lines.[4]

If Mohammed had any idea what prompted this small act of domesticity from Ophelia, he didn't share it with the rest of us. "She takes good care of you," MK remarked, with more than a little sarcasm, when Ophelia had gone. Mohammed, still looking surprised, sheepishly agreed.

Rooms like MK's were the norm at the Brookfields Hotel. While a few of them housed single families, most were occupied by perhaps a half dozen people. Their belongings were stacked neatly in duffle bags against the wall. A simple desk, maybe a few broken chairs, and some thin mattresses were the only furnishings in most quarters. Residents

37. A family meal under the water tank outside Block A, 2001.

slept in shifts through the day and night and sat on their balconies when they weren't moving around the hotel or the city, waiting for orders from above or for something unexpected to change their fortunes for the day. Or, with luck, forever.

My relationship with MK all but ended not long after our conversation about killing as a rite of passage. The atmosphere in the hotel grew more and more tense with rumors of a violent confrontation should the kamajors be evicted. MK was proportionately more difficult and drank more frequently and more heavily. In MK's closet was a small stash of automatic weapons and a pile of ammunition. They added gravity to the claims that the occupants of the room were prepared to defend it. (This didn't prevent someone from breaking into the room one afternoon and stealing the one remaining piece of original furniture—a nonfunctioning toilet.) As MK grew more unpredictable the weapons in the closet became for me and for his roommates a source of great concern.

Jah Kingdom

By this time I had also grown closer to a group of men whose strange little hovel under the hotel swimming pool was becoming a more frequent and much anticipated stop on my rounds of the hotel: Jah Kingdom.

From Block A the least direct but most informative route to the empty swimming pool above Jah Kingdom went through the ruins of the reception center. The glass of the front lobby had long since blown out. The counter of the reception desk remained, but it was staffed only by the chickens that Emmanuel, also known as Cobra, kept to help feed his family. Cobra was the hotel's resident security officer. A former soldier, he was tall, lanky, and heavily tattooed. He seemed always to be in the reception center, perhaps because the kamajors' makeshift jail cell was in the safe room off to one side of the reception desk. I often found him lounging around the desk, playing with a ferret whose home was a bathtub inexplicably sitting in the corner of the hotel lobby. Cobra seemed to have the most reliable information about the upcoming eviction, though it was hard sometimes to know whether he had better sources or whether he simply repeated what he had heard with more conviction.

From the reception area a short corridor led past some of the more in-

38. The entrance to Jah Kingdom, 2001.

triguing corners of the complex. There was the old banquet hall that had become a martial arts dojo in which some of the kamajors trained. The hotel's kitchen now functioned as a medical clinic and infirmary, staffed by a medical student. An auxiliary room served as the hotel mosque, complete with resident imam. A room nearby was the hotel's interdenominational Christian church, presided over by a figure everyone knew as "The Bishop." The Bishop also taught classes at the makeshift hotel school. Traveling past these pockets of community one also walked past the single most bizarre spot on the grounds. Prior to the war the Brookfields Hotel housed the government-run Hotel and Tourism Training Center (HTTC), which was now functioning again, apparently in anticipation of a postwar flood of tourists. A few days a week a group of uniformed young women made their way through the hotel's front gate, past the kamajors sitting on the low wall of the parking lot, past the reception area and Cobra with his chickens and his ferret, and made their way to ruined classrooms where they presumably studied how to run a hotel. As far as I could tell, I alone found this strange.

Beneath the windows of the HTTC classrooms was a never-ending soccer tournament. Teams of a few men collected the entry fee of five hundred leones and challenged one another, playing for the pot. Victory went to the first team to score. Although the matches were refereed, they inevitably ended the same: the winning goal was disputed by the losing side. More often than not, what followed was violent and sometimes bloody as the two five-hundred-leone notes became the object of a brawl. Walking past these matches was a grim reminder that the frontline violence of this war, as profound as it was, was not how most young men encountered violence day in and day out. They did so in more routine and mundane ways, in microencounters made more physical and more confrontational by poverty and the militarized atmosphere that pervaded the hotel just as it pervaded so many other aspects of the kamajors' lived world.

When one rounded the corner into the pool area, Jah Kingdom announced itself in hand-scrawled letters above a set of stairs. In the pool itself a group of children replicated the soccer matches played by their older counterparts on the dirt pitch nearby, but Jah Kingdom was all about life underground, life as lived in the shower stalls, utility closets, and storage rooms down the stairs and underneath the pool.

The name Jah Kingdom made loose reference to what many combatants saw as their connection to a global black underclass of militant male

39. Fighting over the spoils of a soccer game, 2001.

youth. Reggae music was a staple at Jah Kingdom, as was a vaguely Rastafarian inflected vocabulary. "*Tehl Jah tehnki*" ("Tell Jah thank you") replaced the standard Krio "*Tehl Gohd tehnki*" ("Tell God thank you," or "Thanks be to God")[5] in the parlance of Jah Kingdom dwellers. "The Babylonians" described the population outside the hotel, the mass collective of everyone who was not a young man and who conspired to keep the (male) youth of Sierra Leone living underground. One combatant, as we sat in the shower stall in which he slept with his girlfriend, summarized the attitude of the place: "We the youth must tear down Babylon!"

Climbing down the stairs into Jah Kingdom, one first entered a sizable locker room that had been converted to a shebeen. This was King's place, the Nigerian who had allied himself and briefly fought with the kamajors, and now ran both the bar and one of the largest networks of armed robbers in the city. King's girlfriend, Mariama, sold cigarettes, packets of rum, and marijuana as a tinny boombox blasted whatever reggae cassettes were fashionable at the moment. Around her anywhere from two to a dozen young men and a handful of young women played checkers,

40. In the swimming pool, 2001.

smoked, talked, and flirted. King himself would at times emerge to engage the crowd or sit beside his box of wares while Mariama cooked or ran errands, but most often he was in the back room, a narrow storage closet in which he and Mariama slept and in which he conducted his private business. At the far end of the barroom a crawl space led outdoors to an area behind the last block of rooms in the hotel. Though it let in a glimmer of sun, Jah Kingdom functioned in perpetual twilight. A few colored neon bulbs, candles, the ember ends of cigarettes and joints, and constantly striking matches allowed one to read the crude graffiti on the walls. Otherwise Jah Kingdom felt very much like a cave.

When one sat on the uncomfortable wooden benches that lined the walls of the Jah Kingdom shabeen, it was easy to see the humor in a joke that a friend made about the place. Nervousness about the coming eviction had intensified dramatically when in late December Nigerian soldiers appeared outside the hotel. Some of the troops entered the hotel grounds and told the kamajors to pack their things, that they would be coming back soon and would force out anyone who remained. A

41. "Good News" in Jah Kingdom, 2001.

number of the hotel occupants did leave immediately afterward, but the majority stayed, unsure whether the threat would be made good on or even under whose authority it had been issued. There was speculation that this was a freelance operation, that the owners of the hotel had hired the Nigerians to scare everyone away and this was not an official United Nations operation at all. In any case, the Nigerians had not returned, but the incident had everyone rattled. "But," my friend said in recounting the story, "Jah Kingdom was not shaken. Jah Kingdom was dug in." Indeed, it was hard to imagine that the young men collected here would be fazed by anything. Whatever circumstances led them to living in this underground space had long since stripped their ability to be dismayed by what life and the city could bring.

This did not prevent them, however, from being intensely interested and critical thinkers about their own future. A short hallway leading from the locker room and bar ended in the shower room. Four stalls housed a rotating group of about ten people who slept in the cubicles and kept their meager belongings stacked there. The room was never empty and it was rarely quiet. Music spilled over from the boombox next door and provided background to a seemingly continuous and wide-ranging conversation, its participants coming and going. Here some of the better trained and most sought after combatants in the Mano River War sat waiting. Their commentary on what lay ahead could be fascinating.

By late January there was already a great deal of activity in preparation for national elections in May. The SLPP was working to enlist CDF combatants as campaigners, and though few resisted the inducements that party bosses were giving to the young men, there was vocal criticism of the party leadership and the general failure of the SLPP to reward the kamajors for their service to the country. The RUF had formed its political party, the RUFP, and some part of its political strategy seemed to lie in convincing young Sierra Leoneans that it could bring an end to gerontocratic rule. The young men who lived in Jah Kingdom were the target audience of both of these messages, a fact of which they were well aware. Sitting on the floor with four of them I listened as they talked politics and dissected the upcoming political contest.

Mohammed, the most outspoken of the young men, made it clear that while he would happily take the rum, cigarettes, and cash that SLPP bosses were handing out in exchange for mobilizing on rally days, there was no way he would vote for the party. The other three young men agreed when he said that at present, he had no intention of voting at all. When I interjected that I thought it odd that young men who had risked their lives under the banner "we fight for democracy" would sit out the first postconflict vote, all four agreed there was no one to vote for. None of the candidates, they argued, lived up to their expectations. "I vote for God," one of the men, Ibrahim, answered. "My only government is God." Another then explained that if he decided to vote, it would be for the RUFP. Although he had spent years battling the RUF, he still believed that their original intentions were positive. Ridding the country of its elderly elite had been a just cause, even if the tactics that eventually came to dominate the rebel campaign had proved indefensible. Now, as a political party working within an electoral system, the RUFP represented the only force interested in youth progress and change. It was a conversation riddled with the contradictions of a state of emergency. The dialogue, and also the setting, resounded with the idea that, as Simone puts it, "this is a temporality characterized by a lack of gravity that would hold meanings to specific expressions and actions" (2004, 4). A decade-long war that these young men had fought against a brutal rebel force and in the name of democracy bore no relation in their minds to the first postconflict election. The past apparently had no meaning.

The conversation then turned to a more general rumination on the postcolonial condition. "To be a man is not easy in this country," one of the young men said, echoing a sentiment I heard often in the hotel. Sometimes racialized—"the black man is a sufferer"—the idea that it was the condition of the modern Sierra Leonean male to live the hardest of lives was difficult to refute while sitting on the cold dark floor of Jah Kingdom. "I would rather clean toilets or wash clothes in any other country than continue to live in Sierra Leone," he continued. The tragedy in his comment was that his possible futures seemed indeed to lie elsewhere. The kamajors' remaining time at the hotel was short. But the young man's future, and that of many more like him, seemed much more likely to be in even harder and more unstable labor. A few might end up cleaning toilets or washing clothes in Europe, the United States, or the Middle East. But most of these men were bound for the battlefields of Liberia or Côte d'Ivoire, the diamond pits of eastern Sierra Leone, the rubber plantations outside Monrovia, or the streets of Conakry or Freetown.

From Jah Kingdom the simplest way out of the hotel was to climb out the small crawl space at the back of the shebeen. One emerged behind the last of the housing blocks. Some segment of a large family with rooms on the ground floor was invariably seated under the trees. A low hammock was the occasional perch of a young man who at times seemed to be the sentry for the rear entrance of the hotel, and at times seemed simply to have found a convenient place to lounge. I often passed him a few cigarettes as a kind of transit tax, though it never really seemed necessary or required.

There was a narrow gap in the rear wall of the compound. Grabbing hold of a tangle of tree roots, I swung down the five-foot drop into the backyard of the hotel's nearest neighbor. My friend Gleh dropped down after me, and we proceeded with our ritual of exit. It was late, and unlike the Brookfields Hotel the Brookfields neighborhood rarely had electricity. The skinny footpaths that led between houses and across yards were exceptionally dark. The route was heavily populated with neigh-

42. Block A of the Brookfields Hotel, refurbished to house the Truth and Reconciliation Commission, 2003.

borhood residents sitting outside to escape the heat of their homes, and it wound around potholes, piles of trash, and impromptu gardens. Gleh and I talked as we made the ten-minute walk to Old Railway Line Road, the nearest spot to catch a taxi this late at night. I was never allowed to leave the hotel unaccompanied, a small nicety that seemed to upend everything that was commonly said about the hotel by those who lived beyond its walls. The supposedly antisocial kamajor youth were gracious hosts who feared for my safety outside the hotel every bit as much as others feared for my safety inside it. Passing between the hotel and the streets beyond meant passing between order and chaos, though which was which depended upon where one stood.

And yet these spaces were not so different. As we walked from the hotel to the main road Gleh hailed a number of friends in various potes along the way, promising to stop for a chat on his return. Other clusters of young men hanging out by the road sized us up and we them, looking for familiar faces or signs of danger. Some of these men were ex-combatants, many of them not, but they shared the same air of expectancy and waiting that one encountered along the hotel's parking lot wall. These young men lived in small rooms every bit as crowded as those in the hotel, and they, too, spent their days dregging on the city streets, searching for work, trying in vain to master the challenges of the postcolonial city. The streets that surrounded the hotel pulsed with the same potent combination of vibrancy and despair one felt on the hotel grounds. Especially at night, as one wended through these tiny ad hoc communities of barely perceptible youths, it was easy to see the logic in what Hardt and Negri describe as the new terrain of imperial emergency: "The crisis means that today the enclosures that used to define the limited space of the institutions have broken down so that the logic of what once functioned primarily within the institutional walls now spreads across the entire social terrain. Inside and outside are becoming indistinguishable" (2000, 196). It was easy to imagine that these young men populating the many spaces of the city were themselves a potential face of the Mano River war machine.

chapter 7

THE MAGIC OF WAR

Given a certain effect, what machine is capable of producing it?
And given a machine, what can it be used for?
—GILLES DELEUZE AND FÉLIX GUATTARI, *Anti-Oedipus*

BY MID-1994 MOHAMMED ISSA had a problem. Issa and other elders in Bo were searching for ways to protect the city from what seemed an immanent attack by the RUF. The military was untrustworthy. Though ad hoc mobilizations of Bo youth had effectively repelled RUF attackers in the past, it was clear that a more substantial defense of the city was needed.

Issa sent word to Mama Munda Fortune and begged her to come to Bo. Famous in the south for her healing abilities, Mama Munda is an herbalist—her special occult powers come from the use of forest leaves (*tifa*) employed as medicines (hale or *tevi*). A document that Mama Munda keeps with her, issued by the Ministry of Rural Development and Local Governance, describes her as "a native herbalist . . . [who] possesses special superhuman powers in treating and healing all types of sickness by the use of native medicines." It goes on: "Over and above this she is supernaturally gifted in divination and fortune telling for which she has obtained the usual Town Council License."

Mama Munda joined the kamajors when the bush devil Kasela kidnapped her and took her into the bush.[1] When she awoke from the sleep he put her under, she found she had the power to make young men's bodies bulletproof. Incorporating slips of paper with koranic inscriptions that she received from other initiators or directly from Kasela (Mama Munda herself is illiterate), she made men into true kamajor fighters. Because of her association with Kasela, she called her group the Kasela War Council, and her initiates she referred to as Kaselas.

Because she was past the age of reproduction (some say that Kasela

43. Kamajors in protective battle dress, Bo, 2000.

took her womb as the price of power), Mama Munda's gender was less clearly a threat to the secretive men's knowledge of the kamajors. When I asked her, she denied being a *mabɔle*, the one female member of the Poro society and a figure that straddles, albeit precariously, the usual gender divides (see Bledsoe 1984; Ferme 2001b, 74–79; Little [1951] 1967, 245; Rodney 1970, 66). But like the *mabɔle*, Mama Munda seemed to bridge separate worlds. She was an expert practitioner in male knowledge. She was known to travel with her boys to the battlefront, although in theory women and initiators were excluded from that space. She drew on the power of the written word though she was illiterate, and employed the Koran although not herself a Muslim.

Whatever the ambiguities that surrounded her, however, there was little doubt that Mama Munda was powerful and she made the men around her powerful, too. Mama Munda brought her Kasela War Council to Bo, where they achieved some success in fighting the rebels. As the fighting intensified in the regions around the city, the Kasela War Council deployed to villages under attack and manned some of the principal roadways. Mama Munda initiated many of the Bo kamajors, and when the war ended she stayed on there, hoping to reap some reward for her service to the city and the nation.

The bulletproof bodies that resulted from initiations into the kamajor society are a hard reality to grasp. The vast and ever-expanding anthropological literature on the occult in Africa is helpful, of course, but only to a point. The classic approach to occult discourse is to treat it as the index of social conflict, a vernacular expression of social tension, trauma, or economic or political insecurity. This is certainly relevant to understanding not only the kamajors but other aspects of this war. A great deal of discussion, for example, about the occult practices of presidents, rebel leaders, or military commanders has to be seen as critical dialogue on the nature of postcolonial power (an analysis in keeping with seminal recent studies such as Geschiere 1997 and the essays collected in Comaroff

44. The Kasela War Council, Bo, 2000.

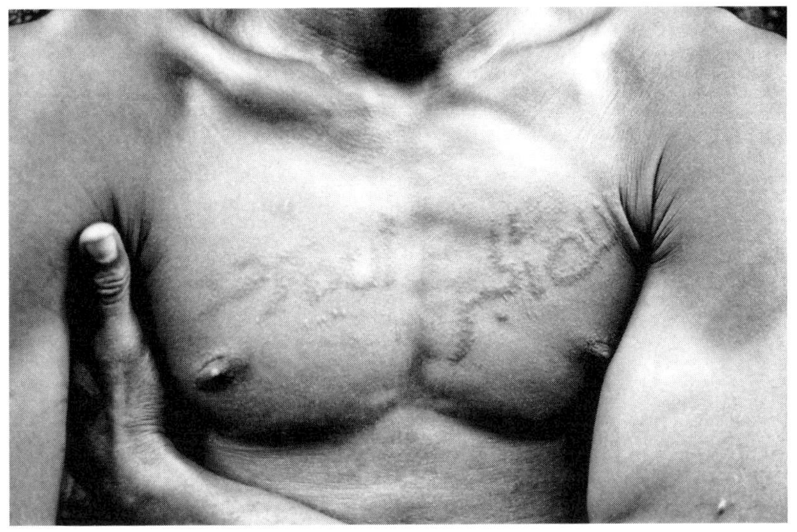

45. CDF and LURD fighter Fumba Kanneh inscribed with koranic text, Monrovia, 2005.

and Comaroff 1993). But this discursive approach goes only so far in accounting for public displays of an initiate's bulletproofed body. It does not address the materiality or immediacy of a kamajor fighter who offers to catch bullets in his teeth, or recounts a tale of having ascended into the sky to escape his enemies. These seem a different order of event, one that cannot be dealt with solely in terms of discourse or social conflict.[2]

Here, therefore, I take a somewhat different approach to the occult dynamics of this war, and to claims of a bulletproof body in particular. The combatants with whom I worked, and especially the initiators responsible for the secret knowledge that makes a body bulletproof, routinely spoke of these practices as a creative technology. The language of experimentation, of creativity, and of military science (not to mention commerce, profit, and intellectual property) ran throughout discussions of bulletproof bodies and other occult dynamics of the war. In this chapter I take that language seriously. I treat occult phenomena as experimental events, and bulletproof bodies as an inventive military tool.

The occult dimensions of this war present us with questions about what is required in the face of incredible violence, about the demands placed on subjects and bodies by violence itself. I contend that one needs some manner of inventive, defensive practice in the context of war. To design a bulletproof body is to operate in a sphere in which questions of efficacy, empiricism, tradition, and belief mean very different things if they mean anything at all. Following on Deleuze's and Guattari's writings on active and reactive forces, I chart here a trajectory of bulletproofing technology that ran from roughly 1995 to 1999. This is a period in which occult technology went from an active to a reactive force in the war, a revolutionary science to an institutional one. What began as a necessary invention, created to deal with specific problems, became a conservative, profitable but nonproductive, noninventive signifying practice used by forces within and outside the militia for different ends. Like any other military technology it grew from an experiment motivated by particular needs into a political tool from which many different actors hoped to profit.

In a recent revisiting of the problem of sorcery, James Siegel writes: "The power of magic . . . is a performative power. It is the power to make something true by saying particular words, those that at least sometimes

46. Mama Munda and the Kasela War Council demonstrating the power of bulletproofing, Bo, 2000.

are thought to create truths via their enunciation" (2003, 148). In the early days of the kamajor movement it was not at all clear what could be made true through enunciating (or inscribing) certain powerful words. All that was clear was a need to confront violence and the need for protection in doing so. By the end of the Mano River War, or at least the Sierra Leone front, those meanings had become less fluid. What had been a certain inventiveness at the heart of this technology was replaced by struggles over the power to wield the sorcerer's magic.

My foray into the vexing problem of the bulletproof body is therefore less informed by the extensive literature on African occult practice than it is by two questions Deleuze and Guattari pose early on in *Capitalism and Schizophrenia*: "Given a certain effect, what machine is capable of producing it? And given a machine, what can it be used for?" (1983, 3). These are the questions that the young men who fought this war and the initiators who made them into combatants seemed to ask themselves.

A Brief History of Bulletproofing

The task of initiating young men into the kamajor society fell largely to specialists who were said to possess one of two kinds of knowledge. Those identified as Muslims practiced an ostensibly Koran-based knowledge and were generally referred to as *kemoh*.[3] Others were herbalists associated with powerful leaf medicines.[4] In practice most of the latter engaged in a form of occult technology similar to Mama Munda's: they blended practices that Mende kamajors referred to as "traditional" leaf medicines with the power of the Koran.

In other words, the kamajor militia was not an Islamic movement, but its occult dimensions drew heavily from Islamic (or purportedly Islamic) symbolism, narrative, and myth. Mama Munda's "controller" (the staff with which she repelled enemy bullets) and the other occult objects she surrounded herself with or gave to her initiates incorporated small pieces of paper with writings in Arabic, allegedly from the Koran. These could be folded and sewn into bundles attached to clothing or planted strategically in vehicles or buildings as a protective mechanism, a technique long associated with Muslim *morimen* in Sierra Leone (see Bledsoe and Robey 1986, 210). The "safe" she created for her initiates, often a necklace or armband made of cowries and thread, was generally washed in holy water that had been blessed by Kasela and in which she had soaked koranic inscriptions. The widespread West African association of literacy and power, and the writings of holy books in particular, pervaded the symbolism associated with kamajor initiation.

Immunization was the central tenet of that initiation, and in many ways a pillar of kamajor identity. The ability to become bulletproof through a process of initiation and then subsequent ritual renewals was one of the singular qualities of the movement. It was a capability pinned to proper conduct on and off the battlefield and it was what separated a kamajor from civilian noncombatants, from the state army, and from the rebels. Initiation and its consequence (the bulletproof body) came through the acquisition of certain privileged knowledge, through the performance of necessary ritual, and through the observation of prescribed behaviors.

If initiation was unique to the kamajors, the use of the occult as a military technology was not. Even among the kamajors, it was widely acknowledged that the most powerful protections and most efficacious military "miracles" belonged to the northern hunters. The tamaboro were the earliest of the so-called hunter militias to mobilize in Sierra Leone, appearing in media accounts as early as 1992. Working with the Sierra Leone Army as trackers and gunners, the tamaboro achieved a remarkable degree of military success and a nationwide reputation for the occult tools they brought to the waging of war.

Michael Jackson (2004) gives two translations of the Kuranko term *tamaboro*. The first, from *ta ma bo aro*, equates roughly with "go and free us (i.e., from this war, this mess, this plight)," a rendering that coincides with the interpretation given to me by a northern defense force leader, Nyamakoro Sesay, at Defence Headquarters in Freetown in 2000: "go and liberate us" or "take us out of this problem." Jackson gives the second meaning as "walk about bag," drawing on the image of the hunter entering the forest without revealing where he is headed—only that he is "walking about" (143). Mohammed Barrie, a former fighter with the tamaboros and later the kamajors, similarly translated tamaboro as a "traveling bag" when I interviewed him in Bo in 2000. "What goes inside," he said, "is known only to [the hunter]," and represents the secret power and knowledge of the hunter-turned-warrior.

The tamaboros' occult power was doubly significant given that in rural areas of Sierra Leone the military's inability to halt the RUF advances was attributed in part to that force's supernatural capabilities. Perhaps because of the Liberian mercenaries and NPFL commandoes fighting with the RUF, the rebels were said to harness powerful extra-human modes of agency in the service of the war. (As they are throughout the global popular imaginary, Liberian fighters are associated by many Sierra Leoneans with extreme brutality mixed with juju practices, including cannibalism.) The RUF's "iron jackets" were thought to make them bulletproof, and their extreme actions seemed to have much in common with destructive bush spirits, a reputation the RUF encouraged (Henry 2000, 35).[5]

Kamajors in various parts of the country told different stories about the origins of the occult dimensions of their own movement. Some focus on an Islamic healer named Mwalimu Saddam Shariff. By the time he was killed in Kenema in September 1996 (allegedly by Sierra Leonean soldiers) Shariff had washed recruits throughout the Bo and Kenema region, making their bodies impenetrable and giving them special abilities to detect the presence of their enemies.

Brima Bangura in Kenema was also an early and prominent developer of the kamajors' occult protections. Like Saddam Shariff he tied his form of initiation and protection to Islam and koranic divination. More than most initiators, however, Brima Bangura associated the kamajors' occult power with an intimate knowledge of the meanings of the Koran and not only to the form of Arabic script.

But it is the kamajors' High Priest, Allieu Kundewa, who figures most prominently in stories of how the immunization against bullets became the foundation of initiation into the kamajors. Kundewa appears in some versions of the bulletproofing story as a humble man of the village.[6] He, along with his brother, a powerful ritual specialist, is captured by the RUF in an attack in the southern Bonthe District.[7] Kundewa's brother is killed by the rebels, but visits Kundewa in a dream and instructs him in the ritual preparation of resistance fighters. Freed from his bonds by his brother's ghost, Kundewa goes on to organize a corps of initiators and combat units.

Joseph Koroma told a slightly different, though not incompatible, version of the story at the CDF headquarters in Bo in 2000. Koroma was a key figure in the Krim Civil Defence organization and in other early mobilizations around Bo. Koroma claimed to have spent time with Kundewa at a village in Bonthe developing the bulletproofing powers. Together they took the medicines associated with the kamajoh hunter and developed a more military use for the magic, experimenting as they went by shooting at dogs.

Allieu Kundewa's own account of the dream at the heart of the kamajors' occult powers also differs somewhat from the stories other people tell about it. Actually, Kundewa's version has changed over time, at least in its details. Who exactly appeared to him and what he did when he woke up varies with different tellings. But the narrative thread of his story is consistent, and the broad strokes of his dream and of the powers he developed as a result of his dream are more or less the same in everyone's recollection.

Allieu Musa Kundewa's dream

The version of Kundewa's story that I recorded in the Special Court detention center in 2006 is haunted by the sounds of prison. On tape our voices echo from the naked cement of the visiting room. Phones ring. The conversations of guards, lawyers, visitors, and the other accused float beneath Kundewa's story, loud enough at times to intrude on the narrative. Everyone stops suddenly to greet Chief Norman as he enters the room, walking with his cane and chatting with the leaders of the other factions and the security detail.

The recordings do not capture Kundewa's bulk but they capture his simplicities. Something in the timbre of his voice conveys the country healer. Kundewa looks more out of place in the Special Court than any of the other accused, though he is the only one of the three who sits in the courtroom dressed formally in a smart suit, a gift from his lawyers, his large family, and his many supporters. In the recordings Kundewa's Mende is the language of the deep south, uninflected by Krio or English. He doesn't speak the urban slang of the RUF or AFRC prisoners and he doesn't exude the easy cosmopolitanism of Hinga Norman. He frames his story in ways that directly refute the charges in his indictment, but they are clumsy and unconvincing allusions. Kundewa's voice is the voice of a man made powerful in small ways by war, a man who does not quite grasp the rules of the postwar conflict he has been caught up in ever since.

> My name is Allieu Musa.[8] My father was Musa Gamanga. Kundewa is just a nickname. It means "You say something and it happens."

I was born in Sierra Leone. No one sent me to school. No one taught me a trade. I simply lived in my village in Yawbeko Chiefdom, Bonthe District, until the war came.

Many people died when the war reached Yawbeko. My father was killed. My brother Kafu was killed. My mother was killed. My wife in Yawbeko, Fati, was injured, and our child starved while we were in the bush running from the rebels.

When the war came to Yawbeko, we fled to the ocean. With food so scarce we moved on to Panguma, but we were attacked there, too, so we again went into hiding in the bush.

It was there in the bush that I had my dream. I saw my father and my mother. They came to me with three people I did not know. "Allieu," my father said, "we have come to see you."

"Why, father?" I asked.

"These three people," my father explained, "have asked us to bring them to you. We have come with them so that you will not be afraid."

The first of the three figures was a man, and he spoke to me about his death and the death of his wife and his children. "We have come," he explained, "so that you, Allieu Musa, can stop the killing. We have come to bring you an herb [tifa] that you can use to stop this violence."

The second figure stood up. She was a woman, pregnant when the war came and when the rebels killed her. She pleaded with me to stop the killing, to take this herb so that I could stop the killing. The third person also told me his story and he, too, asked me to take this herb and to stop the war.

"But how can I do this?" I asked them. "We will show you the herb," they said, "and we will give you our support." They told me the laws that go with this medicine [hale]. "If you accept these laws," they said, "we will show you the herb," and I accepted. They showed me the herb, they told me the laws, and they made clear that anyone who wishes to use this medicine must live by these rules.

The first rule: you may not touch a corpse. If you do not touch a corpse, then you will not be affected by the bullets of your enemies. Even your sweat will carry the power of this medicine, so that if you rub it on another they, too, will be protected.[9] But you must not touch the dead. You must leave even the bodies of your relatives should they die in this war.

A second rule: do not loot. If you loot your safety cannot be guaranteed.

Never taste another person's blood or even your own.[10] When you are immunized against bullets you may not have sex with women. Do not rape.

Do not let a woman cook for you for seven days after you take the herb and do not communicate with women for seven days, either.

There were other rules, but these were some of the ones they showed me before they showed me the herb.

When the herb was given to me, I tested it. First, I tested it on an anthill. Then it was tested on cloth. And again it was tested, this time on a tree. Finally we tested it on dogs before we were willing to test it on a human being. Nothing happened to any of them. As long as you adhere to the rules, nothing will happen to you. And that is why we say that this power comes from God.

You cannot simply give this power to an individual and send him to war.[11] People must come to you and request safety or immunization from enemy fire. That is how it happens. There is a law that you the initiator cannot call for initiates to come. You [the initiators] each have your own district, and when people need you they will call for you. They will take you to their chiefdom and they will arrange for the initiation to take place. That is how the medicine works. This was not the beginning of the kamajor existence. This was in 1995, and the kamajoisia existed long before then. Every chiefdom had its own kamajoh. Even in Yawbeko there was a kamajoh.

We the initiators were given tokens for initiation, but that was not our [the initiators'] doing. That was explained in the dream. The token should be five thousand leones per initiate. Of that five thousand leones, the town chief should be given one thousand. The women of the village should get five hundred. The youth should get five hundred, and the paramount chief of the chiefdom should be given one thousand. That leaves only fifteen hundred [*sic*] for the initiator. This society [the kamajors] does not belong to an individual, it is a society for everyone. So the initiators should receive only their fifteen hundred leones. That is how it happened.

Initiations as we do them today do not take place in the bush. They take place in town. The people of the town build a hut in the middle of town, between the houses so that it can be seen. The initiates are not kept in the hut, they come and go.[12]

When the ceremony is done, the initiate is dressed and we take him to an open field. Everyone gathers and there is a test. Boiling water might be poured on him—nothing will happen. He might be shot at—nothing will happen. We do this in the presence of the paramount chief, the chiefdom speaker, the elders, and so on. When the test is complete, the initiates are handed over to the paramount chief. The rules are explained in the open, so that everyone will hear. They are advised to keep their war garments [*ronkos*]

> in the mosque. When the rules are explained, when the test is done and the initiates are handed over, then the initiator goes home. That is how it was done.
>
> You can see, then, that my being here [at the Special Court] is wrong. You whites manufacture weapons. If someone buys them and says he is going to hunt animals, but kills a human being instead, you do not arrest the manufacturer, do you? Now, if a weapons manufacturer gives a gun to someone and tells him "Go and kill human beings!" *then* the manufacturer will be arrested. Or if you sell someone a car and they get into an accident, people die, will you arrest the seller of that car? The makers of bulletproof vests are not arrested when someone puts one on for his own safety and then kills another person, are they?
>
> I never initiated anyone and told him to go fight a war. I never understood anything about ranks or positions. All I did was protect life. From the day I was born until they brought me to Bo [during the war] I never saw the city. From the day I was born I lived in the bush. My job, my only job, was to heal people.

Whatever its origins, the reputed effects of the bulletproofing technology were widely sought. Kundewa was invited to chiefdoms and IDP camps around the south and east to perform his rituals of purification and defense. Other ritual specialists were drafted by community defense committees to perform similar "miracles" on their own recruits, and soon a cohort of occult practitioners were specializing in the use of hale for military protection. The point at which these rituals of immunization became rituals of initiation is hard to fix. But in the months after the SLPP election victory in 1996 and the appointment of Hinga Norman as the deputy defense minister, Mende communities around the south and east were hearing not only of the occult protections being made available to fighters but of an organization based on those protections that was waging war against the rebels and, when necessary, the military.

Dr. Mohammed Mansaray, an initiator originally from Bonthe, estimates that there were perhaps thirty-six initiators throughout the country, though in practice this number would be impossible to fix. Certain ritual specialists cycled in and out of the movement in the same way combatants did, while others were more clearly identified as kamajor initiators. Convocations of initiators took place at various times during the war, but these never included everyone and had only limited impact regulating the practices of initiators.

As Kundewa indicates, each initiator in the initiator wing of the kamajors and then the CDF had his (or in Mama Munda's case, her) specific set of practices. Some rules and restrictions were universal: the prohibitions on rape, looting, and betrayal were common to every initiator, even if they were not always evident in practice. The initiation process itself and some of the laws were unique to the specialist. Kamajors described being warned against stepping over discarded banana peels or sitting on overturned rice mortars, seemingly esoteric prohibitions that in fact make reference to women's spheres (the world of domestic work symbolized by the rice mortar, for example). One witness before the Special Court described taboos on eating palm kernel oil and snake meat.[13] Other prohibitions were reminiscent of the gendered "laws" of the Poro society.

In some tellings the proscriptions on kamajor behavior evoked not only gendered domains but also the imagery of cleanliness and pollution. "Washing" (in both English and Mende) was a common term for the process of rendering the body bulletproof. Hinga Norman when I interviewed him at the Special Court detention center described the bulletproofing initiation as a practice rooted in the Bible, notably two verses in the Old Testament book of Deuteronomy describing the washing of warriors after sex.[14]

What happened in the kamajor initiation bush (*vaa*) was, of course, a secret. Accounts of the earliest initiations generally describe a longer and more arduous process combining instruction in kamajor knowledge and history, some military training, medicines implanted in the body, and physical ordeals. Initiation in the later phases of the war and by certain initiators reduced the time of the initiation from days and weeks to hours. Kamajors alluded to their experiences in the bush, but most often refused to speak about it directly, claiming that to do so would violate one of the signature kamajor laws: secrecy about the rites of membership. Clearly, however, what took place in the vaa varied greatly depending on who conducted the initiation, where, and at what point in the war.

One of the few consistencies in these initiation processes was a public demonstration at the end in which the newly created kamajors were fired upon in a display of their powers. Mama Munda and other initiators with whom I spoke invariably asserted the same thing—this public performance was not a test of the purity of the kamajors as much as it was a demonstration to the initiates of their newly configured bodies. A witness before the Special Court argued that "for you [the kamajor initiate] to believe that the initiation that you have gone through is the truth, all of you would be shot at and nobody would be affected by the gunshots."[15] CDF fighters themselves didn't always see it this way; a number of them asserted that the final demonstration was an ordeal meant to ensure that the new initiate was worthy of joining the society.

The shortened version of the initiation which began to appear late in the evolution of the CDF, especially in late 1998 and 1999, was of a qualitatively different order from those versions that had come before. Allieu Kundewa began to initiate ever-larger groups of men into new organizations that promised certain advantages over the "traditional" kamajor initiation. These new units required less vigorous screening, initiation, and restriction. They were also more expensive. Just before the 6 January 1999 offensive Kundewa began mass initiations in Bathurst, Bonthe District, and in the town of Bumpe, Bo District. An internal CDF document estimated that five thousand to ten thousand new initiates paid some fifty thousand leones to become what Kundewa called "Avondos," drawing on the Mende term for sweat (the moisture of the Avondo's body was thought to be the locus of his bulletproof potency).[16] Kundewa promised the Avondo initiates that their occult powers exceeded those of the "original" kamajors, and he demarcated these initiates by piercing one of their ears.

Kundeiwa's Avondo initiations angered both community leaders and the national leadership of the organization. Most saw the influx of hastily initiated youth in the same light as the periodic rapid conscriptions by the military—as a dilution of the ranks with untrained thugs who used their semilegitimate security position to prey on the local population. Kundewa was forced by the administrative leaders of the CDF to disband the Avondos and cease making claims to their extraoccult capabilities. From that point claiming Avondo status (or wearing a single earring) was included in the organization's list of "grave offenses."

Although a smaller numerical force (probably no more than a few hundred), Kundewa's second independent mobilization was an even thornier issue for the CDF as a whole. In the wake of the 8 May 2000 incident, Kundewa began to initiate a unit in the Moyamba District called the Banya Moli, derived from a Mende expression meaning "Don't ask me." In this case he distinguished his new force through a red bandana or piece of cloth. As he had with the Avondos, Kundewa claimed that Banya Moli initiates possessed powers in excess of those of other kamajors. "Don't ask me" was described by some kamajors as a warning not to look too carefully into the group's actions. Others maintained that it was a prohibition against asking about the restrictions the unit was supposed to observe. When I asked him about Banya Moli, Dr. Mohammed Mansaray asserted that the name made reference to the fact that Banya Moli's could be protected even without having gone through a traditional initiation: it was a pre-emptive answer to the question "How can you be bulletproof without being bulletproof [i.e., without being made bulletproof through initiation]?" Chiefs in the Moyamba District complained about Kundewa's arrogance and the lack of control over his new force, and the Banya Moli group was quickly shut down by the CDF leadership.

Kundewa's most interesting innovation in kamajor hale was the one that did the most to undermine his credibility both within and outside the CDF. Kundewa developed an initiation that he began to offer recruits—at quite a high price—which he called *ngbɔgbegbɔyei* or "it is finished" (also rendered as *gbe gboyowa* and *kpeh gboryia*, or roughly "everything is finished"). *Ngbɔgbegbɔyei*, Kundewa promised, would relieve the kamajor of any obligation whatsoever to observe restrictions on his

47. Kamajor Murray Agba dressed with protective amulets, Bo, 2000.

behavior and would preclude ever needing a "top up" initiation in the future. It was intended to be the ultimate defensive weapon, though one that changed the very meaning of a kamajor.

Before *ngbɔgbegbɔyei* became standard practice, however, Hinga Norman removed Kundewa as the kamajors' so-called High Priest. The man who represented the occult dimensions of the kamajors had become a liability, the subject of complaints by local leaders and ridicule in the national press. Kundewa was implicated in the hijacking of a government truck and later in stealing a shipment of goods from a Lebanese merchant in Kenema. The man who replaced him, Lahai Bangura, brought an altogether different tone to the position. Literate, cosmopolitan, and unassertive, Bangura was unquestionably part of the CDF hierarchy. He made the Initiator Wing of the CDF in its final days a nonconfrontational part of the CDF bureaucracy.

The Problem of Violence

Patrick Muana has written that one of the weapons that hunter militias brought to the war with the RUF was the heavy artillery of their "superior myth"—the sense that the RUF's command of powerful forces could be matched and defeated only by like forces that the military did not appear to possess (1997, 85, 97). Bringing occult specialists into the militia signified a war fought on multiple fronts.[17]

Muana's phrasing underscores just how difficult and varied understandings of the occult dimensions of war can be. The Mano River War has spawned a whole subgenre of writings on "magic soldiers" (Bergner 2004), writings that tend to play up the war's "Africanness"—and therefore its unfathomability to outsiders. Others have cast occult practice as a primitive form of psychological warfare, a mental game, intentional or otherwise, that makes gullible combatants brazen enough to face the enemy and noncombatants fearful and cooperative.[18] Those writers seeking to understand discourses of the occult in nonexoticized terms tend to emphasize the occult *as discourse*; as meaningful practice, to be sure, but ultimately as a local language of war. A language that gives combatants courage, a language that scares the enemy, a language that legitimates a movement in the eyes of the people, a language that explains the otherwise inexplicable randomness of death in war.

By contrast, when kamajor initiators themselves spoke of bulletproofing they tended not to focus on the occult, or to do so only indirectly. Instead they focused on the problem of violence. The bulletproofing immunizations that came with initiation into the kamajor society were a military technology, developed in response to the problem of violence. It was an invention. What initiators needed to study were not occult traditions but the peculiarities and problems of war.

At a meeting of eastern initiators in Kenema in 2000, I asked Kemoh Brima Bangura about the efficacy of bulletproofing medicines. His response was one I heard echoed by many other initiators and kamajor fighters over the years. In "the West," he argued, you have scientists who develop missile defense shields and bulletproof vests. Whenever there is an innovation in the offensive technologies of war, he explained, there is immediate innovation in the defensive, protective technologies of war as well. This process is no different in Sierra Leone. Initiators are the military scientists of this war, developing the tools to respond to ever-greater threats.

"There was the day of leadership by ability," Norman told me when I asked him the same question about the technology of defense. He went on: "That was survival of the strongest. Unlike today, which is survival of the wittiest. There were those who have the wit to put together missiles to travel thousands of miles to strike their enemies. Now the only challenge to this is the Masonic powers of the people. If and when [that wit is] employed, your dynamite, your mortar bombs, your missiles cannot explode."

"A problem," Claire Colebrook writes in her introduction to the philosophy of Gilles Deleuze, "is a way of creating a future" (2002, 21). To see initiators in the way they asked to be seen would be to see them in the way that Deleuze saw scientists: each as "someone who invents or creates functions" (2006a, 314). By 1995, rural communities in the south and east had very definite problems. Villages were under attack, and the military was in no position to help. Local youth led by kamajoisia and village elders held mostly homemade shotguns and cutlasses against forces armed with military-grade hardware and other less visible weapons. The violence in the countryside was largely ignored in the capital and largely unnoticed anywhere else. These were communities fending for themselves. So they began to experiment.

What this amounts to is a somewhat different starting place from the one that seeks to contextualize occult belief in the nonwar habitus of rural African communities. The focus is not the panoply of beliefs that were put to new uses in a wartime context. Instead it is on the specific problem that needed to be creatively addressed. Rather than beginning with the assumption that occult practice in Africa is inherently conservative and reactive, adapted to new circumstances but essentially the same across contexts, I am suggesting here that *at certain moments* occult practice becomes inventive and active.

Bruce Kapferer's analysis of Sinhala sorcery practices in Sri Lanka draws on Deleuze's and Guattari's chapter on war machines from *A Thousand Plateaus* to argue for exactly this kind of understanding of the creative, productive potential in the occult. In a partial critique of much of the existing literature on witchcraft, rooted as it is in the structural and functionalist origins of modern studies of African witchcraft, Kapferer writes that "sorcery is often seen as the negative anti-social aspects of social and political orders." The occult is generally caste as either the expression of a breakdown in the normal functioning of the social world, or as the idiom for expressing "the negation of human beings" inherent in contemporary political and economic systems—notably, of course, global capitalism and the modern nation-state (see Kapferer 1997, 278–79). Thus, for example, the rash of studies over the past decade that have pointed out the increasing prevalence of witchcraft discourses even as the world becomes more interconnected and less economically equitable.

Read in this way (and this remains the dominant reading both in and outside anthropology) occult practices are inevitably predetermined by the forces against which they are arrayed. They are always reactive, always a negation. They might serve at times as useful weapons of the weak, but they create nothing.

By contrast, sorcery understood as a positive, active force (as, in other words, a war machine) can be understood as an inventive capacity. "The process of change in the war machines is that of metamorphosis," Kapferer writes. "The war machine has the capacity to assume the form of what it overcomes and indeed . . . to continually take new and often original form" (1997, 280). Occult practice confronts problems by creating new possibilities, it does not simply represent or express a problem in different terms. It is not (or at least is not only) a framing of the world. It is an effort to intervene in it.

This is what I take to be the principle that animated initiators' repeated emphasis on the testing of bulletproof powers and the parallels initiators routinely drew between the military technology of the bulletproof body and the high-technology weaponry of United States and European armies. Talk about initiation and about bulletproofing was mostly talk about testing, development, and verification. As Hinga Norman put it when I asked him about the purpose of the live-fire demonstrations at the end of initiation, "Well, professor," he said, "your learning has told you that before knowledge there has always been tests."

Sheikh Walid Kallon at Bandajuma Sowah spent over an hour performing "miracles" for me before he would allow himself to be interviewed. Sitting in his cramped hot quarters, surrounded by the tools of his trade—herbs of various hues, a monkey skull, and in the corner an AK-47—the young initiator was keen to demonstrate the power that had made him famous in the area. When he finished his displays he launched into a lengthy tale about the arrival of the British forces. President Kabbah, he said, wanted to convince the foreigners that the CDF was a powerful ally. So he sent a team of British officers to Bandajuma. While other British soldiers in Freetown monitored satellites to ensure there was no trickery, Kallon invited the officers to fire from six feet away at his magical belt. They could not hit it, of course. Then Kallon took a piece of paper covered in koranic text and stuffed it into his mouth. Again the soldiers fired, emptying an entire magazine. Kallon opened his mouth and out fell the bullets, which he returned to the white men. Finally Kallon himself took up a weapon and fired at a man he had washed in protective medicine. The shots disappeared harmlessly up the man's nose.

It would certainly be possible to read Kallon's story as some kind of metaphor, a collection of local terms through which he (and others) understands the nature of power and violence. But that papers over some of the more interesting details in his story, and what I would suggest are more profound implications. Kallon is careful to put his powers in the same category as those of the British, their weapons, their satellites. These are technologies that can and do interact. It matters to him that power is *demonstrated*. He tells this story after first establishing himself as a performer of miracles, and he tells the story as one of a fantastical invention and the overcoming of doubt. Kallon is not interpreting events, he is creating them.

If, however, occult practice can create new possibilities, if it can be an active, inventive force, that does not necessarily mean that it must always be so. As Kapferer explains it, antisorcery rites in Sinhala, rites that are no less "occult" simply because they are meant to eradicate sorcery, were conservative efforts to reestablish the order of the state and of power. As the rituals of immunization and initiation into the kamajor society were expanded, and as the dynamics of the war changed, they, too, took on a more reactive bent. Allieu Kundewa and a handful of the other initiators responsible for the kamajors' occult weapons began to develop new magics that were defined not by the problem of violence but by the existing, "state" logic of profiteering. The Avondo, Banya Moli, and *ngbɔgbegbɔyei* appeared even as the threat of violence from the AFRC and RUF began to wane. These were technologies that did not confront problems. They were chances for Kundewa and others to take an existing "machine" and see if it could be made profitable in the late-war landscape, an effort to see what else it could do.

A Military Science

Military science is experimental science. It is a response to the demands placed by the reality of violence, the need to exercise violence, or the need to defend against it. Military science creates new machines and reconfigures old ones for new uses. Motivated as it is by specific needs, military science therefore defers certain questions of efficacy. To make room for invention and failure, it cannot definitely settle the question of whether or not a technology works.

As a military technology the bulletproof body therefore revives a set of questions about the empirical realities of occult practices that are easily elided by recent analyses of witchcraft as discourse. When these practices are understood as a local idiom for dealing with social conflict or the uncertainties of global capitalism, witchcraft studies need not take up the problem of "evidence." By contrast, it is hard to think of occult powers as primarily a metaphor for other issues when a young man offers to demonstrate how bullets will bounce from his body, or how he can catch mortar rounds in his teeth.

The materialism of claims to bulletproof the body has generated a slew of interpretations as to what bulletproofing actually is. In the tradition of this earlier anthropology of the occult, the focus is on how it persists even in the face of contrary evidence. Kamajors who were allegedly bulletproof did, in fact, die on the battlefield. At least a few died even in the public demonstrations meant to verify that they were bulletproof.[19]

Kamajors themselves had a variety of explanations for those moments when the occult technology of the bulletproof body fails, explanations that left the validity of bulletproofing itself intact. Violating any of the many taboos surrounding the immunization medicine would render the body vulnerable. At times this was explained as a direct consequence of the violation, akin to a compromised immune system felled by disease. At others it was cast as a punishment from God, a death or injury meted out for violating the society laws. These understandings, however, mirrored the classic explanation Edward Evans-Pritchard (1937) deduced from his work on Azande witchcraft. The fact that witchcraft often *doesn't* work is simply further proof that those who possess real occult knowledge are exceptionally powerful and dangerous.

When I asked a British officer in Sierra Leone what he made of the kamajors' claims to be bulletproof, he offered a two part analysis. The kamajors' faulty weapons and poor training, he said, made it virtually impossible that they could hit anything on the battlefield. Small wonder that they believe they can divert the path of bullets, he argued. And, he added, the incredibly high rate of HIV and AIDS makes them fearless. They have nothing to live for, anyway.[20]

Another popular explanation among expatriates, and even some elite Sierra Leoneans, was that drugs led young men to be reckless on the front line and believe that they were invincible. Cocaine, heroin, marijuana, and alcohol so damaged the brains of fighters from all sides that nothing they believed should be surprising. They were divorced from reality in ways that must have made anything seem possible.

A more sympathetic reading highlights the peculiar nature of a long war in which the casualty rate was nonetheless surprisingly low (which is not to downplay the horror of it's violence.) This was a war in which the goal of attacks on the enemy was as often as not to scare them off as to kill them. Securing weapons and rations from fleeing enemies was generally preferable to having to engage them in open, deadly combat. As Wlordaczyk puts it, this was a war in which firing one's weapon was less about hitting other people than it was about "making noise and displaying firepower" (2009, 115). If the goal of all that shooting wasn't to hit anyone, then it is those instances in which a young man *did* die on the battlefield which requires explanation, not the other way around.

Like the earlier studies of African occult belief, each of these explanations rests on an underlying assumption: that claims to make the body bulletproof might be "subjectively true" (they might make sense given the worldview of the kamajors) but they are "objectively false" (one cannot, in actuality, be made to repel bullets). What all of these explanations mask—including the kamajors' own—is the great deal of uncertainty on the part of many fighters as to what the hale they relied on at the front lines actually did, what its limits were, and how it was related to other forces. Questions of evidence and efficacy elide a great deal of nuance and ambiguity.

This includes the fact that there could be contradictions at the heart of the bulletproofing technology between the demands placed on the technology and the evidence of its efficacy. This was not a static belief system, but a dynamic, ever-changing, and experimental one, at least until it had reached its creative zenith in the aftermath of the SLPP restoration (when it was infrequently tested anyway). Until that point the need to combat the violent power of the RUF and the military generated a constant demand for innovation in protective or defensive powers. These innovations could be tested, and questions of evidence and efficacy were constantly asked about them. But "failure" never alleviated the magical thinking that the violence of war demands. The analogy that the initiators assembled in Kenema drew between the bulletproofing powers of initiation and the so-called Star Wars missile defense shield is apropos. For believers, the system is above all a technology that responds to the demands of new innovations in violence. That it might not work in a specific instance suggests the need for ever greater innovation, and in fact works to reinforce the sense of crisis and need.

This is the essence of modern magical military science: that the final judgment regarding its efficacy is deferred because the need for it is ever present and great. The kinds of violence to which it is a response are themselves always changing, always innovating. The upshot is that no one could speak with certainty about the power of the occult, where its efficacy really comes from, or whether it could always be relied upon. All they could comment on with certainty was the need for defensive innovations to respond to the escalating forms of violence around them. Most kamajors could, and did, speak with great confidence one moment about the bulletproofing technology and could in the next instant underscore its ambiguities. In this sense the way Claude Lévi-Strauss wrote of witchcraft rings at least partly true. Magic thinking and magical pronouncements are a kind of floating signifier, a way to bring into language and to being a reality (in this case the reality of meeting violence head on) that cannot otherwise be spoken or addressed (see Lévi-Strauss 1963; and the analysis of Lévi-Strauss in Siegel 2003).

The testimony before the Special Court regarding bulletproofing, a favorite topic of both witnesses and the prosecution, reflects this simultaneous certainty and ambiguity, a willingness to both act on the knowledge of military science and defer some questions about the efficacy of that technology. A prosecution witness describing his deployments from the Brookfields Hotel after the restoration of the SLPP government in 1998 on the one hand outlines how the immunization gave him great confidence and even the desire to go to war—and then suggests, on the other, that one did not always know if his purity had been compromised or if God (the ultimate source of his power) might abandon him at the front:

Q.: Let's go back. What did you do at the operation you mentioned at Makoro?

A.: We fought war, because, I mean, the immunization which I had never gave me rest. Whenever I heard about war, the more I became serious to go to war, because I knew I was immune. So I had a full confidence about going to war when I heard about it.

. . .

We were shaking because of this immunity. This immunity helped us greatly.

Q.: Describe what you would do while you would be fighting during these [*cut off*]

A.: I was with my AK Dragon [his weapon] and I had a charm. These charms helped me, and I had a special oils [*sic*] which I rubbed. So while in this operation, only what I needed was out of having ammunitions [running out of ammunition] and, when I had a weapon, I was really free and confident of fighting.

. . .

When I went through the process [of initiation], what was important was for me to be pure, as was always the case given the advice given us by the initiators that whenever you are pure in body—that means you have no contamination with a woman—you are free from the bullet. That was one of the major laws we had, and I kept the law into good consideration: to be clean always. So if at all there was any victim in the CDF, it was mainly because the law was spoiled.

Q.: Were you rightfully involved in testing: being shot at?

A.: Yeah, yeah, yeah. I was tested. The cloth I wore was tested—fired, and even myself when I went to war, the bullet never touched me. So I was confident that this immunity was true and realistic.

. . .

Q.: And you believe that you are alive today because of that protection?

A.: With the help of God, also. God is first and protection becomes second, but God worked through these protections.[21]

The witness, in other words, begins by maintaining that without question he was protected from the bullets of his enemies. But in response to the final question he introduces a caveat, a higher order of power that is more capricious and might trump his bulletproof status if it chooses to. This is a power over which he as the kamajor has no control, and no way to predict or appeal its decisions.

A second prosecution witness testified that a number of units were opting for reinitiation either because they were uncertain about the powers of their own initiators or because they did not know if they had inadvertently violated one of the laws.[22] Kamajors I interviewed about the need for continued protection also stressed the uncertainty over how long the protection lasted, and sometimes doubts about particular initiators. A CDF commander I spoke with about initiation admitted at one point that he had no idea if the technology actually worked. He had, however, seen things at the battlefront he could not explain. Better, he argued, to trust in the initiators. No harm was done if he did. Besides, he added, he didn't understand the "magic" of satellite phones either, but he certainly knew they worked.

In 2005 I met a Sierra Leonean in Tubmanburg, Liberia. The young man, nicknamed Protocol, had fought with the CDF and then LURD. He was now stuck in the Liberian countryside, unsure how to earn a living and unable to return home. He feared prosecution by the Special Court, and in any case was unwilling to go back empty-handed. For the past six months, Protocol had been hearing voices. Most of his days he now spent wandering Tubmanburg, searching vainly for the author of the words circulating in his head. At one of his more lucid moments, he told me that he hopes Mama Munda can help him. She initiated him into the kamajor society, and he suspects—but isn't sure—that he broke a society law. "I don't know if it is the society law that affects me. I went to the psychiatric hospital. They kept me for a few days, then discharged me and said I'm OK now. I'm not supposed to touch a body, but I touched a body. An accident happened, and they brought the body. One of my brothers died. A kamajor. We washed the body, we buried him and from that point I started hearing voices but I don't see the people."

Again, these stories suggest that perhaps we need to reverse the usual course of explanation for occult practice and begin with the problem of violence. If bulletproofing is an experimental technology, a military science, then the question of its efficacy is one that is constantly deferred. As the initiators in Kenema put it, every time there is an advance in offensive military technology (and there is *always* an advance in military technology) there is a subsequent process of advancing the science of defense. These innovations proceed in fits and starts, and they proceed through experimentation. Some work, others do not. Most people will

48. Protocol on the streets of Tubmanburg, Liberia, 2005.

admit that they can't be sure. But one thing is never called into question: not the "system," but the need. Violence demands invention, and it demands magic. "Does it work?" is a question we can ask of reactive forces. "What does it do?" is a question for war machines.

"Six Million Dollars' Worth of Ju Ju"

The occult dimensions of this war were further animated by fantasies of otherness and of the power in otherness. The inexplicable powers that "they" brought to the battlefield were always being imitated and matched. The result was a mimetic vortex in which all kinds of parties to the conflict laid claim to powers they did not understand but felt they needed to harness to address the problems that violence posed. As Michael Taussig explored in his study of colonial and postcolonial terror in the Amazon (1987), the presence of the "savage other" produced all manner of extraordinary violence.

From the beginning of the war there was a great deal of discussion in Sierra Leone about the occult practices that made Burkinabe mercenaries especially fearsome and strong. Liberians fighting with the RUF and with ULIMO were said to have access to strength, some of it derived from cannibalism, that made them especially dangerous. The most potent medicines for making the body immune to enemy fire were derived from the Koran but came by way of Malian ritual specialists. The Nigerian soldiers who made up most of the ECOMOG force were credited (or blamed) with uncommon powers for theft, deception, and intrigue that ranged from looting much of the country's wealth to stealing the penises of Sierra Leonean male youth through witchcraft. American gangsta rappers like Tupac Shakur or film icons like the Terminator or Rambo were assigned extraordinary powers that one might harness through imitation, a kind of sympathetic magic very much rooted in fantasies of Otherness.

But most intriguing were the fantasies that this war's combatants and their bulletproof bodies gave rise to in white participant observers, participants who tried to strike an ironic but profitable stance vis-à-vis occult technologies.

The journalist Elizabeth Rubin, in a profile of Executive Outcomes, describes how EO personnel and other white South Africans in Sierra

Leone in the mid-1990s encouraged rumors that they used occult technologies to defeat the rebels or that, as white foreigners, they possessed extrahuman capabilities (1997, 51). Interviewed by another journalist, Corbus Claassens, a white South African employed by EO in Sierra Leone, described EOs plan to attack an RUF stronghold:

> We were also going to use psychology against them. We would only fight at night using blacked-out gunships flying in on night vision, music, and psy-ops from loudspeakers. The FLIR (forward looking, infra red) technology illuminates body heat so no matter where the rebels ran they would glow in the dark through our scopes. We would pop them off one at a time and where they least expected it. At night in their camps, rebels would wake up with their comrades exploding into sprays of blood. They would never sleep. We knew the minds of the rebels. It would be Ju Ju . . . six million dollars' worth of Ju Ju. (Quoted in Pelton 2002, 28–29)

What these discourses of the occult seem to suggest is a belief on the part of these white soldiers that they see through the fantasies that the occult creates in black Africans, and that such false consciousness can be put to work: "We were also going to use psychology against them." But what is fascinating in Claassens's quote is the way he himself mystifies his own power in response to the mystifications of others: "It would be Ju Ju . . . six million dollars' worth of Ju Ju." At the same time that the "hyperrationalism" of FLIR technology and painted helicopter gunships were deployed to rend the veil of the rebels' sense of security, there is an acknowledgment that this violence, too, is mystified. It is military science, an address to the profound requirements of war and violence that demands magical thinking even on the part of those who would simultaneously deny that such things are ever possible.

Both wartime and postwar discourses are shot through with such rhetoric. When I interviewed an investigator with the Truth and Reconciliation Commission in 2003, a young European law student responsible for collecting testimonies regarding the CDF, he complained that the kamajors were not particularly responsive to TRC personnel. At every turn, he argued, kamajor combatants would hide behind claims of society secrets and society laws as a way to avoid telling what they knew about CDF atrocities during the war. But, he argued, the TRC had its own techniques for piercing through these occult prohibitions. Along the way it had uncovered all kinds of activities on the part of the CDF, things about which he could not speak because like the kamajors, the TRC had its own secret knowledge. What happened at Base Zero "is still shrouded in secrecy—or in our case, confidentiality."

During the CDF trial at the Special Court, a former kamajor initiate's refusal to disclose certain aspects of the initiation process prompted two of the judges to repeatedly assert that there could be no secrets before the court, that nothing a witness said in closed session could possibly have any ramifications for him regardless of the oaths he took to guard the secrets of a secret society. The court's powers of protection were construed as supernaturally powerful—precisely because they (unlike local occult belief) were so cleareyed and hyperrational.[23] A few weeks later, the third justice made essentially the same claim to magical omniscience in open court: "Nothing can be hidden, you know, before the law."[24]

What we are left with is an intriguing possibility: that it is impossible in any cultural context to confront the problem of violence without recourse to magical thinking. The innovations that happen in the war zone inevitably become reactive forces: the power to make the body bulletproof is eventually seized on as a profit-making tool at war's end. The need for postwar justice eventually becomes the reactive force of a mythical all-seeing law. But at certain moments, in response to a definite need, there is the space to defer the question of efficacy and undertake radical experiments. Violence becomes the occasion to invent.

conclusion

A LABORATORY OF THE FUTURE

"IT IS ALL TOO EASY to idealize a social upheaval which takes place in some other country than one's own," wrote Edmund Wilson in his 1971 introduction to *To the Finland Station*, his history of European revolution ([1971] 2003, xxi). The social upheaval of the Mano River War may be hard to idealize, but the rise of a community defense militia in rural Sierra Leone, and its successful defense of a democratically elected government, does represent a certain ideal for forces on both the global political right and left. For the latter, the kamajors might be seen as a model of a nonstate social movement prepared to defend itself against the predations of a state military and a corrupt governing elite. For the former, the CDF could be read as a popular defense of neoliberal institutions of governance, a devolution of security functions from the state to the people themselves.

Each of these idealizations is in some sense correct, and in some sense wildly mistaken. The full trajectory of the movement as I have covered it in this book should, I hope, offer a more nuanced and troubling understanding of violent mobilizations under the conditions created by today's regimes of global capital.

Therein lies the larger lesson of the kamajors, the CDF, and LURD. A neoconservative push to outsource violence and security is an integral part of the discourse on global security today. The movements I detailed in this book should offer a warning. Certainly they can tell us a great deal about the logical endpoint of a community mobilization of young men as the agents of security in an unstable political atmosphere. The Mano River region is a laboratory of the future for a certain kind of security privatization. I conclude this book, then, by returning to a point made in the introduction. There is a great deal to be understood about the world after the Cold War, after 11 September 2001, and after the Global War on Terror, by looking to the lessons of the Mano River War.

49. LURD fighter with antiaircraft gun, Voinjama, 2002.

The end of the global Cold War coincided with the outbreak of war in West Africa. To many, the simultaneity of these events was not incidental. In the absence of superpower manipulation, this narrative goes, there is no longer anything to check Africans' primitive tribal animosities. Such thinking has been critiqued as "New Barbarism" (Richards 1996) and a new evolutionism (Lutz 2001). Whatever it is called, the result is the same: Africa is alleged to have noticeably, and violently, departed from the modern world.

There is a certain irony in the fact that as West Africa was being written off in the 1990s Western popular imaginary as hopelessly outside modernity, scholars were making a more and more forceful case that modernity isn't conceivable without it. Modernity as a temporal, intellectual, and aesthetic construct in many ways begins with the ruptures of the slave trade (Gilroy 1993) and the navigational advances required to move African bodies across the southern Atlantic (Seed 1995). Events in the colonial "periphery" are increasingly seen as keys to understanding everything from modern sexuality (Stoler 1995) to Hegelian philosophy (Buck-Morss 2000). At the very least, it now seems that the origins of modernity—in any of the various ways it might be conceived—lie in flows across and around the Atlantic, a world of intercontinental connections from which coastal West Africa cannot be excluded (Thornton 1992).

There is further irony in the fact that those facets of African sociality most often cited as evidence of Africa's premodernity are, in reality, the most modern. Whether kinship structure (Piot 1996), gift exchange (Piot 1999), ritual (Shaw 2002), occult practice (Comaroff and Comaroff 1993, 1999; Geschiere 1997), government corruption (Bond 2006), or even Yorùbá identity (Matory 1999), the particularities of Africans' lived experience is more often indicative of a global connectedness than a timeless isolation.

What was true of West Africa's relation to modernity is no less so of its relation to the postmodern. Rather than constituting a space outside, there may be no location more identifiably "postmodern" than the Mano River region of Sierra Leone and Liberia, no people living a postmodern reality more concretely.

Media images of child combatants in Liberia carrying Mickey Mouse lunchboxes in one hand and AK-47s in the other virtually beg to be labeled "postmodern," though most often by doing so we invoke Mad Max more than Fredric Jameson. Yet the profound sense of rupture, the erasure of any separation between "high" and "low" culture, the seemingly random coupling of all manner of images in a depthless pastiche are certainly consistent with Jameson's definition of the successor to classical modernism (1984). But these are only the most visible (if hardest to comprehend) signifiers of the complex ways in which the region has become enmeshed in the logics and logistics of late global capital.

One could trace any number of other connections between the wars in Sierra Leone and Liberia and postmodern global developments: the rise of neoliberal economic policies and their implementation by international financial institutions like the World Bank and International Monetary Fund; hyperefficient commodity chains that export diamonds and timber from West Africa and import drugs and arms; the globalization of new ideas of accountability and justice epitomized by international criminal courts; the rising importance of diaspora communities and their complex relations to homelands and host communities. I followed a few of these threads in the preceding chapters. But it is in the configuration of the labor of war, and the waging of war as labor, that West Africa might be at the leading edge of global developments.

I conclude this project, then, by making explicit what we might learn by taking seriously the postmodern turn as we see it manifested in West Africa. Even a cursory reading of today's military journals, Pentagon policy papers, and the writings of security theorists suggests that the large troop deployments that characterized the United States wars in Iraq and Afghanistan are not the future of war.[1] Despite the criticism of Secretary of Defense Donald Rumsfeld's minimalist strategy for the Iraq occupation, there is an ever-greater emphasis put on networks, swarming, indirect and counterinsurgency warfare over the conventional models of massive, centralized, and unilateral military operations. "The mission" of state armies is increasingly to deploy indirectly, working with and through more knowledgeable and better positioned surrogate forces and doing so in a way that erodes the divide between war and peace. U.S. Army colonel Gregory Wilson, in a 2006 article on counterinsurgency in *Military Review*, argued that in a successful counterinsurgency operation small units of American Special Forces should work in peacetime and "invisibly" through local forces: "Therefore, the US WOT [war on terrorism] strategy should emphasize working directly 'through, by, and with' indigenous forces and building their capacity to conduct effective operations against common enemies" (2006, 38). The trend is toward finding local partners and outsourcing the labor of war. The language of the 2006 U.S. Department of Defense *Quadrennial Defense Review Report* (QDR) echoes Wilson's—and makes it the "official" view of the United States military.[2]

Two points are crucial here. First, the outsourcing of security envisioned in what Martin Shaw (2005) calls "the new Western way of war" is partly predicated on the idea that local forces are better able to understand appropriate cultural logics of violence. For example, John Arquilla, a professor of defense analysis at the Naval Postgraduate School and one of the chief theorists of netwar (networked warfare), has argued that the United States military should adopt the strategy of recruiting local "pseudo-gangs" that the British used against anticolonial movements like the Mau Mau insurgency in Kenya.[3] Such surrogate forces, the argument goes, are effective because they fight the way the enemy fights. This mirroring approach to counterinsurgency is rendered as military doctrine in the *US Army and Marine Corps Counterinsurgency Field Manual*: "By mid-tour, U.S. forces should be working closely with local forces, training or supporting them and building an indigenous security capability. The natural tendency is to create forces in a U.S. image. This is a mistake. Instead, local HN [host nation] forces need to mirror the enemy's capabilities and seek to supplant the insurgent's role" (United States Department of the Army 2007, 298–99).[4] Local forces, according to the more radical strains of this thinking, are not only better culturally equipped but are free of the legal or moral constraints that prevent the United States military from effectively combating insurgents. This has become something of a cause for the most conservative (but influential) voices in security analysis since 2001. Writers like Michael Rubin of the American Enterprise Institute, journalist and theorist Robert Kaplan, and Richard Perle, head of the Defense Policy Board, argue that it is the nature of asymmetrical warfare as waged by Al Qaeda and other networks to "augment their power relative to Western countries simply by eschewing legal responsibilities" (M. Rubin 2007, 4). Bound by a commitment to the United Nations, the Geneva Conventions, and other international protocols for the conduct of war, the United States and allied state armies, these theorists argue, are hampered in their ability defeat nonstate armies. Local surrogate forces, by contrast, face no such restrictions and are therefore considerably more effective (not to mention cheaper).

The second key point I wish to emphasize here is that the local partners in question might be, but are not necessarily, the official militaries of recognized states. Although Wilson's case study is the Armed Forces of the Philippines, it is worth noting that he repeatedly speaks of alliances with "indigenous or surrogate" forces rather than with allied national militaries. The same holds true for the 2006 *QDR* and the *Counterinsurgency Field Manual*. In fact, the abstract language of partnerships, surrogates, and indigeneity appears throughout both official military publications and the language of security-sector strategists and observers. This is not terribly surprising, given that the United States government views the security services of a number of so-called rogue nations and failed states as complicit in the operations of nonstate networks like Al Qaeda. The upshot is that a great deal of the investment of United States military resources is currently dedicated to the cultivation of local forces, with no a priori assumption that the army of the state is the force most suitable for that aid. What this amounts to in cases where the official state army is not the most reliable or desirable partner for the United States military is the militarization of other sociopolitical formations, or the creation of new, militarized sodalities.

The Awakening movement in Iraq is the most high-profile recent exemplar. Begun in the summer of 2005 in Anbar Province, Awakening groups amount to the arming of local militias to patrol neighborhoods, guard sensitive infrastructure, and hunt insurgent fighters and cells. United States military personnel in Iraq have referred to Awakening units as "security contractors" and even as "little Iraqi Blackwaters" (the private security company infamous for the September 2007 massacre at Nisour Square in Baghdad).[5] By the end of 2007, there were estimated to be between sixty-five thousand and eighty thousand members of such ad hoc militarized formations.[6] Most often these Awakening units are organized along ethnic or "tribal" lines, or what amounts to the arming of sectarian factions to fight other ethnically affiliated insurgent groups. In his summary of the lessons learned from the United States military's engagement with Iraq's social structures, Lieutenant Colonel Michael Eisenstadt writes that if Iraq is ever stabilized, it will be in large measure do to the "leveraging of Iraq's tribes and tribal networks" in mobilizations such as the Anbar Awakening (2007, 29).

There is every reason to think that these mobilizations, working in conjunction with or on behalf of small units of United States security operatives, will be the primary actors in counterinsurgency operations of the future. As the administration of President Barack Obama shifts the emphasis from the occupation of Iraq to the war in Afghanistan, it, too, has put a great deal of support behind local militia forces, in this case known as the Afghan Public Protection Force (APPF).[7] Understanding the subcontracted mode of warfare represented by the Awakening movement and the APPF will be critical to understanding the foreseeable future of global security—and the new common ground of social and military science.

The militia movements with which I worked in Sierra Leone and Liberia and which I analyze in these chapters are exactly the kind of indigenous force envisioned as partners in the current strategic thinking of United States military planners and commentators. They were without question the faction most "loyal" to the democratically elected (and friendly to the United States) government after 1996—certainly more so than the state army, which was notoriously corrupt and widely known to be colluding with the rebels. These same fighters made up a significant proportion of the forces which overthrew Charles Taylor in Liberia, ridding the region of a despot whom the United States regarded as a destabilizing presence with financial links to "terrorist" groups like Al Qaeda (see Farah 2004). As social actors in the local cultural landscape, these militia fighters had the respect and support of local communities (at least in the beginning). The "kamajor" was an already recognizable figure, literally and figuratively, whose role it was to protect villages from outside threats. Kamajors were a logical choice around which to base a counterinsurgency strategy, well positioned to act on the kind of "ethnographic intelligence" seen as key to the new way of war.[8] What's more, these fighters could by definition "mirror the enemy's capabilities" (in the language of the Army counterinsurgency manual). Everything from their occult powers to their particular modes of violence was crafted in response to the perceived threats posed by the rebels and the mutinous army.

Perhaps even more important, these irregular forces were structured along exactly the lines that the network theorists of war envision as

50. "War don don" ("War is over") monument outside Kono, 2003.

most effective for counterinsurgency operations. The militia combined its "ethnographic intelligence" with a decentralized organization that allowed it to mobilize quickly wherever necessary. A truly grassroots organization, it materialized as needed throughout the country in response to specific threats. Though the CDF became more institutionalized as the Sierra Leone war went on, local units never lost the capability to act independently, move quickly, and adjust themselves to rapidly changing circumstances and new threats. As a community-based outfit structured according to an existing social logic, the CDF could be wherever it needed to be. What the CDF amounted to was the militarization of everyday life and local communities such that they could be quickly mobilized and deployed as necessary in the interest of security.

Recent trends in the reorganization of global security are laying the groundwork for continued mobilizations of exactly the kind represented by the Mano River War. Beyond developments like those in Afghanistan and Iraq, we are witnessing a more generic discourse on African security that would like to see so-called African solutions to African problems. In other words, local and regional forces, with minimal advising, financial and logistical support from the United States, the United Nations, and contracted private security companies are increasingly tasked with war fighting, peace enforcing, and peacekeeping. If experience is anything to judge by, these forces will not receive the levels of support necessary to operate effectively even as the demands on them grow. The upshot is that they will have to work with local surrogate forces like those I discuss in this book. In fact, since it is in keeping with the United States military's culturalist turn to work with local surrogates, it is easy to imagine United States and European trainers and security advisors encouraging African partner forces to do just that. Jeremy Keenan in his review of the United States military's new Africa Command writes that "the indications are that AFRICOM's mission will be outsourced to 'contractors'," notably private military companies (2008, 20; see also McFate 2008, 118–19). No doubt he is correct, but it is the subcontractors of war like these militia irregulars who will likely do most of the fighting. More than any other region of the world, the temptation to outsource war will likely prevail in Africa. In the two-decade history of the Mano River War, we see that project's devastating effects.

notes

preface

1. The phrase *war don don* in Sierra Leonean Krio translates as "the war is over."

2. Ron Lieber, "Minimizing Your Own Exposure to Risk," *New York Times*, 20 September 2008, C1.

3. Stephen Lubkemann (2008, 27–29, 103–9) makes this argument as part of a more detailed history of Africanist anthropology's examinations of war on the continent.

4. This is a critique Veena Das has made of the anthropology of violence in general, at least as it relates to non–North American contexts. See Das (2007, 240–41).

5. *Warscapes* is a term I borrow from Carolyn Nordstrom (1997), who in turn added it to the various regimes of "-scapes" proposed by Arjun Appadurai (1996) for understanding the flows that constitute the modern world.

6. See Gberie (2005, 146–47) for a critique of anthropological "deeper cultural readings" of the war in Sierra Leone, especially those extrapolated from work in a single locale.

introduction: War Machines

1. The Special Court for Sierra Leone (SCSL) was the war crimes tribunal backed by the United Nations and set up in the aftermath of the war to prosecute the leaders of various factions. For more on the court, and in particular the CDF trial from which this transcript was taken, see Kelsall (2009) and the website of the SCSL, http://www.sc-sl.org/ (available online as of 15 May 2009).

2. From transcript of *The Prosecutor of the Special Court v. Sam Hinga Norman, Moinina Fofana, Allieu Kondewa* (SCSL-2004–14-T), 27 January 2006, 95–96. This exchange was in English.

3. At this point in the war the military had joined forces with the rebels of the RUF to form the People's Army. As will become clear in the chapters to follow, this meant that the kamajors were a pro-government militia fighting against the official army of the state.

4. Testimony of witness TF2–022, case no. SCSL-2004–14-T, 18 February 2005, 46–47.

5. As François Cusset argues in his overview of "French theory" in the United States, it is exactly this erasure of the political critique of capital in Deleuze's and Guattari's writing (as well as that of Derrida, Foucault, and others) that has allowed them to be parodied as removed from real world considerations. See Cusset (2008, xvi, 160).

6. Roitman actually distances herself somewhat from such a reading. Though she cites Deleuze and Guattari at various points, she also insists that when she writes of "deterritorializing practice" in the Chad Basin she is "limiting [herself] to situations where the ultimate reference is the nation-state" and "refraining from conclusions as to its significance as 'nomadology', an alternative mode of representation (or even non-representation) and power" (1998, 310, n. 28).

7. This is also the mode of authority that Hardt and Negri explore in the first section of *Multitude*, and that Foucault introduced in his 1975–76 lectures at the Collège de France (2003), the latter being one of Mbembe's inspirations. For a more ethnographically oriented examination of the blurred boundary between war and peace, see the essays in Richards (2005a).

8. Jeffrey Gettleman, "Mai Mai Fighters Third Piece in Congo's Violent Puzzle," *New York Times*, 21 November 2008, A13.

9. Nina Bernstein, "The Strategists Fight a War about the War," *New York Times*, 6 April 2003, Week in Review, 5.

10. Robert M. Gates, United States secretary of defense, quoted in Thom Shanker, "Command for Africa Established by Pentagon," *New York Times*, 5 October 2008, 10. See also the "About AFRICOM" section of the command's website, http://www.africom.mil/.

11. Quoted in Shanker, "Command for Africa Established by Pentagon," 10. See also William McMichael, "AfriCom Goes Operational," *Army Times*, 2 October 2008.

12. According to Weizman's interviews, IDF theorists were also reading the work of anthropologists Gregory Bateson and Clifford Geertz (Weizman 2006, 10). I am grateful to David Giles for drawing my attention to Weizman's work on Deleuze and the IDF.

13. Apparently this Deleuzian contingent in the IDF suffered a severe blow in a general backlash against postmodern theory in Israeli security circles. The devastating violence Israeli troops unleashed in the later incursions in Nablus can apparently be attributed to the rise of old-fashioned modernists within the IDF who opposed what they saw as the epistemological confusion of military postmodernism. I am grateful to Eyal Ben-Ari for conversations on this point.

14. For additional examples, see Cusset (2008, 291) on new social movements of the Left and their readings of Deleuze and Guattari.

15. On the importance of the philosophical context in which Deleuze in particular is writing, see Hardt (1993, xviii–xix).

16. Among the most notable critiques are those of Harvey (1990, 350–52) on actual schizophrenics, Spivak (1988) on actual subalterns, and Young (1995, 172–73) on actual nomads.

chapter 1: The Mano River War

1. Paul Richards, who has worked extensively in both Sierra Leone and Liberia, has similarly written of the "Mano River conflicts" in, for example, Richards (2005a).

2. The most comprehensive histories of the past two decades in the region include, for Sierra Leone, Gberie (2005), Keen (2005), the No Peace without Justice Conflict Mapping Report (Smith, Gambette, and Longley 2004), and the pieces collected in the volume edited by Ibrahim Abdullah (2004). Abdullah (1998), Patrick Muana (1997), and Paul Richards (1996) have each written excellent accounts of the early phases of the war. The website Focus on Sierra Leone is an extraordinary archive of events and commentary from the period in Sierra Leone from 1994 to 2001, which at the time of this writing was still available online (http://www.focus-on-sierra-leone.co.uk/). Among the most complete histories of the early phases of the war in Liberia are Ellis (1999), Huband (1998), Levitt (2005), and Williams (2002). Both countries conducted truth and reconciliation commissions, which offer historical narratives of these wars, though in neither case are these records complete. (The Sierra Leone TRC records are available online at http://www.sierra-leone.org/TRCDocuments.html; the Liberian TRC is ongoing at the time of this writing, but its archives to date are available online at https://www.trcofliberia.org/.) The same is true of the Special Court for Sierra Leone, which collected years of testimony, much of which is available online (http://www.sc-sl.org/).

3. These included the Firestone Company, which holds an infamous rubber concession at Harbel, not far from the Liberian capital.

4. For more on the ECOWAS decision and the deployment of ECOMOG, see Aboagye (1999) and Adebajo (2002).

5. These incidents are detailed in Gberie (2005, 58–59); Human Rights Watch, "The Cycle of Abuse," 21 October 1991 (www.hrw.org/); and Musa and Musa (1993, 21).

6. Keen (2005, 38–39), Muana (1997, 80), and Richards (1996, 8) catalogue a number of other factors prompting Taylor's withdrawal of Liberian forces from the RUF. These include tensions within the RUF over Liberian fighters' execution of occult specialists, conflict between Sankoh and Taylor over payments to mercenaries, and the amount of looting in which Liberian forces were engaged.

7. The Bo uprising is described in detail in Gberie (2005, 87–88) and Richards (1996, 152–55; 2005b, 388–92).

8. David Keen (2005, 141–47) describes these attacks; see also Gberie (2005, 88–89).

9. The AFRC is sometimes listed as the Armed Forces Ruling Council.

10. One of the more interesting outsiders' accounts of the environment in Sierra Leone during the junta period is Voeten (2002).

11. See Harris (1999) and Moran (2006, 101–23) for analyses of Taylor's electoral victory.

12. Gberie (2005, 121) has suggested that the main justification for the attack was an effort by Sam "Maskita" Bockarie, then the RUF field commander, to free Foday Sankoh from Pademba Road Prison.

13. Howe uses the example of the Ukranian presence in Sierra Leone to underscore just how cynical—and profitable—wars in West Africa are to outsiders. At a time when an estimated three hundred Ukranians were fighting on behalf of the

RUF, the Ukranian government was selling attack helicopters to the Sierra Leone government. See Howe (2001, 81).

14. Two extraordinary eyewitness accounts document the 6 January invasion. Omoru David's photocopied booklet *The Coming of the Killers* and Sorious Samura's film *Cry Freetown* record each author's harrowing experiences during the invasion and cover in detail the heavy damage to the city and the activities of the various factions.

15. For more on the West Side Boys, see Utas and Jörgel (2008).

16. For Human Rights Watch accounts, see, for example, the series of media statements cataloged over the summer of 2000 at http://www.hrw.org/ (accessible as of 30 June 2009).

17. The extent to which United States officials were aware of the redirection of resources to LURD is unclear, though it seems highly unlikely that this was unknown.

18. 30 November 30 1996 was the date on which the Abidjan Accords were signed. The SCSL website includes a more detailed history of the court, background on the cases, and at least some of the transcripts of court testimony. See http://www.sc-sl.org/. For an in-depth analysis of the CDF trial and the workings of the Special Court, see Kelsall (2006, 2009).

chapter 2: Hunters, Lumpens, and War Boys

1. "The Time of History and the Times of the Gods" is the title of Dipesh Chakrabarty's essay on "the problems a secular subject like history faces in handling imaginations in which gods, spirits, or the supernatural have agency in the world" (1997, 35).

2. This narrative is paraphrased.

3. There are a number of variations in spelling and pronunciation of the original term, reflecting dialect differences in spoken Mende: *kamajoi*, *kamajo*, *kamajoh*, and *kamasoi* (sing.) and *kamajoisia*, *kamajesia*, or *kamasesia* (pl.). Anthropologists suggest different English equivalents. Patrick Muana (1997) proposes that a more accurate translation would read "a past master at doing mysterious things." Muana gives the Mende origins of the term as follows: "[T]he word itself comprises two components: Kama and Joi. 'Kama' is usually used in an adjectival position as in Kama kama hinda: 'something mysterious'. 'Joi' is the clipped form of the word sowei meaning a 'past master, an expert'. With consonant mutation in southern and southwestern Mende dialects, 's' is mutated in intervocalic positions to 'J'" (78, n. 2). Caspar Fithen translates the name as "master of mysteries" (1999, 11, n. 1) and Doug Henry describes it as the combination of terms for "wonder" or "marvel" and that for "something hidden" or "capable of disappearing" (2000, 39).

4. *Mande* refers to a historical community of related languages and ethnic and cultural groups that span West Africa. Mende is understood to be one of many Mande subgroupings. (See Alie 1990, 6–9; Fyfe 1962, 6).

5. As Moran (1995) has argued, this excessiveness can at times be usefully co-

opted or deployed by men. This might help to explain the use of the markers of the feminine—dresses, wigs—by male fighters, especially on the Liberian side of the border.

6. John Nunley in a detailed ethnographic study of Freetown Ode-lay troupes puts the earliest records of hunting masquerades in Freetown at 1838. See Nunley (1987, 27).

7. Ibrahim Abdullah and Ismail Rashid have done the most extensive research on this political youth culture over the past four decades. See, in particular, Abdullah (2002, 2005) and Rashid (2004).

8. Muana (1997, 92), for example, notes the role of *tutunjiangamui*, or spies operating at night, and my own conversations with fighters sometimes covered the ambush as a Mende technique for both hunting and war.

9. For more on Lavalie, see Abdullah and Muana (1998, 185), Henry (2000, 38), and Reno (2003, 2004).

10. Testimony before the Special Court, my own interviews, and the work of a number of other researchers underscore the importance of recruitment in the IDP camps. See, for example, the testimony of Albert Nallo, 11 March 2005, 50, lines 13–18, and Ishmael Koroma, 22 February 2006, 24–34, 38, as well as accounts in Henry (2000) and Peters and Richards (1997).

11. For more on the chieftaincy system in Sierra Leone, see Abraham (1978), Fanthorpe (1998, 2001, 2005), P. Jackson (2007), Tangri (1976), and Wylie (1969).

12. *Ndogboyosoi* is a Mende "bush devil" (see Gittins 1987). The Ndogboyosoi affair and other local conflicts are described in greater detail in Gberie (2005, 66), Kandeh (1999), Keen (2005, 18), Massaquoi and Fortune (2000), and Richards (1996, 22).

13. For other examples, see Hoffman (2007b).

14. In fact many of these restrictions aimed to keep separate male and female domains. A number of them resonated with Poro restrictions or those of other men's associations.

15. See Ferme and Hoffman (2004) for more on the significance of the phrase *baa woteh* and its relevance in the militia's ethical discourse.

16. The Poro is only one, though the most widespread and significant, of the men's secret societies. Others, including the Wunde and Humui, generally serve more limited roles. The female equivalent of the Poro is the Sande, which is discussed in Bledsoe (1984), Boone (1986), Ferme (2001b), and Phillips (1995).

17. See Douglas (1986). I have in mind here Paul Richards's writings on the RUF (especially 1996) and the work of two of Richards's occasional collaborators: Krijn Peters (2007), whose excellent study of the RUF is similarly neo-Durkheimian and Douglassian, and Caspar Fithen (1999), whose ethnography of the diamond trade during the war offers invaluable insights into the early days of the kamajors and the CDF. See also Fithen and Richards (2005) and Peters and Richards (1997).

18. Transcript of testimony before the Special Court in the case against the CDF (case no. SCSL-03-14-I), 14 June 2005, 31, lines 22–23.

19. I have done a more detailed analysis of Iron's report in Hoffman (2007b).

20. Transcript of testimony in case SCSL-4–14-T, 3 June 2004, 12–13.

chapter 3: States of Conflict

1. This appears to be a typographic error. President Kabbah was elected in 1996.

2. Again, the use of this date is confusing. The significant event in November 1996 was the signing of the peace agreement in Abidjan between Kabbah and the RUF leader Foday Sankoh.

3. As Richards notes, many of these activities were in violation of the cease-fire declared to facilitate the Abidjan peace talks. See Richards (1999, 436).

4. Sierra Leone Broadcasting Service broadcast, 25 May 1997, as quoted in Abdullah (1998, 231).

5. I write more extensively about Mohammed in chapter 4 and in Hoffman (2007a, 2008).

6. Norman's plans for the postjunta period were relayed to me by a number of persons close to him and were also the subject of Special Court testimony. See, for example, the testimony in case SCSL 03–14-I, witness TF2–008, 16 November 2004, 87–88; witness TF2–199, 23 November 2004, 109–10; and Albert Nallo (TF2–014), 11 March 2005, 29; as well as closed-session testimony from witnesses at Base Zero, where Norman apparently discussed his plans for the CDF publicly.

7. See Bøås and Dunn (2007, 13) and Keen (2005, 65) for more extensive critique of the "lumpen" hypothesis.

8. The quintessential ethnographic account of this moment and its ruptures is Michael Taussig's *The Devil and Commodity Fetishism in South America* (1980).

9. It is worth noting that my characterization of West Africa's condition of real labor subsumption runs against the grain, both as Marx understood capital's progression and as it has been subsequently interpreted. The model for labor's real subsumption was, for Marx, the factory floor. And it is advanced industrial capital in the Fordist and post-Fordist mode which most theorists have in mind when they suggest that "this passage [to real subsumption] has only come to be generalized in the most completely capitalist countries in our time" (Hardt 1995, 38). What's more, the forms of labor most commonly associated with the Mano River region's economic life (farming and mining) correspond to earlier moments in capital's development as articulated by Marx and subsequent thinkers. At this point, however, it would be difficult to argue that the Mano River region—or any part of the African continent—is somehow "less completely capitalist" than any other part of the world (a point made forcefully by Bond [2006]; Ferguson [2006]; and Piot [2010]).

10. This is an example more fully explored in Ferme and Hoffman (2004, 80–81).

11. For one such account from Bo, see the Special Court testimony of witness TF2–008, 16 November 2004, 114–15.

12. The "greed versus grievance" formulation began with economists Paul Collier and Anke Hoeffler (2000) and is explored, among many other sources, in the chapters collected in Berdal and Malone (2000) and in Reno (2004).

13. Massalley was the best known of the Pujehun CDF commanders. Prior to the war he was a driver for an international NGO, a respectable position but hardly one that would make him a leading figure in the region.

14. Andrea Elliott, "A Call to Jihad, Answered in America: F.B.I. Investigates Ties between Somali-Americans and Faction Linked to Al-Qaeda," *New York Times*, 12 July 2009, A1, A14–15.

chapter 4: Big Men, Small Boys

1. As I have argued elsewhere, this is the fallacy at the heart of the Special Court for Sierra Leone's accusations against the CDF—that "traditional" mechanisms of control were superseded in war time by the need for a military hierarchy of command. See Hoffman (2007b), from which parts of this chapter are taken.

2. This idea of youth in Africa today as a kind of social stagnation is explored more fully in Barrett (2004), Vigh (2006), and the essays collected in Christiansen, Utas, and Vigh (2006).

3. Testimony of Samuel Hinga Norman, 30 January 2006, 55, line 29, and 56, line 1.

4. See chapters 5 and 6 for more on Jah Kingdom and the Brookfields Hotel in general.

5. For a more extended discussion of these overlapping developments across West Africa in the post–Cold War, neoliberial period, see Piot (2010).

6. The DDR process for adults included a cash payout for weapons, whereas the procedure for children did not. The result was that many militia leaders and other local elites attempted to enter children in the adult DDR program. For more on this dynamic and what it suggests about conceptions of child soldiers and childhood in general, see Hoffman (2003).

7. The SSD (previously called the Internal Security Unit and known colloquially as "Siaka Stevens' Dogs") was a major force in the suppression of student political movements in the 1970s and 1980s (see Conteh-Morgan and Dixon-Fyle 1999, 114; Cox 1976, 216; Kpundeh 2004, 92; Rashid 2004, 75–78).

8. See transcript of the Special Court for Sierra Leone, 11 May 2006, 29–30.

9. Testimony of Albert Nallo (translated from Krio), SCSL transcript, 10 March 2005, 68–69.

10. Quote given to a Human Rights Watch investigator.

11. This perception that I was a journalist covering the war was one I confronted repeatedly over the course of my work on the region's militias. The distinction between ethnographer and journalist was one that mattered little to the people with whom I interacted.

12. Nunie claimed in his own Special Court testimony that he received the title of general from Maxwell Khobe of ECOMOG (see SCSL transcript, 11 May 2006, 65). No one I have spoken to about Nunie backed up this claim, and a number of people asserted that Nunie simply insisted on being referred to as "General Joe."

chapter 5: The Barracks

1. "Ghetto" is the Liberian equivalent of the Sierra Leonean pote described earlier.

2. The spatialization and organization at work here is a gendered one. Although I do not deal with it in this chapter, one facet of the processes I describe is the way in which women's labor is increasingly organized into a "service" economy. In the barracks, "female" is defined by the performance of duties that sustain the barracks itself. Although employing different terminology, Chris Coulter (2005, 2009), Doug Henry (2000, 2005), Mary Moran (1995, 2006), Susan Shepler (2002), and Mats Utas (2005) have each done work on some of the important gender and sexuality questions posed by the Mano River War.

3. This is a configuration described in particularly graphic detail by Lorna Rhodes (2004) in her work on maximum-security prisons in the United States.

4. Although mining is obviously the starkest example, the same argument could be said for the economies of timber production and even rubber tapping, which has increasingly become a wildcat operation on the grounds of once-established plantations.

5. As Rosalind Shaw points out, there were a number of other reasons as well why Sierra Leoneans were hesitant to engage the TRC, including a reluctance to "reproduce the war by discussing it publicly" (2007, 68).

6. Tellingly, Koolhaas himself claims that he achieves such a comprehensive vision only when he rents the helicopter of Nigeria's president and flies over Lagos, a pointed illustration of the "God's eye" perspective of postcolonial power.

chapter 6: The Hotel Kamajor

1. "Featuring: The Kama Boyz," *Pool*, 10 July 2000, http://poolnewspaper.tripod.com/.

2. This gendered aspect of kamajor knowledge is dealt with in more detail in Ferme (2001b), Leach (2000), and Muana (1997).

3. This facet of the kamajors' approach to the war is actually belied by the number of RUF "captives" who ended up fighting with the CDF, a reasonably common occurrence. (See chapter 4.)

4. There are a number of excellent studies of cross-gender relationships, the shifting meaning of marriage, and what Utas has called "girlfriending" during the Mano River War. See in particular Coulter (2009), Gale (2007), and Utas (2005).

5. The phrase is a common Krio response to, among other things, "How are you?"

chapter 7: The Magic of War

1. Innes defines a "kasela" as "a spirit said to live in the Bonthe area, and whose boat is said to be seen from time to time at night with lights on" (1969, 40). Both Mama Munda and Hinga Norman described Kasela as a riverine devil and noted the importance of water to the Kasela spirits and to the Kasela War Council initiates.

2. For more extensive summary and critique of the literature on the occult in Africanist anthropology, see Ashforth (2005) and West (2007).

3. *Kemoh* is a Mende synonym for *karamoko*, an Arabic term meaning roughly a teacher-scholar (lit., "one who can read") (Bledsoe and Robey 1986, 223, n. 5). Less often initiators associated specifically with the Koran were referred to by the title "Mualimu" or "Sheik." A witness before the Special Court testified that any initiator might be referred to as a kemoh (testimony of Ishmael Koroma, 22 February 2006, 32), though in practice only a few routinely used the title.

4. Henry (2000) offers a useful discussion of the differences between these two types of *hale-mui*, or "medicine person."

5. According to Krijn Peters, by 1995 the RUF had renounced the use of occult protections, declaring all "superstition" counterrevolutionary. See Peters (2007, 73).

6. As Muana points out, the origin story of kamajor bulletproofing is very much shaped by conventions in Mende oral narrative. See Muana (1997). For a detailed analysis of how these conventions impacted the way the history of the CDF movement—and its occult dimensions—was narrated before the Special Court, see Kelsall (2009).

7. In one version of this story Kundewa's brother's name is Kposowai and the attack occurs in Jong Chiefdom (see Muana 1997, 87–88; see also Alie 2005, 57). In other versions of the story the occult power was developed by Kundewa in the village of Kale (see SCSL transcript from 10 February 2005, 85; Wlodarczyk 2009, 95).

8. The interview on which this account is based was conducted on 19 April 2006. I paraphrase the story here based on translation from the original Mende.

9. This detail was significant in that Kundewa was accused by others within the CDF, and by the Special Court, of running a group of initiates known as the Avondo, from the Mende for "sweat." Other initiators and CDF leaders argued that the Avonodos were a perversion of the original kamajors and outlawed Avondo membership in 2000. By making reference here to the early importance of sweat, Kunde was presumably attempting to counter the idea that the Avondo were a later, perverse form of the original kamajor society.

10. This detail, too, was significant in that one of the most inflammatory charges made by the court was that the CDF, and Kundewa in particular, engaged in cannibalism as one of the rites of the movement.

11. Again, command responsibility was the crux of the prosecution case against the three CDF accused, as I outline in more detail in Hoffman (2007b). Kundewa was in essence claiming that as an initiator he had no authority to send fighters into battle.

12. At one point in the Special Court testimony against the CDF, Kundewa was accused of having killed an initiate in the bush after keeping him secluded. The secrecy of the *vaa* (initiation bush) was therefore a loaded issue in the context of Kunde's telling.

13. See Special Court transcript of testimony of Ishmael Koroma, 22 February 2006, 36–37.

14. In the King James translation, those verses are: "When the host goeth forth against thine enemies, then keep thee from every wicked thing. / If there be among

you any man, that is not clean by reason of uncleanness that chanceth him by night, then shall he go abroad out of the camp, he shall not come within the camp. / But it shall be, when evening cometh on, he shall wash himself with water: and when the sun is down, he shall come into the camp again" (Deut. 23: 9–11). Norman made reference to the same verses in his Special Court testimony. See transcript of the Special Court, 27 January 2006, 47–48.

15. Testimony at SCSL, 16 February 2006, 67.

16. Both figures are drawn from RSLCDF (2000) and are probably overstated.

17. This occult (or what Ellis calls "religious") aspect of the Sierra Leone front of the war is explored more fully in Wlodarczyk (2009) and, on the Liberian side, Ellis (1999).

18. This psychological warfare approach ran through the prosecution case against the CDF at the Special Court: that claims to make young men bulletproof were a psychological technique intended to convince unarmed men to take on much more heavily armed opponents. See, for example, transcript of testimony by Joe Demby, the former vice-president, 15 February 2006, 12–15. One of the most fascinating efforts to cast occult practice in terms of psychological warfare has to be a 1964 study by the Special Operations Research Office on behalf of the U.S. Department of the Army (part of the Department of Defense) titled *Witchcraft, Sorcery, Magic, and other Psychological Phenomena and Their Implications on Military and Paramilitary Operations in the Congo* (Price and Jureidini 1964). In addition to detailing the occult powers claimed by insurgent forces, the report weighs the merits of United States military personnel attempting to employ occult discourses in a counterinsurgency campaign.

19. Doctors working with emergency medical teams in the southeast reported a high number of young men brought to hospitals with gut wounds that they suspected had been from failed initiation tests. In a closed session before the Special Court, a highly placed kamajor commander also describes an incident in which three initiates were killed and six wounded during an initiation ceremony in Bonthe. Some initiated kamajors and a few of the initiators with whom I spoke verified that a number of initiates failed these tests.

20. The pop sociological theory of contemporary African warriors made fearless through HIV circulates through a surprising variety of military and policy circles. Besides being logically bizarre, it rests on what can only be described as a nakedly racist assumption that most African men are HIV positive.

21. Testimony of prosecution witness TF2–140, a child soldier who first fought with the RUF and then went on to become a bodyguard to Hinga Norman, 14 September 2004, 98–99, 162, 163. The testimony was given in English and is taken from the official transcript.

22. I do not quote this testimony verbatim because it came from a closed court session in which the identity of the witness was masked and the testimony was not made public.

23. This exchange took place as part of closed, nonpublic testimony and therefore I do not reproduce the conversation here.

24. Presiding Justice Benjamin Itoe, from the transcript of testimony in SCSL-2004–14-T, 17 November 2004, 16.

conclusion: A Laboratory of the Future

1. I take the United States as exemplary here, because it both offers the most concrete recent examples, and what the US military does has perhaps the greatest impact globally on the future of military (and militarized) thought.

2. *Quadrennial Defense Review Report*, 6 February 2006, http://www.defense.gov/.

3. John Arquilla, "9/11: Yesterday and Tomorrow; How We Could Lose the War on Terror," *San Francisco Chronicle*, 7 September 2003.

4. The manual goes on to state that "this does not mean that they should be irregular in the sense of being brutal or outside proper control," though it is not clear where that line of brutality is to be drawn or what being "under proper control" means if the force is not operating "in a U.S. image."

5. See Ann Scott Tyson, "U.S. Widens Push to Use Armed Iraqi Residents: Irregulars to Patrol Own Neighborhoods," *Washington Post*, 28 July 2007, A1, 16.

6. See Alissa Rubin and Damien Cave, "In a Force for Iraqi Calm, Seeds of Conflict," *New York Times*, 23 December 2007, A1, 14–15.

7. Graeme Smith, "Afghan Militia Gears Up to Fight the Taliban," *Globe and Mail*, 9 April 2009, http://www.theglobeandmail.com/.

8. "Ethnographic intelligence" is the term Fred Renzi, a Lieutenant Colonel in the United States Army writing in the journal *Military Review* (Renzi 2006), uses to describe militarily useful understandings of local culture.

bibliography

Abdullah, Ibrahim. 1998. "Bush Path to Destruction: The Origin and Character of the Revolutionary United Front / Sierra Leone." *Journal of Modern African Studies* 36, no. 2: 203–35.

———. 2002. "Youth Culture and Rebellion: Understanding Sierra Leone's Wasted Decade." *Critical Arts* 16, no. 2: 19–37.

———, ed. 2004. *Between Democracy and Terror: The Sierra Leone Civil War*. Dakar: CODESRIA.

———. 2005. "'I Am a Rebel': Youth, Culture, and Violence in Sierra Leone." In *Makers and Breakers: Children and Youth in Postcolonial Africa*, edited by Alcinda Honwana and Filip de Boeck, 172–87. Trenton, N.J.: Africa World Press.

Abdullah, Ibrahim, and Patrick Muana. 1998. "The Revolutionary United Front of Sierra Leone: A Revolt of the Lumpenproletariat." In *African Guerrillas*, edited by Christopher Clapham, 172–94. Bloomington: Indiana University Press.

Aboagye, Festus. 1999. *ECOMOG: A Sub-Regional Experience in Conflict Resolution, Management and Peacekeeping in Liberia*. Accra: SEDCO.

Abraham, Arthur. 1976. *Topics in Sierra Leone History: A Counter-Colonial Interpretation*. Freetown: Leone.

———. 1978. *Mende Government and Politics under Colonial Rule*. Freetown: Sierra Leone University Press.

Adebajo, Adekeye. 2002. *Liberia's Civil War: Nigeria, ECOMOG, and Regional Security in West Africa*. Boulder, Colo.: Lynne Rienner.

Agamben, Giorgio. 1993. *The Coming Community*. Translated by Michael Hardt. Minneapolis: University of Minnesota Press.

———. 1998. *Homo Sacer: Sovereign Power and Bare Life*. Stanford, Calif.: Stanford University Press.

Alie, Joe A. D. 1990. *A New History of Sierra Leone*. New York: St. Martin's Press.

———. 2005. "The Kamajor Militia in Sierra Leone: Liberators or Nihilists?" In *Civil Militia: Africa's Intractable Security Menace?* edited by David J. Francis, 51–70. Aldershot: Ashgate.

Appadurai, Arjun. 1996. *Modernity at Large: Cultural Dimensions of Globalization*. Minneapolis: University of Minnesota Press.

———. 2006. *Fear of Small Numbers: An Essay on the Geography of Anger*. Durham, N.C.: Duke University Press.

Apter, Andrew. 1999. "IBB=419: Nigerian Democracy and the Politics of Illusion." In *Civil Society and the Political Imagination in Africa*, edited by John Comaroff and Jean Comaroff, 267–307. Chicago: University of Chicago Press.

Arquilla, John, and David Ronfeldt, eds. 2001. *Networks and Netwars: The Future of Terror, Crime, and Militancy*. Santa Monica, Calif.: RAND.

Ashforth, Adam. 2005. *Witchcraft, Violence, and Democracy in South Africa*. Chicago: University of Chicago Press.

Bangura, Yusuf. 1997. "Understanding the Political and Cultural Dynamics of the Sierra Leone War: A Critique of Paul Richards' *Fighting for the Rainforest*." *African Development* 22, no. 3/4: 117–48.

———. 2004. "The Political and Cultural Dynamics of the Sierra Leone War: A Critique of Paul Richards." In *Between Democracy and Terror: The Sierra Leone Civil War*, edited by Ibrahim Abdullah, 13–40. Dakar: CODESRIA.

Barber, Karin. 2007. "When People Cross Thresholds." *African Studies Review* 50, no. 2: 111–24.

Barrett, Michael. 2004. "Paths to Adulthood: Freedom, Belonging and Temporalities in Mbunda Biographies from Western Zambia." PhD Dissertation, Uppsala University.

Bateson, Gregory. [1972] 2000. *Steps to an Ecology of Mind*. Chicago: University of Chicago Press.

Bayart, Jean-François. 1993. *The State in Africa: The Politics of the Belly*. New York: Longman.

Bayart, Jean-François, Stephen Ellis, and Beatrice Hibou. 1999. *The Criminalization of the State in Africa*. Bloomington: Indiana University Press.

Bellman, Beryl. 1984. *The Language of Secrecy*. New Brunswick, N.J.: Rutgers University Press.

Berdal, Mats, and David Malone, eds. 2000. *Greed and Grievance: Economic Agendas in Civil Wars*. Boulder, Colo.: Lynne Rienner.

Bergner, Daniel. 2004. *In the Land of Magic Soldiers: A Story of White and Black in West Africa*. New York: Farrar, Straus, and Giroux.

Berman, Bruce. 1998. "Ethnicity, Patronage, and the African State: The Politics of Uncivil Nationalism." *African Affairs* 97, no. 388: 305–41.

Bledsoe, Caroline. 1980. *Women and Marriage in Kpelle Society*. Stanford, Calif.: Stanford University Press.

———. 1984. "The Political Use of Sande Ideology and Symbolism." *American Ethnologist* 11, no. 3, no. 1: 455–72.

———. 1990. "'No Success without Struggle': Social Mobility and Hardship for Foster Children in Sierra Leone." *Man* 25:70–88.

Bledsoe, Caroline, and Kenneth Robey. 1986. "Arabic Literacy and Secrecy among the Mende of Sierra Leone." *Man* 21, no. 2: 202–26.

Bøås, Morten, and Kevin C. Dunn. 2007. "African Guerrilla Politics: Raging Against the Machine?" In *African Guerrillas: Raging Against the Machine*, edited by Morten Bøås and Kevin C. Dunn, 9–37. Boulder, Colo.: Lynne Rienner.

Boltanski, Luc, and Eve Chiapello. 2005. *The New Spirit of Capitalism*. New York: Verso.

Bond, Patrick. 2006. *Looting Africa: The Economics of Exploitation*. New York: Zed Books.

Boone, Sylvia. 1986. *Radiance from the Waters*. New Haven: Yale University Press.

Broch-Due, Vigdis, ed. 2005. *Violence and Belonging: The Quest for Identity in Post-Colonial Africa*. New York: Routledge.

Buck-Morss, Susan. 2000. "Hegel and Haiti." *Critical Inquiry* 26:821–65.

Bujra, Janet, Lionel Cliffe, Morris Szeftel, Rita Abrahamsen, and Tunde Zack-Williams. 2004. "Agendas, Past and Future." *Review of African Political Economy* 31, no. 102: 557–69.

Bundu, Abass. 2001. *Democracy by Force? A Study of International Military Intervention in the Conflict in Sierra Leone from 1991–2000*. Parkland, Fla.: Universal.

Chakrabarty, Dipesh. 1997. "The Time of History and the Time of the Gods." In *The Politics of Culture in the Shadow of Capital*, edited by Lisa Lowe and David Lloyd, 35–60. Durham, N.C.: Duke University Press.

Chatterjee, Partha. 2004. *The Politics of the Governed: Reflections on Popular Politics in Most of the World*. New York: Columbia University Press.

Christensen, Maya, and Mats Utas. 2008. "Mercenaries of Democracy: The 'Politricks' or Remobilized Combatants in the 2007 General Elections, Sierra Leone." *African Affairs* 107, no. 429: 515–39.

Christiansen, Catrine, Mats Utas, and Henrik Vigh, eds. 2006. *Navigating Youth, Generating Adulthood: Social Becoming in an African Context*. Uppsala: Nordic Africa Institute.

Clastres, Pierre. 1989. *Society Against the State: Essays in Political Anthropology*. Translated by Robert Hurley. New York: Zone Books.

———. 1994. *Archeology of Violence*. New York: Semiotext(e).

Clausewitz, Carl von. [1832] 2007. *On War*. Translated by Michael Howard and Peter Paret, Oxford World's Classics. New York: Oxford University Press.

Cohen, Abner. 1981. *The Politics of Elite Culture: Explorations in the Dramaturgy of Power in a Modern West African Society*. Berkeley: University of California Press.

Colebrook, Claire. 2002. *Gilles Deleuze*. New York: Routledge.

Collier, Paul, and Anke Hoeffler. 2000. "Greed and Grievance in Civil War." World Bank Policy Research Working Paper, WPS 2355. Washington: World Bank Development Research Group.

Comaroff, Jean, and John L. Comaroff, eds. 1993. *Modernity and Its Malcontents: Ritual and Power in Postcolonial Africa*. Chicago: University of Chicago Press.

———. 1999. "Occult Economies and the Violence of Abstraction: Notes from the South African Postcolony." *American Ethnologist* 26, no. 2: 279–303.

Conteh-Morgan, Earl, and Mac Dixon-Fyle. 1999. *Sierra Leone at the End of the Twentieth Century: History, Politics, and Society*. New York: Peter Lang.

Cosentino, Donald. 1989. "Midnight Charters: Musa Wo and Mende Myths of Chaos." In *Creativity of Power: Cosmology and Action in African Societies*, edited by William Arens and Ivan Karp, 21–37. Washington: Smithsonian Institution Press.

Coulter, Chris. 2005. "Reflections from the Field: A Girl's Initiation Ceremony in Northern Sierra Leone." *Anthropological Quarterly* 78, no. 2: 431–41.

———. 2009. *Bush Wives and Girl Soldiers: Women's Lives through War and Peace in Sierra Leone*. Ithaca, N.Y.: Cornell University Press.

Cox, Thomas. 1976. *Civil-Military Relations in Sierra Leone: A Case Study of African Soldiers in Politics*. Cambridge, Mass.: Harvard University Press.

Cusset, François. 2008. *French Theory: How Foucault, Derrida, Deleuze, and Co.*

Transformed the Intellectual Life of the United States. Minneapolis: University of Minnesota Press.

Das, Veena. 2007. *Life and Words: Violence and the Descent into the Ordinary*. Berkeley: University of California Press.

David, Omoru. 1999. *The Coming of the Killers*. Freetown.

d'Azevedo, Warren. 1962. "Common Principles of Variant Kinship Structures among the Gola of Western Liberia." *American Anthropologist* 64, no. 3: 504–20.

de Boeck, Filip. 2002. "Domesticating Diamonds and Dollars: Identity, Expenditure, and Sharing in Southwestern Zaire (1984–1997)." *Development and Change* 29, no. 4: 777–810.

de Boeck, Filip, and Marie-Françoise Plissart. 2005. *Kinshasa: Tales of the Invisible City*. Ghent: Ludion.

Deleuze, Gilles. 1995. *Negotiations: 1972–1990*. Translated by Martin Joughin. Edited by Lawrence Kritzman. European Perspectives. New York: Columbia University Press.

———. 2004. *Desert Islands and Other Texts, 1953–1974*. Los Angeles: Semiotext(e).

———. 2006a. *Two Regimes of Madness: Texts and Interviews, 1975–1995*. New York: Semiotext(e).

———. 2006b. *Nietzsche and Philosophy*. New York: Columbia University Press.

Deleuze, Gilles, and Félix Guattari. 1983. *Anti-Oedipus*. Vol. 1, *Capitalism and Schizophrenia*. Translated by Brian Massumi. Minneapolis: University of Minnesota Press.

———. 1987. *A Thousand Plateaus*. Vol. 2, *Capitalism and Schizophrenia*. Translated by Brian Massumi. Minneapolis: University of Minnesota Press.

Demissie, Fassil, ed. 2007. *Postcolonial African Cities: Imperial Legacies and Postcolonial Predicaments*. New York: Routledge, 2007.

Douglas, Mary. 1986. *How Institutions Think*. Syracuse, N.Y.: Syracuse University Press.

Eisenstadt, Lieutenant Colonel Michael. 2007. "Iraq: Tribal Engagement Lessons Learned." *Military Review* September–October: 16–31.

Ellis, Stephen. 1999. *The Mask of Anarchy: The Destruction of Liberia and the Religious Dimensions of an African Civil War*. New York: New York University Press.

Enwezor, Okwui. 2006. *Snap Judgments: New Positions in Contemporary African Photography*. New York: International Center of Photography.

Evans-Pritchard, Edward. 1937. *Witchcraft, Oracles, and Magic among the Azande*. Oxford: Clarendon Press.

Fabian, Johannes. 2007. *Memory Against Culture*. Durham, N.C.: Duke University Press.

Fanon, Frantz. [1961] 2005. *The Wretched of the Earth*. Translated by Richard Philcox. New York: Grove Press.

Fanthorpe, Richard. 1998. "Locating the Politics of a Sierra Leonean Chiefdom." *Africa* 68, no. 4: 558–84.

———. 2001. "Neither Citizen nor Subject? 'Lumpen' Agency and the Legacy of Native Administration in Sierra Leone." *African Affairs* 100, no. 400: 363–86.

———. 2005. "On the Limits of Liberal Peace: Chiefs and Democratic Decentralization in Post-War Sierra Leone." *African Affairs* 105, no. 418: 27–49.

Farah, Douglas. 2004. *Blood from Stones: The Secret Financial Network of Terror*. New York: Broadway Books.

Feldman, Allen. 1991. *Formations of Violence: The Narrative of the Body and Political Terror in Northern Ireland*. Chicago: University of Chicago Press.

Ferguson, James. 2006. *Global Shadows: Africa in the Neoliberal Order*. Durham, N.C.: Duke University Press.

Ferme, Mariane. 1999. "Staging Politisi: The Dialogics of Publicity and Secrecy in Sierra Leone." In *Civil Society and the Political Imagination in Africa*, edited by John Comaroff and Jean Comaroff, 160–91. Chicago: University of Chicago Press.

———. 2001a. "La Figure du chasseur et les chasseurs-miliciens dans le confit Sierra-Léonais." *Politique africaine* 82:119–32.

———. 2001b. *The Underneath of Things: Violence, History, and the Everyday in Sierra Leone*. Berkeley: University of California Press.

Ferme, Mariane, and Danny Hoffman. 2004. "Hunter Militias and the New Human Rights Discourse in Sierra Leone and Beyond." *Africa Today* 50, no. 4: 73–95.

Fischer, Michael M. J. 2003. *Emergent Forms of Life and the Anthropological Voice*. Durham, N.C.: Duke University Press.

Fithen, Caspar. 1999. "Diamonds and War in Sierra Leone: Cultural Strategies for Commercial Adaptation to Endemic Low-Intensity Conflict." PhD Dissertation, University College.

Fithen, Caspar, and Paul Richards. 2005. "Making War, Crafting Peace: Militia Solidarities and Demobilization in Sierra Leone." In *No War, No Peace: An Anthropology of Contemporary Armed Conflicts*, edited by Paul Richards, 117–36. Athens: Ohio University Press.

Fofana, Lansana. 1998. "Facing the Future without the Military." *BBC Focus on Africa* 9, no. 2: 12–14.

Foucault, Michel. 2003. *Society Must Be Defended: Lectures at the College De France, 1975–1976*. New York: Picador.

Fyfe, Christopher. 1962. *A History of Sierra Leone*. Oxford: Oxford University Press.

Gale, Lacey. 2007. "Bulgur Marriages and Big Women: Navigating Relatedness in Guinean Refugee Camps." *Anthropological Quarterly* 80, no. 2: 355–79.

———. 2008. "Beyond *Men Pikin*: Improving Understanding of Post-Conflict Child Fostering in Sierra Leone." Feinstein International Center Briefing Paper. Boston: Tufts University.

Gberie, Lansana. 2005. *A Dirty War in West Africa: The RUF and the Destruction of Sierra Leone*. Bloomington: Indiana University Press.

Geschiere, Peter. 1997. *The Modernity of Witchcraft: Politics and the Occult in Postcolonial Africa*. Charlottesville: University of Virginia Press.

Gibson-Graham, J. K. [1996] 2006. *The End of Capitalism (as We Knew It): A Feminist Critique of Political Economy*. Minneapolis: University of Minnesota Press.

Gilligan, James. 1999. *Violence: Reflections on a National Epidemic*. New York: Vintage.

Gilroy, Paul. 1993. *The Black Atlantic: Modernity and Double Consciousness*. Cambridge, Mass.: Harvard University Press.

Gittins, Anthony. 1987. *Mende Religion*. Nettetal: Steyler.

Gluckman, Max. 1963. *Order and Rebellion in Tribal Africa*. New York: Free Press.

Guattari, Félix, 2004. "On Capitalism and Desire." In *Desert Islands and Other Texts 1953–1974*, by Gilles Deleuze, 262–73. Los Angeles: Semiotext(e)

Guha, Ranajit. 1999. *Elementary Aspects of Peasant Insurgency in Colonial India*. Durham. N.C.: Duke University Press.

Guyer, Jane. 1995. *Money Matters: Instability, Values, and Social Payments in the Modern History of West African Communities*. Portsmouth, N.H.: Heinemann.

———. 2004. *Marginal Gains: Monetary Transactions in Atlantic Africa*. Chicago: University of Chicago Press.

Hansen, Thomas Blom. 2001. *Wages of Violence: Naming and Identity in Postcolonial Bombay*. Princeton: Princeton University Press.

Hardt, Michael. 1993. *Gilles Deleuze: An Apprenticeship in Philosophy*. Minneapolis: University of Minnesota Press.

———. 1995. "The Withering of Civil Society." *Social Text* 14, no. 4: 27–44.

———. n.d. "Reading Notes on Deleuze and Guattari, *Capitalism and Schizophrenia*."

Hardt, Michael, and Antonio Negri. 1994. *Labor of Dionysus: A Critique of the State-Form*. Minneapolis: University of Minnesota Press.

———. 2000. *Empire*. Cambridge: Harvard University Press.

———. 2004. *Multitude: War and Democracy in the Age of Empire*. New York: Penguin Press.

Harris, David. 1999. "From 'Warlord' to 'Democratic' President: How Charles Taylor Won the 1997 Liberian Elections." *Journal of Modern African Studies* 37, no. 3: 431–55.

Harvey, David. 1990. *The Condition of Postmodernity: An Enquiry into the Origins of Cultural Change*. Cambridge, Mass.: Blackwell.

———. 2003. *The New Imperialism*. New York: Oxford University Press.

Hecht, David, and AbdouMaliq Simone. 1994. *Invisible Governance: The Art of African Micro-Politics*. Brooklyn: Autonomedia.

Hellweg, Joseph, ed. 2004. "Security, Socioecology, Polity: Mande Hunters, Civil Society, and Nation-States in Contemporary West Africa." Special issue, *Africa Today* 50, no. 4.

Henry, Doug. 2000. "Embodied Violence: War and Relief Along the Sierra Leone Border." PhD Dissertation, Southern Methodist University.

———. 2005. "The Legacy of the Tank: The Violence of Peace." *Anthropological Quarterly* 78, no. 2: 443–56.

Hill, Matthew. 1984. "Where to Begin? The Place of the Hunter Founder in Mende Histories." *Anthropos* 79:653–56.

Hirsch, John. 2001. *Sierra Leone: Diamonds and the Struggle for Democracy*. Boulder, Colo.: Lynne Reinner.

Hoffman, Danny. 2003. “Like Beasts in the Bush: Synonyms of Childhood and Youth in Sierra Leone.” *Postcolonial Studies* 6, no. 3: 295–308.

———. 2004. “The Civilian Target in Sierra Leone and Liberia: Political Power, Military Strategy, and Humanitarian Intervention.” *African Affairs*, no. 103, no. 411: 211–26.

———. 2006. “Despot Deposed: Charles Taylor and the Challenge of State Reconstruction in Liberia.” In *Legacies of Power: Leadership Change and Former Presidents in African Politics*, edited by Roger Southall and Henning Melber, 308–31. Pretoria: HSRC Press.

———. 2007a. “The Disappeared: Images of the Environment at Freetown’s Urban Margins,” *Visual Studies* 22, no. 2: 104–19.

———. 2007b. “The Meaning of a Militia: Understanding the Civil Defense Forces of Sierra Leone,” *African Affairs* 106, no. 425: 639–62.

———. 2008. “Rocks: A Portrait of Mohammed. “ In *Telling Young Lives: Portraits of Global Youth*, edited by Craig Jeffrey and Jane Dyson, 123–35. Philadelphia: Temple University Press.

———. 2011. “The Sub-Contractors: Counterinsurgency, Militias and the New Common Ground in Military and Social Science.” In *Dangerous Liasons: Anthropologists and the National Security State*, edited by Laura McNamara and Robert Rubenstein. Santa Fe, N.M.: SAR Press.

———. n.d. “The Mano River Sketches.” Unpublished manuscript.

Holland, Eugene. 1999. *Deleuze and Guattari’s Anti-Oedipus: Introduction to Schizoanalysis*. New York: Routledge.

Höller, Christian. 2002. “Africa in Motion: An Interview with the Post-Colonialism Theoretician Achille Mbembe.” *Springerin* 3, http://www.springerin.at/.

Howe, Herbert. 2001. *Ambiguous Order: Military Forces in African States*. Boulder, Colo.: Lynne Rienner.

Huband, Mark. 1998. *The Liberian Civil War*. New York: Routledge.

Human Rights Watch. 1998. *Sowing Terror: Atrocities against Civilians in Sierra Leone*. New York: Human Rights Watch.

———. 1999. *Getting Away with Murder, Mutilation, and Rape: New Testimony from Sierra Leone*. New York: Human Rights Watch.

———. 2003. *“We’ll Kill You If You Cry”: Sexual Violence in the Sierra Leone Conflict*. New York: Human Rights Watch.

———. 2005. *Youth, Poverty and Blood: The Lethal Legacy of West Africa’s Regional Warriors*. New York: Human Rights Watch.

Innes, Gordon. 1969. *A Mende-English Dictionary*. London: Cambridge University Press.

Iron, Richard. 2005. “Military Expert Witness Report on the Civil Defense Force of Sierra Leone.” Freetown: Special Court for Sierra Leone.

Jackson, Michael. 1998. *Minima Ethnographica: Intersubjectivity and the Anthropological Project*. Chicago: University of Chicago Press.

———. 2004. *In Sierra Leone*. Durham, N.C.: Duke University Press.

———. 2005. “Custom and Conflict in Sierra Leone: An Essay on Anarchy.” In

Existential Anthropology: Events, Exigencies and Effects, 53–74. New York: Berghahn Books.

Jackson, Paul. 2007. "Reshuffling an Old Deck of Cards? The Politics of Local Government Reform in Sierra Leone." *African Affairs* 106, no. 422: 95–111.

Jaganathan, Ganase. 2005. *21 Days: A True Story of a Malaysian Hostage in Sierra Leone*. Kuala Lumpur: Silverfishbooks.

Jameson, Fredric. 1984. "Postmodernism, or the Cultural Logic of Late Capitalism." *New Left Review* 146:53–92.

Jędrej, M. C. 1974. "An Analytical Note on the Land and Spirits of the Sewa Mende." *Africa* 44, no. 1: 38–45.

Kandeh, Jimmy. 1999. "Ransoming the State: Elite Origins of Subaltern Terror in Sierra Leone." *Review of African Political Economy* 78:349–66.

Kapferer, Bruce. 1997. *The Feast of the Sorcerer: Practices of Consciousness and Power*. Chicago: University of Chicago Press.

Keen, David. 2000. "Incentives and Disincentives for Violence." In *Greed and Grievance: Economic Agendas in Civil Wars*, edited by Mats Berdal and David Malone, 19–42. Boulder, Colo.: Lynne Rienner.

———. 2005. *Conflict and Collusion in Sierra Leone*. New York: Palgrave.

Keenan, Jeremy. 2008. "US Militarization in Africa: What Anthropologists Should Know About Africom." *Anthropology Today* 24, no. 5: 16–20.

Kelsall, Tim. 2006. "Politics, Anti-Politics, International Justice: Language and Power in the Special Court for Sierra Leone." *Review of International Studies* 32:587–602.

———. 2009. *Culture under Cross-Examination: International Justice and the Special Court for Sierra Leone*. New York: Cambridge University Press.

Kilson, Martin. 1969. *Political Change in a West African State: A Study of the Modernization Process in Sierra Leone*. New York: Atheneum.

Klein, Naomi. 2007. *The Shock Doctrine: The Rise of Disaster Capitalism*. New York: Metropolitan Books.

Koolhaas, Rem. 2002. "Fragments of a Lecture on Lagos." In *Under Siege: Four African Cities, Freetown, Johannesburg, Kinshasa, Lagos*, edited by Okwui Enwezor, Carlos Basualdo, Ute Meta Bauer, Susanne Ghez, Sarat Maharaj, Mark Nash, and Octavio Zaya, 173–83. Ostfildern-Ruit: Hatje Cantz.

Kpundeh, Sahr. 2004. "Corruption and Political Insurgency in Sierra Leone." In *Between Democracy and Civil War: The Sierra Leone Civil War*, edited by Ibrahim Abdullah, 90–103. Dakar: CODESRIA.

Kumar, Krishnan. 1995. *From Post-Industrial to Post-Modern Society: New Theories of the Contemporary World*. Cambridge, Mass.: Blackwell.

Lan, David. 1985. *Guns and Rain: Guerillas and Spirit Mediums in Zimbabwe*. Berkeley: University of California Press.

Lavalie, Alpha. 1985. "Government and Opposition in Sierra Leone, 1968–1978." In *Proceedings of the Fourth Conference, Birmingham Sierra Leone Studies Symposium, 13–15 July 1985*, edited by Adam Jones and Peter Mitchell. Birmingham: University of Birmingham.

Leach, Melissa. 1994. *Rainforest Relations: Gender and Resource Use among the Mende of Gola, Sierra Leone*. Washington: Smithsonian Institution Press.

———. 2000. "New Shapes to Shift: War, Parks and the Hunting Person in Modern West Africa." *Journal of the Royal Anthropological Institute* 6, no. 4: 577–95.

Lévi-Strauss, Claude. 1963. "The Sorcerer and His Magic." In *Structural Anthropology*. New York: Basic Books.

Levitt, Jeremy. 2005. *The Evolution of Deadly Conflict in Liberia: From 'Paternaltarianism' to State Collapse*. Durham, N.C.: Carolina Academic Press.

Little, Kenneth. 1965. "The Political Function of the Poro, Part 1." *Africa* 35, no. 4: 349–65.

———. 1966. "The Political Function of the Poro, Part 2." *Africa* 36, no. 1: 62–71.

———. [1951] 1967. *The Mende of Sierra Leone: A West African People in Transition*. London: Routledge and Kegan Paul.

Lizza, Ryan. 2000. "Sierra Leone, the Latest Clinton Betrayal: Where Angels Fear to Tread." *New Republic*, 24 July, 22–27.

Lubkemann, Stephen. 2008. *Culture in Chaos: An Anthropology of the Social Condition in War*. Chicago: University of Chicago.

Lutz, Catherine. 2001. "The Wars Less Known." *South Atlantic Quarterly* 101, no. 2: 285–96.

Malcolm, J. M. 1939. "Mende Warfare." *Sierra Leone Studies* 21:47–52.

Mamdani, Mahmood. 2001. *When Victims Become Killers: Colonialism, Nativism, and the Genocide in Rwanda*. Princeton: Princeton University Press.

Marx, Karl. [1857] 1973. *The Grundrisse*. New York: Vintage.

———. [1850] 1974. "The Class Struggles in France: 1848 to 1850." In *Surveys from Exile: Political Writings*, 2:35–142. New York: Vintage.

———. [1867] 1977. *Capital: A Critique of Political Economy*. Vol. 1. New York: Vintage.

Marx, Karl, and Friedrich Engels. 1978. *The Marx-Engels Reader*. Edited by Robert Tucker. New York: Norton.

Massaquoi, John, and Frances Fortune. 2000. "Grassroots Peacebuilding in Pujehun." *Accord: An International Review of Peace Initiatives*. London: Conciliation Resources.

Massumi, Brian. 1992. *A User's Guide to Capitalism and Schizophrenia: Deviations from Deleuze and Guattari*. Cambridge, Mass.: MIT Press.

Matory, Lorand. 1999. "The English Professors of Brazil: On the Diasporic Roots of the Yoruba Nation." *Comparative Studies in Society and History* 41, no. 1: 72–103.

May, Todd. 2001. "The Ontology and Politics of Gilles Deleuze." *Theory and Event* 5, no. 3.

Mbembe, Achille. 1992. "The Banality of Power and the Aesthetics of Vulgarity in the Postcolony." *Public Culture* 4, no. 2: 1–30.

———. 2003. "Necropolitics." *Public Culture* 15, no. 1: 11–40.

———. 2006. "On Politics as a Form of Expenditure." In *Law and Disorder in the Postcolony*, edited by Jean Comaroff and John L. Comaroff, 299–335. Chicago: University of Chicago Press.

Mbembe, Achille, and Sarah Nuttall. 2004. "Writing the World from an African Metropolis" *Public Culture* 16, no. 3: 347–72.

Mbembe, Achille, and Janet Roitman. 1995. "Figures of the Subject in Times of Crisis." *Public Culture* 7, no. 2: 323–52.

McFate, Sean. 2008. "U.S. Africa Command: Next Step or Next Stumble?" *African Affairs* 107, no. 426: 111–20.

McNaughton, Patrick. 1982. "The Shirts That Mande Hunters Wear." *African Arts* 15, no. 3: 54–58, 91.

———. 1988. *The Mande Blacksmiths: Knowledge, Power, and Art in West Africa*. Bloomington: Indiana University Press.

Miller, Christopher. 1998. *Nationalists and Nomads: Essays on Francophone African Literature and Culture*. Chicago: University of Chicago Press.

Mitchell, Timothy. 1991. "The Limits of the State: Beyond Statist Approaches and Their Critics." *American Political Science Review* 85:77–96.

Mitchell, W. J. T. 1994. *Picture Theory: Essays on Verbal and Visual Representation*. Chicago: University of Chicago Press.

Moore, Sally Falk. 1994. *Anthropology and Africa: Changing Perspectives on a Changing Scene*. Charlottesville: University of Virginia Press.

Moran, Mary. 1995. "Warriors or Soldiers? Masculinity and Ritual Transvestism in the Liberian Civil War." In *Feminism, Nationalism, and Militarism*, edited by Constance R. Sutton, 73–88. Arlington, Va.: American Ethnological Society.

———. 2006. *Liberia: The Violence of Democracy*. Philadelphia: University of Pennsylvania Press.

Muana, Patrick. 1997. "The Kamajoi Militia: Civil War, Internal Displacement and the Politics of Counter-Insurgency." *African Development* 22, no. 3/4: 77–100.

Murphy, Willam P. 2003. "Military Patrimonialism and Child Soldier Clientalism in the Liberian and Sierra Leonean Civil Wars." *African Studies Review* 46, no. 2: 61–87.

Musa, Sorie, and John Lansana Musa. 1993. *The Invasion of Sierra Leone: A Chronicle of Events of a Nation under Siege*. Washington: Sierra Leone Institute for Policy Studies.

Nietzsche, Friedrich. [1872] 1956. *The Birth of Tragedy and the Genealogy of Morals*. New York: Doubleday.

Njami, Simon. 2001. "The Spores of the Stamen." In *Africas: The Artist and the City, a Journey and an Exhibition*, edited by Pep Subirós, 72–75. Barcelona: Centre de Cultura Contemporània de Barcelona.

Nordstrom, Carolyn. 1997. *A Different Kind of War Story*. Philadelphia: University of Pennsylvania Press.

———. 1999. "Requiem for the Rational War." In *Deadly Developments: Capitalism, States and War*, edited by S. P. Reyna and R. E. Downs, 153–75. Amsterdam: Gordon and Breach.

———. 2004. *Shadows of War: Violence, Power, and International Profiteering in the Twenty-First Century*. Berkeley: University of California Press.

Nunley, John. 1983. "Urban Ode-Lay Masquerades of Sierra Leone: A Theoretical

Explanation of Failure, an Answer to Success." *Sierra Leone Studies at Birmingham* 3:363–82.

———. 1987. *Moving with the Face of the Devil: Art and Politics in Urban West Africa*. Urbana: University of Illinois Press.

Ong, Aihwa, and Stephen J. Collier, eds. 2005. *Global Assemblages: Technology, Politics, and Ethics as Anthropological Problems*. Malden, Mass.: Blackwell.

Opala, Joseph. 1994. "'Ecstatic Renovation!': Street Art Celebrating Sierra Leone's 1992 Elections." *African Affairs*, no. 93, no. 371: 195–218.

Ortner, Sherry. 2006. *Anthropology and Social Theory: Culture, Power, and the Acting Subject*. Durham, N.C.: Duke University Press.

Osagie, Iyunolu. 1997. "Historical Memory and a New National Consciousness: The Amistad Revolt Revisited in Sierra Leone." *Massachusetts Review* Spring: 63–68.

———. 2000. *The Amistad Revolt: Memory, Slavery, and the Politics of Identity in the United States and Sierra Leone*. Athens: University of Georgia Press.

Owusu, Maxwell. 1989. "Rebellion, Revolution, and Tradition: Reinterpreting Coups in Ghana." *Society for Comparative Study of Society and History* 31, no. 2: 372–97.

Patton, Paul. 1984. "Conceptual Politics and the War-Machine in *Mille Plateaux*." *SubStance*, no. 44/45: 61–80.

———. 1997. "The World Seen from Within: Deleuze and the Philosophy of Events." *Theory and Event* 1, no. 1.

———. 2000. *Deleuze and the Political*. New York: Routledge.

Pauw, Jacques. 2006. "Pappy and Captain Cut-Hand." In *Dances with Devils: A Journalist's Search for Truth*, 199–217. Cape Town: Zebra Press.

Pelton, Robert Young. 2002. *The Hunter, the Hammer, and Heaven: Journeys to Three Worlds Gone Mad*. Guilford, Conn.: Lyons Press.

Peters, Krijn. 2007. "Footpaths to Reintegration: Armed Conflict, Youth and the Rural Crisis in Sierra Leone." PhD Dissertation. Wageningen University.

Peters, Krijn, and Paul Richards. 1997. "Why We Fight: Voices of Youth Ex-Combatants in Sierra Leone." *Africa* 68, no. 1: 183–210.

Phillips, Ruth. 1995. *Representing Woman: Sande Masquerades of the Mende of Sierra Leone*. Los Angeles: UCLA Fowler Museum of Cultural History.

Physicians for Human Rights. 2000. *War-Related Sexual Violence in Sierra Leone: A Population-Based Assessment*. Boston: Physicians for Human Rights.

Piot, Charles. 1996. "Of Slaves and the Gift: Kabre Sale of Kin during the Era of the Slave Trade." *Journal of African History* 37:31–49.

———. 1999. *Remotely Global: Village Modernity in West Africa*. Chicago: University of Chicago Press.

———. 2010. *Nostalgia for the Future: West Africa after the Cold War*. Chicago: University of Chicago Press.

Price, James R., and Paul Jureidini. 1964. *Witchcraft, Sorcery, Magic, and Other Psychological Phenomena and Their Implications on Military and Paramilitary Operations in the Congo*. Washington: Special Operations Research Office, American University Counterinsurgency Information Analysis Center.

Rashid, Ismail. 1997. "Subaltern Reactions: Lumpens, Students, and the Left." *African Development* 22, no. 3/4: 19–44.

———. 2004. "Student Radicals, Lumpen Youth, and the Origins of Revolutionary Groups in Sierra Leone, 1977–1996." In *Between Democracy and Terror: The Sierra Leone Civil War*, edited by Ibrahim Abdullah, 66–89. Dakar: CODESRIA.

Reno, William. 1995. *Corruption and State Politics in Sierra Leone*. Cambridge: Cambridge University Press.

———. 1998. *Warlord Politics and African States*. Boulder, Colo.: Lynne Rienner.

———. 2001. "How Sovereignty Matters: International Markets and the Political Economy of Local Politics in Weak States." In *Intervention and Transnationalism in Africa*, edited by Thomas Callaghy, Ron Kassimir, and Robert Latham, 197–215. New York: Cambridge University Press.

———. 2003. "Political Networks in a Failing State: The Roots and Future of Violent Conflict in Sierra Leone." *Internationale Politik und Gesellschaft* [*International Politics and Society*] 2:44–66.

———. 2004. "Greed or Grievance: Why Some Armed Groups Care and Why Others Do Not." Paper presentation, Micropolitics of Armed Groups conference. Humboldt University, Berlin, 18–19 June.

———. 2007. "Liberia: The Lurds of the New Church." In *African Guerrillas: Raging Against the Machine*, edited by Morten Bøås and Kevin C. Dunn, 69–80. Boulder, Colo.: Lynne Rienner.

Renzi, Fred. 2006. "Networks: Terra Incognita and the Case for Ethnographic Intelligence." *Military Review* September–October: 16–22.

Republic of Sierra Leone Civil Defence Forces (RSLCDF). 1999. *Recommended Values and Standards*. Freetown: Republic of Sierra Leone Civil Defence Forces.

———. 2000. *Report on the National Consultative Conference for the Restructuring of the Republic of Sierra Leone Civil Defense Forces, 12–14 September*. Freetown: Republic of Sierra Leone Civil Defence Forces.

Revolutionary United Front, Sierra Leone (RUF/SL). 1995. *Footpaths to Democracy*. Freetown: Revolutionary United Front, Sierra Leone.

Rhodes, Lorna. 2004. *Total Confinement: Madness and Reason in the Maximum Security Prison*. Berkeley: University of California Press.

Richards, Paul. 1996. *Fighting for the Rainforest: War, Youth and Resources in Sierra Leone*. Portsmouth, N.H.: Heinemann.

———. 1998. "Postscript: On Hunters and Martyrs." *Fighting for the Rainforest: War, Youth and Resources in Sierra Leone*. 2nd edition. Portsmouth, N.H.: Heinemann.

———. 1999. "New Political Violence in Africa: Secular Sectarianism in Sierra Leone." *GeoJournal* 47:433–42.

———, ed. 2005a. *No Peace No War: An Anthropology of Contemporary Armed Conflicts*. Athens: Ohio University Press.

———. 2005b. "War as Smoke and Mirrors: Sierra Leone 1991–2, 1994–5, 1995–6." *Anthropological Quarterly* 78, no. 2: 377–402.

Riley, Stephen. 1996. "The 1996 Presidential and Parliamentary Elections in Sierra Leone." *Electoral Studies* 15, no. 4: 537–45.

Rodney, Walter. 1970. *A History of the Upper Guinea Coast, 1545 to 1800*. Oxford: Clarendon Press.

Roitman, Janet. 1998. "The Garrison-Entrepôt." *Cahiers d'Études Africaines* 38, no. 2–4: 297–329.

———. 2005. *Fiscal Disobedience: An Anthropology of Economic Regulation in Central Africa*. Princeton: Princeton University Press.

———. 2006. "The Ethics of Illegality in the Chad Basin." In *Law and Disorder in the Postcolony*, edited by Jean Comaroff and John L. Comaroff, 247–72. Chicago: University of Chicago Press.

RSLCDF. See Republic of Sierra Leone Civil Defence Forces.

Rubin, Elizabeth. 1997. "An Army of One's Own: In Africa, Nations Hire a Corporation to Wage War." *Harper's* February: 44–55.

Rubin, Michael. 2007. "Asymmetrical Threat Concept and Its Reflections on International Security." Presentation to the Strategic Research and Study Center (SAREM) under the Turkish General Staff, 31 May. Istanbul, Turkey. Available on the American Enterprise Institute website.

RUF/SL. See Revolutionary United Front, Sierra Leone.

Samura, Sorious. 2000. *Cry Freetown*. Documentary film. London: Insight News TV.

Sawyer, Amos. 2005. *Beyond Plunder: Toward Democratic Governance in Liberia*. Boulder, Colo.: Lynne Rienner.

Scarry, Elaine. 1985. *The Body in Pain: The Making and Unmaking of the World*. New York: Oxford.

Schama, Simon. 2006. *Rough Crossings: Britain, the Slaves, and the American Revolution*. New York: Ecco.

Seed, Patricia. 1995. *Ceremonies of Possession in Europe's Conquest of the New World, 1492–1640*. Cambridge: Cambridge University Press.

Shaw, Martin. 2005. *The New Western Way of War: Risk-Transfer War and Its Crisis in Iraq*. Cambridge: Polity.

Shaw, Rosalind. 1997. "Secret Societies." In *Encyclopedia of Africa South of the Sahara*, edited by John Middleton, 44–48. New York: Macmillan.

———. 2001. "Cannibal Transformations: Colonialism and Commodification in the Sierra Leone Hinterland." In *Magical Interpretations, Material Realities: Modernity, Witchcraft and the Occult in Postcolonial Africa*, edited by Henrietta Moore and Todd Sanders, 50–70. New York: Routledge.

———. 2002. *Memories of the Slave Trade: Ritual and the Historical Imagination in Sierra Leone*. Chicago: University of Chicago Press.

———. 2007. "Displacing Violence: Making Pentecostal Memory in Postwar Sierra Leone." *Cultural Anthropology* 22, no. 1: 66–93.

Shearer, David. 1998. "Outsourcing War." *Foreign Policy* Fall: 68–81.

Shepler, Susan. 2002. "Les Filles-Soldat: Trajectories d'apres-Guerre en Sierra Leone." *Politique africaine* 88, December: 49–62.

Siegel, James. 2003. "The Truth of Sorcery." *Cultural Anthropology* 18, no. 2: 135–55.

Simone, AbdouMaliq. 2001. "The Worlding of African Cities." *African Studies Review* 44, no. 2: 15–41.

———. 2002. "The Visible and the Invisible: Remaking Cities in Africa." In *Under Siege: Four African Cities: Freetown, Johannesburg, Kinshasa, Lagos*, edited by Okwui Enwezor, 23–44. Ostfildern-Ruit: Hatje Cantz.

———. 2004. *For the City Yet to Come: Changing Life in Four African Cities*. Durham, N.C.: Duke University Press.

Simons, Anna. 2005. "Seeing the Enemy (or Not)." In *Rethinking the Principles of War*, edited by Anthony McIvor, 323–44. Annapolis, Md.: Naval Institute Press.

Simons, Anna, and David Tucker. 2004. *Improving Human Intelligence in the War on Terrorism: The Need for an Ethnographic Capability*. Washington: Office of Net Assessment, Office of the Secretary of Defense.

Smillie, Ian, Lansana Gberie, and Ralph Hazelton. 2000. *The Heart of the Matter: Sierra Leone, Diamonds and Human Security*. Ottawa: Partnership Africa Canada.

Smith, L. Alison, Catherine Gambette, and Thomas Longley. 2004. *Conflict Mapping in Sierra Leone: Violations of International Humanitarian Law from 1991 to 2002*. New York: No Peace without Justice.

Southall, Roger, Neo Simutanyi, and John Daniel. 2006. "Former Presidents in African Politics." In *Legacies of Power: Leadership Change and Former Presidents in African Politics*, edited by Roger Southall and Henning Melber, 1–25. Pretoria: HSRC Press.

Spivak, Gayatri. 1988. "Can the Subaltern Speak?" In *Marxism and the Interpretation of Culture*, edited by Cary Nelson and Lawrence Grossberg, 271–313. Urbana: University of Illinois Press.

Stoler, Ann. 1995. *Race and the Education of Desire: Foucault's History of Sexuality and the Colonial Order of Things*. Durham, N.C.: Duke University Press.

Strachan, Hew. 2007. *Clausewitz's on War: A Biography*. Books That Changed the World. New York: Grove.

Tangri, Roger. 1976. "Conflict and Violence in Contemporary Sierra Leone Chiefdoms." *Journal of Modern African Studies* 14, no. 2: 311–21.

Taussig, Michael. 1980. *The Devil and Commodity Fetishism in South America*. Chapel Hill: University of North Carolina Press.

———. 1987. *Shamanism, Colonialism and the Wild Man: A Study in Terror and Healing*. Chicago: University of Chicago Press.

Taylor, Christopher. 1999. *Sacrifice as Terror: The Rwandan Genocide of 1994*. New York: Berg.

Thornton, Robert. 1992. *Africa and Africans in the Making of the Atlantic World, 1400–1680*. Cambridge: Cambridge University Press.

Tostevin, Matthew. 1993. "Sinking to the Depths." BBC World Service, *Focus on Africa*, July–September, 23–26.

United States Department of the Army. 2007. *The U.S. Army / Marine Corps*

Counterinsurgency Field Manual. Vol. 324, U.S. Army Field Manual. Chicago: University of Chicago Press.

Utas, Mats. 2003. "Sweet Battlefields: Youth and the Liberian Civil War." PhD Dissertation, Uppsala University.

———. 2005. "Victimcy, Girlfriending, Soldiering: Tactic Agency in a Young Woman's Social Navigation of the Liberian War Zone." *Anthropological Quarterly* 78, no. 2: 403–30.

Utas, Mats, and Magnus Jörgel. 2008. "The West Side Boys: Military Navigation in the Sierra Leone Civil War." *Journal of Modern African Studies* 46:487–511.

Vigh, Henrik. 2006. *Navigating Terrains of War: Youth and Soldiering in Guinea-Bissau*. Oxford: Berghahn Books.

Virilio, Paul, and Sylvère Lotringer. 1997. *Pure War*. Los Angeles: Semiotext(e).

Voeten, Teun. 2002. *How De Body? One Man's Terrifying Journey through an African War*. Translated by Roz Vatter-Buck. New York: Thomas Dunne Books, St. Martin's Press.

Wainaina, Binyavanga. 2005. "How to Write about Africa: Some Tips: Sunsets and Starvation Are Good." *Granta*, no. 92: 91–96.

Watts, Michael. 2004. "Resource Curse? Governmentality, Oil and Power in the Niger Delta, Nigeria." *Geopolitics* 9, no. 1: 50–80.

Weizman, Eyal. 2002. "The Politics of Verticality." www.opendemocracy.net/, April.

———. 2006. "Walking through Walls: Soldiers as Architects in the Isreali-Palestinian Conflict." *Radical Philosophy* 136:8–22.

West, Harry G. 2007. *Ethnographic Sorcery*. Chicago: University of Chicago Press.

Williams, Gabriel I. H. 2002. *Liberia, the Heart of Darkness: Accounts of Liberia's Civil War and Its Destabilizing Effects in West Africa*. Victoria, B.C.: Trafford.

Wilson, Edmund. [1971] 2003. *To the Finland Station*. New York: New York Review of Books.

Wilson, Gregory. 2006. "Anatomy of a Successful Coin Operation: OEF-Philippines and the Indirect Approach." *Military Review* November–December: 38–48.

Wlodarczyk, Nathalie. 2009. *Magic and Warfare: Appearance and Reality in Contemporary African Conflict and Beyond*. New York: Palgrave.

Wylie, Kenneth. 1969. "Innovation and Change in Mende Chieftaincy, 1880–1896." *Journal of African History* 10, no. 2: 295–308.

Young, Robert J. C. 1995. *Colonial Desire: Hybridity in Theory, Culture and Race*. New York: Routledge.

Zack-Williams, A. B. 1999. "Sierra Leone: The Political Economy of Civil War, 1991–1998." *Third World Quarterly* 20, no. 1: 143–62.

———. 2002. "Freetown: From the 'Athens of West Africa' To a City under Siege: The Rise and Fall of Sub-Saharan Africa's First Municipality." In *Under Siege: Four African Cities, Freetown, Johannesburg, Kinshasa, Lagos*, edited by Okwui Enwezor, Carlos Basualdo, Ute Meta Bauer, Susanne Ghez, Sarat Maharaj, Mark Nash and Octavio Zaya, 287–315. Ostfildern-Ruit: Hatje Cantz.

Žižek, Slavoj. 2008. *Violence: Six Sideways Reflections*. New York: Picador.

index

Danny Hoffman is an assistant professor
of anthropology at the University of Washington.

Library of Congress Cataloging-in-Publication Data
Hoffman, Danny, 1972–
The war machines : young men and violence in Sierra Leone
and Liberia / Danny Hoffman.
p. cm. — (Cultures and practice of violence series)
ISBN 978-0-8223-5059-0 (cloth : alk. paper)
ISBN 978-0-8223-5077-4 (pbk. : alk. paper)
1. Sierra Leone—History—Civil War, 1991–2002—Participation, Juvenile.
2. Liberia—History—Civil War, 1989–1996—Participation, Juvenile.
3. Liberia—History—Civil War, 1999–2003—Participation, Juvenile.
4. Militia movements—Sierra Leone—History.
5. Militia movements—Liberia—History.
I. Title. II. Series: Cultures and practice of violence series.
DT516.826.H644 2011
966.404—dc22 2011006446